Cupcakes

More than 100 sweet and simple
recipes for every occasion

WILEY

John Wiley & Sons, Inc.

Meredith Corporation

Editor: Jessica Saari Christensen

Contributing Editors:
Mary Williams, Spectrum
Communication Services Inc.

Recipe Development and Testing:
Better Homes and Gardens Test
Kitchen

John Wiley & Sons, Inc.

Publisher: Natalie Chapman

Executive Editor: Anne Ficklen

Senior Editorial Assistant:
Heather Dabah

Senior Production Editor:
Marina Padakis Lowry

Production Director: Diana Cisek

Interior Design: Tai Blanche

Layout: Indianapolis Composition
Services

Manufacturing Manager:
Tom Hyland

Library of Congress Cataloging-in-Publication Data

Better homes and gardens cupcakes : more than 100 sweet and simple recipes for every occasion.

   pages cm

Includes index.

ISBN 978-1-118-29269-3 (pbk.); 978-1-118-29270-9 (ebk.); 978-1-118-29271-6 (ebk.); 978-1-118-29272-3 (ebk.)

1. Cupcakes. I. Better homes and gardens.

TX771.B525 2013

641.86'53--dc23

              2012015858

Printed in the United States of America

10 9 8 7 6 5 4 3 2 1

PB and Jelly Cupcakes, page 124

Brownie Surprise Cupcakes, page 134

Table of Contents

Introduction

No other confection shares the cupcake's uncanny ability to warm hearts while pleasing palates. What is it about a cupcake that garners such happiness? Perhaps the teensy treat brings out our inner child. Or maybe its petite size makes it the perfect individual-size indulgence. Or possibly it's that cupcakes are just so adorable.

No matter what sort of cupcake tickles your fancy—classic or trendy, playful or sophisticated, swirled, sprinkled, dipped, glazed or embellished—you'll find it here.

And you'll find it along with everything you need to make your own custom cupcakes—from go-to recipes for basic cakes, frostings, and toppings to ideas for making cupcakes the star attraction at weddings, showers, birthday parties, and holidays year around.

Think of this book's contents as "big ideas for little things." Let the cupcakes on these pages inspire you to scoop sweet thoughts into cupcake papers and to bake up your very own creations— batch after batch after batch. Here's to making sweet somethings!

Dark Chocolate-Raspberry Cakes, page 101

Cupcake Toolbox

Cupcake Central at your service! Here's a handy guide to basic recipes, frostings, and toppings, plus a sweet treasure trove of fantastic flavor variations. Mix and match, pick and choose, and customize your cupcakes to suit everyone's taste.

Vanilla Cupcakes

Prep: 30 minutes **Stand:** 30 minutes **Bake:** 20 minutes at 350°F
Cool: 45 minutes **Makes:** 12 (2½-inch) or 48 (1¾-inch) cupcakes

½ cup butter	1½ cups all-purpose flour
1 egg	1½ teaspoons baking powder
2 egg yolks	¼ teaspoon salt
1 vanilla bean, split lengthwise, or 1 teaspoon vanilla	¾ cup sugar
	½ teaspoon vanilla
	½ cup whipping cream

1. Allow butter, egg, and egg yolks to stand at room temperature for 30 minutes. Meanwhile, line twelve 2½-inch muffin cups or forty-eight 1¾-inch muffin cups with paper bake cups. If using vanilla bean, use a small sharp knife to scrape the seeds from the vanilla bean. Set seeds aside. In a small bowl stir together flour, baking powder, and salt. Set aside.

2. Preheat oven to 350°F. In a large mixing bowl beat butter with an electric mixer on medium to high speed for 30 seconds. Add sugar. Beat on medium to high speed for 1 minute, scraping sides of bowl. Add egg, egg yolks, vanilla bean seeds (or 1 teaspoon vanilla extract), and ½ teaspoon vanilla extract; beat until combined. Alternately add flour mixture and whipping cream to butter mixture, beating on low speed after each addition just until combined (batter will be thick).

3. Spoon batter into prepared muffin cups, filling each about three-fourths full. Use the back of a spoon to smooth out batter in cups.

4. Bake about 20 minutes for 2½-inch cupcakes, about 15 minutes for 1¾-inch cupcakes, or until a wooden toothpick inserted in centers comes out clean. Cool cupcakes in muffin cups on wire racks for 5 minutes. Remove cupcakes from muffin cups. Cool completely on wire racks. Spread desired frosting onto tops of cupcakes.

Per cupcake: 224 cal., 13 g total fat (8 g sat. fat), 87 mg chol., 144 mg sodium, 25 g carb., 0 g dietary fiber, 13 g sugar, 3 g protein.

Yellow Cupcakes

Prep: 40 minutes **Stand:** 30 minutes **Bake:** 18 minutes at 350°F
Cool: 45 minutes **Makes:** 24 to 30 (2½-inch) cupcakes

¾ cup butter	½ teaspoon salt
3 eggs	1¾ cups sugar
2½ cups all-purpose flour	1½ teaspoons vanilla
2½ teaspoons baking powder	1¼ cups milk

1. Allow butter and eggs to stand at room temperature for 30 minutes. Meanwhile, line twenty-four to thirty 2½-inch muffin cups with paper bake cups. In a medium bowl stir together flour, baking powder, and salt. Set aside.

2. Preheat oven to 350°F. In a large mixing bowl beat butter with an electric mixer on medium to high speed for 30 seconds. Gradually add sugar, about ¼ cup at a time, beating on medium speed until combined. Scrape sides of bowl; beat about 2 minutes more or until light and fluffy. Add eggs, one at a time, beating well after each addition. Beat in vanilla. Alternately add flour mixture and milk to butter mixture, beating on low speed after each addition just until combined.

3. Spoon batter into prepared muffin cups, filling each one-half to two-thirds full. Use the back of a spoon to smooth out batter in cups.

4. Bake for 18 to 22 minutes or until a wooden toothpick inserted in centers comes out clean. Cool cupcakes in muffin cups on wire racks for 5 minutes. Remove cupcakes from muffin cups. Cool completely on wire racks. Spread desired frosting onto tops of cupcakes.

Per cupcake: 171 cal., 7 g total fat (4 g sat. fat), 43 mg chol., 129 mg sodium, 25 g carb., 0 g dietary fiber, 15 g sugar, 3 g protein.

Chocolate Cupcakes

Prep: 40 minutes **Stand:** 30 minutes **Bake:** 18 minutes at 350°F
Cool: 45 minutes **Makes:** 24 to 30 (2½ inch) cupcakes

¾ cup butter	¾ teaspoon baking powder
3 eggs	½ teaspoon salt
2 cups all-purpose flour	2 cups sugar
¾ cup unsweetened cocoa powder	2 teaspoons vanilla
1 teaspoon baking soda	1½ cups milk

1. Allow butter and eggs to stand at room temperature for 30 minutes. Meanwhile, line twenty-four to thirty 2½-inch muffin cups with paper bake cups. In a medium bowl stir together flour, cocoa powder, baking soda, baking powder, and salt. Set aside.

2. Preheat oven to 350°F. In a large mixing bowl beat butter with an electric mixer on medium to high speed for 30 seconds. Gradually add sugar, about ¼ cup at a time, beating on medium speed until combined. Scrape sides of bowl; beat about 2 minutes more or until light and fluffy. Add eggs, one at a time, beating well after each addition. Beat in vanilla. Alternately add flour mixture and milk to butter mixture, beating on low speed after each addition just until combined. Beat on medium to high speed for 20 seconds more.

3. Spoon batter into prepared muffin cups, filling each one-half to two-thirds full. Use the back of a spoon to smooth out batter in cups.

4. Bake for 18 to 22 minutes or until a wooden toothpick inserted in centers comes out clean. Cool cupcakes in muffin cups on wire racks for 5 minutes. Remove cupcakes from muffin cups. Cool completely on wire racks. Spread desired frosting onto tops of cupcakes.

Per cupcake: 177 cal., 7 g total fat (4 g sat. fat), 43 mg chol., 165 mg sodium, 27 g carb., 1 g dietary fiber, 18 g sugar, 3 g protein.

Simple White Cupcakes

Prep: 30 minutes **Stand:** 30 minutes **Bake:** 18 minutes at 350°F
Cool: 1 hour **Makes:** 12 (2½-inch) cupcakes

⅓ cup butter	⅛ teaspoon salt
2 eggs	⅔ cup sugar
1 cup all-purpose flour	1 teaspoon vanilla
1 teaspoon baking powder	⅓ cup buttermilk or sour milk*
¼ teaspoon baking soda	

1. Allow butter and eggs to stand at room temperature for 30 minutes. Grease twelve 2½-inch muffin cups or line with paper bake cups. In a medium bowl stir together flour, baking powder, baking soda, and salt. Set aside.

2. Preheat oven to 350°F. In a large mixing bowl beat butter with an electric mixer on medium to high speed for 30 seconds. Add sugar and vanilla. Beat on medium to high speed about 2 minutes or until light and fluffy, scraping sides of bowl occasionally. Add eggs, one at a time, beating well after each addition. Alternately add flour mixture and buttermilk to butter mixture, beating on low speed after each addition just until combined.

3. Spoon batter into prepared muffin cups, filling each about half full. Bake for 18 to 20 minutes or until a wooden toothpick inserted in centers comes out clean. Cool cupcakes in muffin cups on wire racks for 5 minutes. Remove cupcakes from muffin cups. Cool completely on wire racks.

Per cupcake: 411 cal., 18 g total fat (12 g sat. fat), 71 mg chol., 225 mg sodium, 58 g carb., 1 g dietary fiber, 46 g sugar, 3 g protein.

Tip: To make ½ cup sour milk, place 1½ teaspoons lemon juice or vinegar in a glass measuring cup. Add enough milk to equal ½ cup total liquid; stir. Let stand 5 minutes before using.

Cupcake Convert

Most butter-style cake recipes (those that start with beating butter and sugar together) can easily be turned into cupcakes. Here's how:

○ Choose a recipe for a butter-style cake. Most two-layer cakes will yield 24 to 30 cupcakes.

○ Line muffin cups with paper bake cups. Fill cups half to two-thirds full. (You can start by baking a couple cups with different amounts to see which height you like best.)

○ Bake cupcakes at the same temperature called for in the cake recipe, but reduce the baking time by one-third to one-half. Most cupcakes bake for 15 to 22 minutes. Check doneness of cupcakes by inserting a toothpick in the center of a middle cupcake; if the toothpick comes out clean, the cupcakes are done. If toothpick has wet crumbs on it, you'll need to continue baking for a couple of minutes and then check again. Let cupcakes cool in pan for 5 minutes; remove cupcakes from pan and cool completely.

Vanilla Cupcake   Chocolate Cupcake   Simple White Cupcake   Yellow Cupcake

Mix It Up!

Now that you've got the basic cupcakes down, it's time to add a little life and love to your next batch. Try any of these tasty toppings on the Yellow Cupcake recipe (page 10) or cut the topping ingredients in half and try them on Vanilla Cupcakes (page 10) or Simple White Cupcakes (page 11).

Coconut Cupcakes

2   cups flaked coconut, toasted

Prepare Yellow Cupcakes as directed and frost with Butter Frosting (page 14) or Creamy White Frosting (page 15). Sprinkle frosted cupcakes with coconut.

Raspberry Cupcakes

Fresh raspberries

Prepare Yellow Cupcakes as directed, except place 2 to 3 raspberries on top of batter in each cup. Bake and cool as directed. After frosting with Butter Frosting (page 14) or Creamy White Frosting (page 15), top each cupcake with a raspberry.

Hawaiian Cupcakes

1   cup chopped macadamia nuts
1   cup tropical blend mixed dried fruit bits

Prepare Yellow Cupcakes as directed and frost with Butter Frosting (page 14) or Creamy White Frosting (page 15). Sprinkle tops with macadamia nuts and dried fruit bits.

Cinnamon-Orange Cupcakes

¼   cup orange marmalade
½   teaspoon ground cinnamon

Prepare Yellow Cupcakes as directed. Prepare Butter Frosting (page 14) or Creamy White Frosting (page 15) as directed, except stir marmalade and cinnamon into frosting. Frost cupcakes.

Lemon Cupcakes

1   tablespoon finely shredded lemon peel
½   cup purchased lemon curd

Prepare Yellow Cupcakes as directed, except add lemon peel to butter. Prepare Butter Frosting (page 14) or Creamy White Frosting (page 15) as directed. Frost cupcakes. Top each with 1 teaspoon lemon curd; swirl with frosting. If desired, sprinkle with additional lemon peel.

Candy Cupcakes

24   bite-size chocolate-covered peanut butter cups, unwrapped
1   cup crushed crunchy chocolate-covered peanut butter candy bar

Prepare Yellow Cupcakes as directed as directed, except top batter in each cup with 1 peanut butter cup. Bake as directed. Frost with Butter Frosting (page 14) or Creamy White Frosting (page 15). Sprinkle with crushed candy bar.

Chocolate Chip Cupcakes

1   tablespoon finely shredded orange peel
1   cup miniature semisweet chocolate pieces

Prepare Yellow Cupcakes as directed, except add orange peel with the butter. Fold chocolate pieces into batter. Bake as directed. Frost with Butter Frosting (page 14) or Creamy White Frosting (page 15).

Espresso Cupcakes

1   tablespoon espresso powder
1   cup chopped chocolate-covered espresso beans

Prepare Yellow or Vanilla Cupcakes as directed. Prepare Butter Frosting (page 14) or Creamy White Frosting (page 15) as directed, except add espresso powder to butter. Sprinkle frosted cupcakes with espresso beans.

Cranberry-Pistachio Cupcakes

1   cup chopped dried cranberries
1   cup shelled pistachio nuts

Prepare Yellow Cupcakes as directed and frost with Butter Frosting (page 14) or Creamy White Frosting (page 15). Sprinkle frosted cupcakes with dried cranberries and pistachio nuts.

Toffee Cupcakes

1   cup chopped cashews
1   cup toffee pieces
1   cup caramel ice cream topping

Prepare Yellow Cupcakes as directed and frost with Butter Frosting (page 14) or Creamy White Frosting (page 15). Sprinkle with cashews and toffee bits. Drizzle with ice cream topping.

Almond Cupcakes

½   to 1 teaspoon almond extract
½   teaspoon almond extract
1   cup sliced almonds, toasted

Prepare Yellow Cupcakes as directed, except reduce vanilla to 1 teaspoon and add ½ to 1 teaspoon almond extract. Prepare Butter Frosting (page 14) or Creamy White Frosting (page 15) as directed, except reduce vanilla to 1 teaspoon and add ½ teaspoon almond extract. Frost cupcakes. Sprinkle with toasted sliced almonds.

Peppermint Cupcakes

Grated white chocolate
Coarsely crushed peppermint candies

Prepare Yellow Cupcakes as directed and frost with Butter Frosting (page 14) or Creamy White Frosting (page 15). Sprinkle frosted cupcakes with grated white chocolate and peppermint candies.

Butter Frosting

Prep: 20 minutes **Stand:** 30 minutes **Makes:** About 4½ cups

¾	cup butter	2	teaspoons vanilla
2	pounds powdered sugar (about 8 cups)		Milk
⅓	cup milk		Food coloring (optional)

Allow butter to stand at room temperature for 30 minutes. In a very large mixing bowl beat butter with an electric mixer on medium speed until smooth. Gradually add 2 cups of the powdered sugar, beating well. Slowly beat in ⅓ cup milk and vanilla. Gradually beat in remaining powdered sugar. Beat in additional milk until frosting reaches spreading consistency. If desired, tint with food coloring.

Per tablespoon: 67 cal., 2 g total fat (1 g sat. fat), 5 mg chol., 14 mg sodium, 13 g carb., 0 g dietary fiber, 12 g sugar, 0 g protein.

Milk Chocolate Butter Frosting:

Prepare as above, except melt 1 cup milk chocolate pieces; cool. Beat into the butter before adding powdered sugar.

Chocolate Butter Frosting:

Prepare as above, except substitute ½ cup unsweetened cocoa powder for ½ cup of the powdered sugar.

Strawberry Butter Frosting:

Prepare as above, except beat ⅓ cup strawberry jam into butter before adding powdered sugar.

Irish Cream Butter Frosting:

Prepare as above, except substitute Irish cream liqueur for the milk.

Coffee Butter Frosting:

Prepare as above, except add 1 tablespoon instant espresso powder or coffee crystals to butter or substitute strong brewed coffee for milk.

Per tablespoon and variations: 68 cal., 2 g total fat (1 g sat. fat), 5 mg chol., 16 mg sodium, 12 g carb., 0 g dietary fiber, 15 g sugar, 0 g protein.

Classic Buttercream

Prep: 20 minutes **Stand:** 30 minutes **Cool:** 10 minutes
Makes: 3 cups

1½	cups unsalted butter	6	egg yolks, lightly beaten
1	cup sugar	2	tablespoons desired-flavor liqueur or water
¼	cup water	1½	teaspoons vanilla

1. Allow butter to stand at room temperature for 30 minutes. In a heavy medium saucepan combine sugar and the water. Bring to boiling; remove from heat. Gradually whisk about half of the hot sugar mixture into egg yolks. Gradually whisk egg yolk mixture back into the remaining sugar mixture in saucepan. Bring to a gentle boil; reduce heat. Cook and stir for 2 minutes. Remove from heat. Stir in liqueur and vanilla.

2. Transfer yolk mixture to a bowl. Fill a larger bowl with cold water and ice. Place the smaller bowl into the larger bowl. Stir frequently until mixture is cooled to room temperature.

3. In a large mixing bowl beat butter with an electric mixer on high speed until fluffy. Add cooled sugar mixture, beating until combined. If necessary, chill until mixture reaches spreading consistency.

Chocolate Buttercream:

Prepare as above, except melt 4 ounces semisweet or bittersweet chocolate; cool. Add chocolate to butter with sugar mixture.

Per tablespoon: 77 cal., 6 g total fat (4 g sat. fat), 41 mg chol., 2 mg sodium, 5 g carb., 0 g dietary fiber, 5 g sugar, 0 g protein.

Cream Cheese Frosting

Prep: 20 minutes **Stand:** 30 minutes **Makes:** About 3½ cups

1	8-ounce package cream cheese	2	teaspoons vanilla
½	cup butter	5½	to 6 cups powdered sugar

Allow cream cheese and butter to stand at room temperature for 30 minutes. In a large mixing bowl beat cream cheese, butter, and vanilla with an electric mixer on medium speed until light and fluffy. Gradually beat in powdered sugar until frosting reaches spreading consistency.

Cocoa and Cream Cheese Frosting:

Prepare as above, except beat ½ cup unsweetened cocoa powder into the cream cheese mixture and reduce powdered sugar to 5 to 5½ cups.

Per tablespoon: 75 cal., 3 g total fat (2 g sat. fat), 9 mg chol., 25 mg sodium, 12 g carb., 0 g dietary fiber, 12 g sugar, 0 g protein.

Creamy White Frosting

Start to Finish: 20 minutes
Makes: About 3 cups

- 1 cup shortening
- 1½ teaspoons vanilla
- ½ teaspoon almond extract
- 1 pound powdered sugar (about 4 cups)
- 3 to 4 tablespoons milk

In a large mixing bowl beat shortening, vanilla, and almond extract with an electric mixer on medium speed for 30 seconds. Gradually add 2 cups of the powdered sugar, beating well. Beat in 2 tablespoons of the milk. Gradually beat in the remaining powdered sugar. Beat in enough of the remaining milk until frosting reaches spreading consistency.

Per tablespoon: 74 cal., 4 g total fat (1 g sat. fat), 0 mg chol., 1 mg sodium, 9 g carb., 0 g dietary fiber, 9 g sugar, 0 g protein.

creamy white frosting

ganache

sweetened whipped cream frosting

classic buttercream

cream cheese frosting

butter frosting

Easy Homemade Fondant

Start to Finish: 25 minutes **Makes:** 1 pound

- 3 cups tiny marshmallows
- ½ ounce white baking chocolate with cocoa butter, finely chopped
- 1 tablespoon butter, cut up
- 1½ teaspoons milk or whipping cream
- 1 teaspoon clear vanilla
- 3 cups powdered sugar
- Paste food coloring (optional)

1. In a medium microwave-safe bowl combine marshmallows, white chocolate, butter, and milk. Microwave on 100% power (high) about 1 minute or until marshmallows begin to melt and are puffy. Stir the marshmallow mixture until smooth (if necessary, return to the microwave oven to continue melting).

2. Stir vanilla into marshmallow mixture. Add 1½ cups of the powdered sugar; stir to combine.

3. Sprinkle a work surface with about ½ cup of the remaining powdered sugar; scrape marshmallow mixture onto prepared surface and knead. Sprinkle with additional powdered sugar as needed, kneading until fondant is smooth and no longer sticky (this will take about 10 minutes).

4. If desired, knead food coloring into fondant. To use, roll fondant on a surface coated with additional powdered sugar according to directions in recipe. If working with the fondant a portion at a time, keep any remaining portions tightly covered with plastic wrap.

Per ounce: 137 cal., 1 g total fat (1 g sat. fat), 2 mg chol., 20 mg sodium, 32 g carb., 0 g dietary fiber, 29 g sugar, 0 g protein.

Ganache

Start to Finish: 35 minutes **Makes:** About 2 cups

- 1 cup whipping cream
- 12 ounces milk chocolate, semisweet chocolate, or bittersweet chocolate, chopped

In a medium saucepan bring whipping cream just to boiling over medium-high heat. Remove from heat. Add chocolate (do not stir). Let stand for 5 minutes. Stir until smooth. Cool for 15 minutes.

Per tablespoon: 82 cal., 6 g total fat (4 g sat. fat), 13 mg chol., 14 mg sodium, 6 g carb., 0 g dietary fiber, 6 g sugar, 1 g protein.

Sweetened Whipped Cream Frosting

Start to Finish: 25 minutes **Makes:** 4 cups

- 2 tablespoons cold water
- 1 teaspoon unflavored gelatin
- 2 cups whipping cream
- ¼ cup sugar

1. In a large saucepan bring about 1 inch water to boiling over high heat. Meanwhile, in a 1-cup heatproof glass measuring cup combine the cold water and gelatin. Let stand for 2 minutes. Place measuring cup in the saucepan of boiling water. Cook and stir about 1 minute or until the gelatin is completely dissolved. Remove measuring cup from water; cool for 5 minutes.

2. In a chilled large mixing bowl beat whipping cream and sugar with the chilled beaters of an electric mixer on medium speed while gradually drizzling the gelatin mixture into the cream mixture. Continue beating the cream mixture until stiff peaks form (tips stand straight).

Per tablespoon: 29 cal., 3 g total fat (2 g sat. fat), 10 mg chol., 3 mg sodium, 1 g carb., 0 g dietary fiber, 1 g sugar, 0 g protein.

How to Make Cupcake Batter

Preparing homemade butter-style cake and cupcake batter is a piece of cake. Follow these steps and you'll get amazing results—first time, every time.

Step 1: Beat butter with an electric mixer on medium speed until light.

Step 2: Gradually add sugar, beating until mixture is fluffy. Scrape sides of bowl occassionally.

Step 3: Add eggs one at a time, beating well after each addition.

Step 4: Alternately add flour mixture and liquid, beating after each addition just until combined.

How to Prepare Muffin Tins

The best way to prepare your muffin tins for cupcakes is to line them with paper bake cups. But if you don't have bake cups, you can grease and flour each cup of the muffin tin.

Paper muffin cups: Place paper bake cups in muffin tins.

Customize Your Cupcake

Here are some fun ways to tweak any basic cake recipe (or a cake mix) to come up with something deliciously new.

○ To spice up the batter, stir in 1 teaspoon ground cinnamon, ground ginger, or pumpkin pie spice or apple pie spice.

○ Add a little liquid flavoring by replacing ¼ cup of the milk or cream called for in the recipe or mix with ¼ cup flavored liqueur, fruit juice, or melted ice cream.

○ After baking, lightly sprinkle hot cupcakes with chocolate, butterscotch, or peanut butter pieces; chopped chocolate-covered raisins or peanuts; or chopped candy bars or caramels.

Or grease and flour: Lightly brush shortening over sides and bottom of cups using a pastry brush or paper towel.

Spoon flour into each cup. Shake muffin tin to coat sides of cups. Tap pan upside down to discard remaining flour.

Techniques & Tools

Part of the fun of cupcake decorating is all the gadgets and goodies you can find on the market. Here are some of our top must-haves in pastry bags, tips, and other tools.

Closed Star Tip

This closed star tip has tines that curve in more than those of an open star tip (below), creating stars, shells, and rosettes with deeper, more pronounced grooves.

Open Star Tip

Star tips come in a variety of sizes for all your decorating needs (see large star tip, below). Depending on what size you have, these are great for borders, small stars (see page 129), long stars (see page 104), and basket weave (see page 188).

Leaf Tip

This tip does just what its name says—makes perfect little leaves for frosting flowers. If you connect the leaves together (as in photo for open star tips, above left), they also make a lovely border on a cupcake. The leaf tips come in many sizes.

Multiopening Tip

While this tip is most commonly used to make grass (see page 261), it also can be used to make fur, hair, and a lion's mane (see page 273).

Large Star Tip

The classic cupcake swirl—looking like soft-serve ice cream—depends on this very large open star tip. To make this swirl, start at the edge of the cupcake, turning cupcake and piping around entire outside edge. When you make it back to your starting point, start overlapping the first rim and building up frosting to reach a peak at the top.

1. Spatulas

Both angled- and straight-blade spatulas make frosting a breeze. They range in size from 8 inches to 15 inches.

2. Pastry Wheel

This pastry wheel has many applications outside of cupcake baking (piecrusts, cookies, ravioli dough), including making decorative-edge fondant cutouts (see page 243).

3. Coupler

To easily switch out piping tips (opposite), insert this coupler into a pastry bag, add a tip, and screw it on tightly. When you're ready for a different tip, just unscrew and replace.

4. Sprinkles

Buy sprinkles in every shape, size, and color! While most grocery stores carry some sugars and sprinkles, you can find even more in hobby stores.

5. Paper Baking Cups

Paper baking cups come in a variety of colors and designs, so you can customize them to match any theme. If you don't have paper baking cups on hand, in a pinch, you can simply grease and flour your muffin cups.

6. Pastry Bags

Piping is a piece of cake with these strong polyurethane bags. They're easy to clean—just use hot water and soap.

7. Disposable Pastry Bags

Plastic bags are great when time is short. When you're done piping, simply discard. Disposable bags are great for piping meringue mixtures (see page 44), since oils may remain in reusable bags even after washing which could cause meringue to deflate.

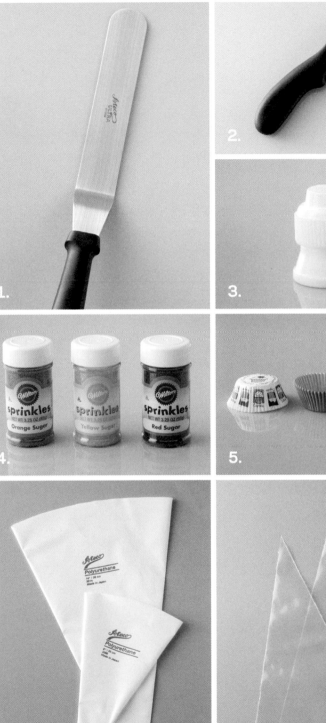

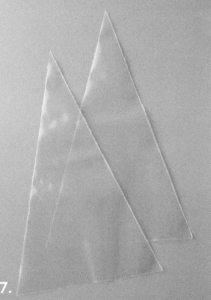

Neapolitan Cupcakes, page 30

Remakes on Favorite Flavors

Trendy and contemporary always take a backseat to nostalgia, especially when it brings back the comfort of best-loved flavors from the past. It was smooth sailing to concoct cupcake ringers of top soda parlor picks (such as floats, shakes, and splits) and bakery beauties (like pies, doughnuts, and cinnamon rolls) for your reminiscing enjoyment. These are calories worth every blissful bite!

Hot Fudge Sundae Cupcakes

Prep: 40 minutes **Bake:** 16 minutes at 350°F **Cool:** 45 minutes

Makes 24 (2½-inch) cupcakes

1 package 2-layer-size chocolate cake mix

1 12-ounce jar hot fudge ice cream topping, at room temperature

1 to two 16-ounce cans creamy white frosting

½ cup semisweet chocolate pieces*

1 teaspoon shortening*

Chopped nuts

1 10-ounce jar maraschino cherries with stems, well drained

1. Line twenty-four 2½-inch muffin cups with paper bake cups. Preheat oven to 350°F. Prepare cake mix according to package directions.

2. Spoon batter into prepared muffin cups, filling each about two-thirds full. Use the back of a spoon to smooth out batter in cups. Place 1 scant tablespoon fudge topping on the top center of each cupcake.

3. Bake for 16 to 20 minutes or until tops spring back when lightly touched. Cool cupcakes in muffin cups on wire racks for 5 minutes. Remove cupcakes from muffin cups. Cool completely on wire racks.

4. Spread some of the frosting onto tops of cupcakes. Spoon the remaining frosting into a pastry bag fitted with a star tip.

5. In a small saucepan melt chocolate pieces and shortening over low heat; cool slightly. Spoon melted chocolate into a small heavy resealable plastic bag. Snip off a small piece from one corner of bag. Drizzle melted chocolate on top of frosted cupcakes.

6. Sprinkle cupcakes with nuts. Pipe the remaining frosting onto cupcakes. Place a cherry on top of each cupcake.

*Test Kitchen Tip:
If desired, use Smucker's Magic Shell instead of melting the semisweet chocolate pieces and shortening.

Per cupcake: 291 cal., 11 g total fat (4 g sat. fat), 27 mg chol., 220 mg sodium, 46 g carb., 1 g dietary fiber, 33 g sugar, 3 g protein.

Cupcake Shakes

Here's a creative way to use up past-prime cupcakes: Place 1 pint vanilla or desired-flavor ice cream, softened; 1 frosted cupcake; and 2 tablespoons milk in a blender. Cover and blend until combined. Pour into glasses. Makes 2 (1-cup) servings.

Orange Cream Pop Cupcakes

Prep: 40 minutes Bake: 18 minutes at 350°F Cool: 45 minutes
Makes 27 (2½-inch) cupcakes

1 3-ounce package orange-flavor gelatin
1 package 2-layer-size white cake mix
1 4-serving-size package cheesecake instant pudding and pie filling mix
1¼ cups orange juice
4 eggs
⅓ cup vegetable oil
1 teaspoon vanilla
1 recipe Cream Pop Frostings
   Wooden craft sticks (optional)

1. Preheat oven to 350°F. Line twenty-seven 2½-inch muffin cups with paper bake cups. Set aside 2 teaspoons of the gelatin for the Cream Pop Frostings. In a large mixing bowl beat remaining gelatin, cake mix, pudding mix, orange juice, eggs, oil, and vanilla with an electric mixer on medium speed until combined.

2. Spoon batter into prepared muffin cups, filling each about two-thirds full. Use the back of a spoon to smooth out batter in cups.

3. Bake for 18 to 20 minutes or until a toothpick inserted in centers comes out clean. Cool cupcakes in muffin cups on wire racks for 5 minutes. Remove cupcakes from muffin cups. Cool completely on wire racks.

4. Spoon orange-flavor Cream Pop Frosting into a pastry bag fitted with a large round tip. Spoon vanilla-flavor Cream Pop Frosting into another pastry bag fitted with a small star tip. Pipe orange frosting onto tops of cupcakes. Pipe a medium-size star of white frosting onto each cupcake. If desired, insert a craft stick into top of each cupcake.

Cream Pop Frostings
Prepare 1 recipe Cream Cheese Frosting (see recipe, page 14). Transfer one-fourth of the frosting to a small bowl. Beat in an additional ¼ teaspoon vanilla with an electric mixer on medium speed. To the remaining bowl of Cream Cheese Frosting add reserved 2 teaspoons orange gelatin from the cupcakes and 1 teaspoon finely shredded orange peel. If desired, add a few drops orange food coloring. Beat to combine.

Per cupcake: 304 cal., 12 g total fat (5 g sat. fat), 50 mg chol., 255 mg sodium, 47 g carb., 0 g dietary fiber, 41 g sugar, 3 g protein.

Cream Soda–Toffee Cupcakes

Prep: 30 minutes **Stand:** 30 minutes **Bake:** 18 minutes at 350°F **Cool:** 45 minutes
Makes 18 (2½-inch) cupcakes

½ cup butter
3 eggs
2 cups all-purpose flour
1½ teaspoons baking powder
½ teaspoon baking soda
¼ teaspoon salt
¾ cup granulated sugar
¼ cup packed brown sugar
1 tablespoon molasses
1½ teaspoons vanilla
½ cup buttermilk or sour milk (see tip, page 11)
½ cup cream soda (not diet)
½ cup almond toffee bits
1 recipe Browned-Butter Frosting
 Almond toffee bits

1. Allow butter and eggs to stand at room temperature for 30 minutes. Meanwhile, line eighteen 2½-inch muffin cups with paper bake cups. In a medium bowl stir together flour, baking powder, baking soda, and salt. Set aside.

2. Preheat oven to 350°F. In a large mixing bowl beat butter with an electric mixer on medium to high speed for 30 seconds. Add granulated sugar and brown sugar. Beat until combined, scraping sides of bowl occasionally. Add eggs, one at a time, beating well after each addition. Beat in molasses and vanilla.

3. Alternately add flour mixture, buttermilk, and cream soda to butter mixture, beating on low speed after each addition just until combined. Stir in ½ cup toffee bits. Spoon batter into prepared muffin cups, filling each about three-fourths full. Use the back of a spoon to smooth out batter in cups.

4. Bake about 18 minutes or until tops spring back when lightly touched. Cool in muffin cups on wire racks for 5 minutes. Remove cupcakes from muffin cups. Cool completely on wire racks. Spread Browned-Butter Frosting onto tops of cupcakes. Place additional toffee bits on a small plate. Roll frosted edges of cupcakes in toffee bits to coat.

Browned-Butter Frosting

In a small saucepan heat ¼ cup butter over medium-low heat about 8 minutes or until butter turns a light golden brown; cool. In a medium bowl beat ¼ cup softened butter with an electric mixer on medium to high speed for 30 seconds. Beat in browned butter until combined. Add 2 cups powdered sugar, ½ teaspoon vanilla, ⅛ teaspoon ground nutmeg, and a pinch salt, beating well. Beat in 1 to 2 tablespoons buttermilk until frosting reaches spreading consistency. Use immediately. (If frosting starts to set up, stir in a small amount of boiling water.)

Per cupcake: 307 cal., 14 g total fat (8 g sat. fat), 69 mg chol., 241 mg sodium, 42 g carb., 0 g dietary fiber, 31 g sugar, 3 g protein.

Root Beer Float Cupcakes

Prep: 45 minutes **Stand:** 30 minutes **Bake:** 15 minutes at 350°F **Cool:** 45 minutes

Makes 24 (2½-inch) cupcakes

¾ cup butter

3 eggs

2½ cups all-purpose flour

2½ teaspoons baking powder

½ teaspoon salt

1½ cups sugar

1 tablespoon root beer extract

½ teaspoon vanilla

1¼ cups root beer

1 recipe Float Frosting

24 root beer–flavor hard candies (optional)

12 colorful straws, cut in half (optional)

1. Allow butter and eggs to stand at room temperature for 30 minutes. Meanwhile, line twenty-four 2½-inch muffin cups with paper bake cups. In a medium bowl stir together flour, baking powder, and salt. Set aside.

2. Preheat oven to 350°F. In a large mixing bowl beat butter with an electric mixer on medium to high speed for 30 seconds. Gradually add sugar, about ¼ cup at a time, beating on medium speed until combined. Scrape sides of bowl; beat on medium speed about 2 minutes more or until light and fluffy. Add eggs, one at a time, beating well after each addition. Beat in root beer extract and vanilla. Alternately add flour mixture and root beer to butter mixture, beating on low speed after each addition just until combined.

3. Spoon batter into prepared muffin cups, filling each two-thirds to three-fourths full. Use the back of a spoon to smooth out batter in cups.

4. Bake for 15 to 17 minutes or until a wooden toothpick inserted in centers comes out clean. Cool cupcakes in muffin cups on wire racks for 10 minutes. Remove cupcakes from muffin cups. Cool completely on wire racks.

5. If desired, spoon Float Frosting into a pastry bag fitted with a large star tip. Pipe or spread Float Frosting onto tops of cupcakes. If desired, top each cupcake with a root beer–flavor candy and a straw half.

Float Frosting

Allow ¼ cup butter to stand at room temperature for 30 minutes. Allow ¾ cup ice cream to stand at room temperature for 10 minutes. In a large mixing bowl beat butter with an electric mixer on medium speed until fluffy. Beat in ½ cup of the ice cream and ½ teaspoon vanilla. Gradually beat in 4 cups powdered sugar. If necessary, stir in additional ice cream, 1 tablespoon at a time, until frosting reaches piping or spreading consistency.

Per cupcake: 268 cal., 9 g total fat (5 g sat. fat), 49 mg chol., 155 mg sodium, 45 g carb., 0 g dietary fiber, 35 g sugar, 2 g protein.

Neapolitan Cupcakes

Prep: 45 minutes **Bake:** 15 minutes at 350°F **Cool:** 45 minutes
Makes 22 to 26 (2½-inch) cupcakes

1 package 2-layer-size white cake mix

½ teaspoon vanilla

1 tablespoon unsweetened cocoa powder

1 ounce semisweet or bittersweet chocolate, melted

¼ cup strawberry preserves
  Red food coloring

1 recipe Ice Cream Frosting
  Desired sprinkles, such as jimmies

1. Line twenty-two to twenty-six 2½-inch muffin cups with paper bake cups.* Preheat oven to 350°F. Prepare cake mix according to package directions.

2. Divide cake batter evenly among three bowls. Stir vanilla into batter in one bowl. Stir cocoa powder and melted chocolate into batter in second bowl. Stir in strawberry preserves and enough red food coloring to turn batter pink in third bowl.

3. Spoon 1 tablespoon of the strawberry batter into the bottom of each prepared muffin cup. Add 1 tablespoon chocolate batter to each muffin cup. Top each muffin cup with 1 tablespoon vanilla batter. (Cups will be one-half to two-thirds full.)

4. Bake about 15 minutes or until a toothpick inserted in centers comes out clean. Cool cupcakes in muffin cups on wire racks for 5 minutes. Remove cupcakes from muffin cups. Cool completely on wire racks.

5. Tint half of the Ice Cream Frosting pink with red food coloring. Spoon pink and white frostings side by side into a pastry bag fitted with a star tip. Pipe frosting onto tops of cupcakes to look like soft-serve ice cream; decorate as desired with sprinkles. Chill until ready to serve.

Ice Cream Frosting

Allow half of an 8-ounce package cream cheese and ⅓ cup butter to stand at room temperature for 30 minutes. If desired, allow ¼ cup vanilla ice cream to stand at room temperature for 10 minutes. In a large mixing bowl beat cream cheese and butter with an electric mixer on medium speed until fluffy. Beat in 2 teaspoons vanilla. Gradually beat in 5½ cups powdered sugar. Beat in ice cream (if using) or ¼ cup whipping cream until frosting reaches piping consistency. Chill until ready to use.

*Test Kitchen Tip:

To make cupcake cones, wrap the bases of 24 to 30 flat-bottom ice cream cones in foil. Place one cone in each cup of a muffin pan. If necessary, press foil into cups around the cones to secure in place. Layer batter in cones as directed in step 3, using about 3 tablespoons batter total (no more than one-half full); let batter settle in cones. (Before filling all cones, bake one pan to double-check batter amounts.) Bake at 350°F for 25 to 30 minutes or until a toothpick inserted in centers comes out clean. Cool completely. Frost as directed.

Per cupcake: 322 cal., 11 g total fat (5 g sat. fat), 43 mg chol., 210 mg sodium, 54 g carb., 1 g dietary fiber, 44 g sugar, 2 g protein.

Shamrock Milk Shake Cupcakes

Prep: 50 minutes **Stand:** 30 minutes **Bake:** 15 minutes at 350°F **Cool:** 45 minutes
Makes 20 to 22 (2½-inch) cupcakes

4   egg whites
2   cups all-purpose flour
1   teaspoon baking powder
½   teaspoon baking soda
½   teaspoon salt
1   cup buttermilk or sour milk (see tip, page 11)
¼   cup green crème de menthe*
½   cup shortening
1¾ cups sugar
1   teaspoon vanilla
1   recipe White Chocolate Frosting
    Green food coloring

1. Allow egg whites to stand at room temperature for 30 minutes. Meanwhile, line twenty to twenty-two 2½-inch muffin cups with paper bake cups. In a medium bowl stir together flour, baking powder, baking soda, and salt. In a 2-cup glass measuring cup combine buttermilk and crème de menthe. Set aside.

2. Preheat oven to 350°F. In a large mixing bowl beat shortening with an electric mixer on medium to high speed for 30 seconds. Gradually add sugar, about ¼ cup at a time, beating on medium speed until light and fluffy. Beat in vanilla. Add egg whites, one at a time, beating well after each addition. Alternately add flour mixture and buttermilk mixture to shortening mixture, beating on low speed after each addition just until combined.

3. Spoon batter into prepared muffin cups, filling each about two-thirds full. Use the back of a spoon to smooth out batter in cups.

4. Bake for 15 to 18 minutes or until tops spring back when lightly touched. Cool cupcakes in muffin cups on wire racks for 5 minutes. Remove cupcakes from muffin cups. Cool completely on wire racks.

5. Divide White Chocolate Frosting between two bowls. Tint one portion with green food coloring. Spoon each frosting into a separate pastry bag fitted with a large star tip. Pipe white and green frostings onto tops of cupcakes to resemble four-leaf clovers.

White Chocolate Frosting

Allow 1 cup butter, cut up, to stand at room temperature for 30 minutes. Meanwhile, place 6 ounces white baking chocolate with cocoa butter, chopped, in a large mixing bowl. In a small saucepan heat ⅓ cup whipping cream just until simmering. Pour over white chocolate (do not stir). Let stand for 5 minutes. Stir until smooth. Cool for 15 minutes. Gradually add butter to white chocolate mixture, beating with an electric mixer on medium to high speed until combined. Gradually beat in 1½ to 2 cups powdered sugar until frosting reaches piping or spreading consistency.

*Test Kitchen Tip:

If you prefer not to use crème de menthe, substitute a mixture of ¼ cup milk, 1 teaspoon mint extract, and several drops green food coloring.

Per cupcake: 358 cal., 18 g total fat (10 g sat. fat), 32 mg chol., 208 mg sodium, 43 g carb., 0 g dietary fiber, 33 g sugar, 3 g protein.

Red Velvet Cupcakes

Prep: 40 minutes **Stand:** 30 minutes **Bake:** 20 minutes at 350°F **Cool:** 45 minutes

Makes 26 (2½-inch) cupcakes

¾ cup butter

3 eggs

3 cups all-purpose flour

1 tablespoon unsweetened cocoa powder

¾ teaspoon salt

2¼ cups sugar

1 1-ounce bottle red food coloring (2 tablespoons)

2 tablespoons raspberry liqueur or milk

1 teaspoon vanilla

1⅓ cups buttermilk or sour milk (see tip, page 11)

1½ teaspoons baking soda

1½ teaspoons vinegar

1 recipe Cream Cheese-Raspberry Frosting

Fresh raspberries (optional)

1. Allow butter and eggs to stand at room temperature for 30 minutes. Meanwhile, line twenty-six 2½-inch muffin cups with paper bake cups or parchment paper. In a medium bowl stir together flour, cocoa powder, and salt. Set aside.

2. Preheat oven to 350°F. In a very large mixing bowl beat butter with an electric mixer on medium to high speed for 30 seconds. Gradually add sugar, about ¼ cup at a time, beating on medium speed until combined. Scrape sides of bowl; beat on medium speed about 2 minutes more or until light and fluffy. Add eggs, one at a time, beating well after each addition. Beat in red food coloring, liqueur, and vanilla. Alternately add flour mixture and buttermilk to butter mixture, beating on low speed after each addition just until combined. In a small bowl combine baking soda and vinegar; fold into batter.

3. Spoon batter into prepared muffin cups, filling each about three-fourths full. Use the back of a spoon to smooth out batter in cups.

4. Bake about 20 minutes or until tops spring back when lightly touched. Cool cupcakes in muffin cups on wire racks for 5 minutes. Remove cupcakes from muffin cups. Cool completely on wire racks.

5. Spread Cream Cheese-Raspberry Frosting onto tops of cupcakes. If desired, top with fresh raspberries.

Cream Cheese-Raspberry Frosting

Allow half of an 8-ounce package cream cheese and ⅓ cup butter to stand at room temperature for 30 minutes. In a large mixing bowl beat cream cheese, butter, 2 tablespoons raspberry liqueur or milk, and 1 teaspoon vanilla with an electric mixer on medium speed until light and fluffy. Gradually beat in 4 cups powdered sugar. If necessary, beat in milk, 1 teaspoon at a time (1 to 3 teaspoons total), until frosting reaches spreading consistency.

Per cupcake: 298 cal., 10 g total fat (6 g sat. fat), 50 mg chol., 230 mg sodium, 49 g carb., 0 g dietary fiber, 37 g sugar, 3 g protein.

Liner Lesson

Making your own cupcake liners with parchment paper or waxed paper is easy and stylish. To start, cut out 6-inch squares of parchment or waxed paper. Press one paper square at a time into a muffin cup so the paper forms a flat bottom. Press the folds in the paper flat against the sides of the cup to create pleats. To avoid splattering batter on the liner's sides spoon batter into a large resealable plastic bag and snip a small hole in one corner. While holding onto the paper liner with one hand, pipe batter into liner (about 3 tablespoons). Repeat with remaining liners and batter.

Boston Cream Pies

Prep: 30 minutes **Chill:** 3 to 25 hours
Makes 12 (2½-inch) cupcakes

3 egg yolks
⅓ cup sugar
3 tablespoons cornstarch
1⅓ cups milk
2 tablespoons butter
1 teaspoon vanilla
12 2½-inch Vanilla Cupcakes (see recipe, page 10)
1 6-ounce package semisweet chocolate pieces (1 cup)
½ cup whipping cream

1. For vanilla cream, in a small bowl lightly beat egg yolks. Set aside. In a medium saucepan combine sugar and cornstarch. Whisk in milk. Cook and stir over medium heat until thickened and bubbly. Cook and stir for 2 minutes more.

2. Gradually add about 1 cup of the hot mixture to the egg yolks, stirring constantly. Return all of the mixture to the saucepan. Cook and stir until bubbly. Cook and stir for 2 minutes more. Remove from heat. Stir in butter until melted. Stir in vanilla. Cover surface with plastic wrap. Chill in the refrigerator for at least 2 hours or up to 24 hours.

3. To assemble, remove paper liners from cupcakes, if present. Using a serrated knife, cut each Vanilla Cupcake horizontally in half. Spoon 1 heaping tablespoon of the vanilla cream onto the cut side of each cupcake bottom. Replace cupcake tops. Place cupcakes on a wire rack set over waxed paper.

4. For ganache, in a medium microwave-safe bowl microwave chocolate pieces and whipping cream on 100% power (high) for 1 to 2 minutes or until chocolate is almost melted. Stir until smooth.

5. Spoon ganache over cupcakes. Let stand just until ganache is set. Chill in the refrigerator for at least 1 hour before serving.

Per cupcake: 401 cal., 24 g total fat (14 g sat. fat), 160 mg chol., 177 mg sodium, 43 g carb., 1 g dietary fiber, 28 g sugar, 5 g protein.

Malibu Rum Baby Cakes

Prep: 40 minutes Stand: 15 minutes Bake: 20 minutes at 350°F Cool: 5 minutes
Makes 6 baby cakes

¼ cup butter

1 egg

1 8-ounce can pineapple slices (juice pack)

¼ cup Malibu rum or light rum

¼ cup dried apricots, quartered

½ cup packed brown sugar

3 tablespoons butter
   Nonstick cooking spray

1⅓ cups all-purpose flour

¼ cup flaked coconut

2 teaspoons baking powder

½ cup granulated sugar
   Whipped cream (optional)

1. Allow ¼ cup butter and egg to stand at room temperature for 30 minutes. Meanwhile, drain pineapple well, reserving juice (you should have about ⅓ cup juice). Set pineapple slices aside. In a small saucepan combine reserved pineapple juice, rum, and apricots. Bring just to boiling; remove from heat. Let stand for 15 minutes. Strain, reserving both the juice mixture and the apricots. In the same saucepan combine brown sugar, 3 tablespoons butter, and 1 tablespoon of the reserved juice mixture. Cook and stir over medium heat until butter is melted and sugar is dissolved.

2. Lightly coat the insides of six 10-ounce ramekins or custard cups with cooking spray. Spoon the brown sugar mixture evenly into the prepared ramekins. Cut each pineapple slice into six pieces. Arrange pineapple and apricots on top of brown sugar mixture. Set aside.

3. Preheat oven to 350°F. In a small bowl stir together flour, coconut, and baking powder. Set aside. Measure the remaining juice mixture, adding water to equal ⅔ cup total liquid. Set aside. In a medium mixing bowl beat ¼ cup butter with an electric mixer on medium to high speed for 30 seconds. Add granulated sugar. Beat until fluffy, scraping sides of bowl occasionally. Add egg, beating until combined. Alternately add juice mixture and flour mixture to butter mixture, beating on low speed after each addition just until combined. Gently spoon batter over fruit in ramekins.

4. Bake for 20 to 25 minutes or until a wooden toothpick inserted near centers comes out clean. Cool cupcakes in ramekins on wire racks for 5 minutes. Loosen cupcakes from ramekins; invert onto a serving platter. If desired, top each cake with whipped cream. Serve warm.

Test Kitchen Tip:
To reheat cakes, preheat oven to 350°F. Wrap cakes loosely in foil and bake about 10 minutes or until heated through. Or microwave, uncovered, on 50% power (medium) for 1 to 2 minutes or until heated through.

Per baby cake: 446 cal., 16 g total fat (10 g sat. fat), 67 mg chol., 233 mg sodium, 67 g carb., 2 g dietary fiber, 44 g sugar, 5 g protein.

Berry Shortcakes

Prep: 40 minutes **Cool:** 30 minutes
Makes 12 (2½-inch) cupcakes

1 cup fresh strawberries, cut up; blueberries; and/or raspberries

¼ cup water

½ cup sugar

12 Yellow Cupcakes (see recipe, page 10)

1 cup whipping cream

¼ cup sour cream

2 tablespoons sugar or honey

2½ cups fresh strawberries, halved; blueberries; and/or raspberries

White chocolate shavings and/or curls*

1. In a small saucepan bring 1 cup berries and the water to boiling; reduce heat. Simmer, covered, for 5 minutes. Press the mixture through a fine-mesh sieve; discard any solids. Return juice to saucepan. Stir in ½ cup sugar. Bring mixture to boiling, stirring to dissolve sugar. Boil gently, uncovered, for 2 minutes. Transfer to a bowl; cool about 30 minutes.

2. Using a fork, poke holes in tops of Yellow Cupcakes. Slowly spoon juice mixture over cupcakes. Set aside.

3. In a medium mixing bowl beat whipping cream, sour cream, and 2 tablespoons sugar with an electric mixer on medium speed until soft peaks form (tips curl). If desired, spoon cream mixture into a pastry bag fitted with a large star tip. Generously spoon or pipe mixture onto tops of cupcakes. Serve immediately or chill in the refrigerator for up to 4 hours.

4. To serve, garnish tops of cupcakes with 2½ cups berries. Sprinkle with white chocolate shavings and/or curls.

*Test Kitchen Tip:

To make white chocolate shavings or curls, pull a vegetable peeler along one edge of a 1-ounce square of white baking chocolate or white candy coating.

Per cupcake: 316 cal., 16 g total fat (10 g sat. fat), 73 mg chol., 142 mg sodium, 41 g carb., 1 g dietary fiber, 30 g sugar, 4 g protein.

Sweet Potato Pie Cupcakes

Prep: 45 minutes Stand: 30 minutes Bake: 20 minutes at 350°F Cool: 45 minutes
Makes 24 (2½-inch) cupcakes

1 cup butter

3 eggs

2 cups all-purpose flour

2 teaspoons baking powder

1 teaspoon ground cinnamon

½ teaspoon baking soda

¼ teaspoon salt

1½ cups sugar

1 17.2-ounce can vacuum-pack whole sweet potatoes (unsweetened), mashed

½ teaspoon vanilla

1 recipe Bourbon-Cream Cheese Frosting

Finely shredded orange peel

1. Allow butter and eggs to stand at room temperature for 30 minutes. Meanwhile, line twenty-four 2½-inch muffin cups with paper bake cups. In a medium bowl stir together flour, baking powder, cinnamon, baking soda, and salt. Set aside.

2. Preheat oven to 350°F. In a large mixing bowl beat butter with an electric mixer on medium to high speed for 30 seconds. Gradually add sugar, about ¼ cup at a time, beating on medium speed until combined. Scrape sides of bowl; beat about 2 minutes more or until light and fluffy. Add eggs, one at a time, beating well after each addition. Beat in sweet potatoes and vanilla. Add flour mixture. Beat until combined (batter will be thick).

3. Spoon batter into prepared muffin cups, filling each about three-fourths full. Use the back of a spoon to smooth out batter in cups.

4. Bake about 20 minutes or until tops spring back when lightly touched. Cool cupcakes in muffin cups on wire racks for 1 minute. Remove cupcakes from muffin cups. Cool completely on wire racks.

5. Spoon Bourbon-Cream Cheese Frosting into a large resealable plastic bag. Snip off a ¼-inch piece from one corner of bag. Pipe frosting onto tops of cupcakes. Sprinkle with orange peel.

Bourbon-Cream Cheese Frosting

Allow one 8-ounce package cream cheese and ⅔ cup butter to stand at room temperature for 30 minutes. In a large mixing bowl beat cream cheese and butter with an electric mixer on medium speed until light and fluffy. Beat in 2 tablespoons bourbon or milk. Gradually beat in 8 cups powdered sugar until frosting reaches piping consistency.

Make-Ahead Directions:

Place unfrosted cupcakes in a single layer in an airtight container; seal. Store at room temperature for up to 3 days. Or freeze for up to 1 month. Thaw cupcakes at room temperature before frosting.

Per cupcake: 400 cal., 17 g total fat (10 g sat. fat), 71 mg chol., 210 mg sodium, 60 g carb., 1 g dietary fiber, 48 g sugar, 3 g protein.

Lemon Meringue Pie Cupcakes

Prep: 35 minutes **Stand:** 30 minutes **Bake:** 22 minutes at 350°F **Cool:** 45 minutes

Makes 15 (2½-inch) cupcakes

4	eggs
½	cup butter
1½	cups all-purpose flour
1½	teaspoons baking powder
¼	teaspoon salt
⅔	cup milk
¼	cup lemon curd
¾	cup granulated sugar
1½	teaspoons vanilla
2	tablespoons lemon curd
¼	teaspoon cream of tartar
⅔	cup granulated sugar
	Powdered sugar

Piping Meringue

If you choose to pipe meringue onto the cupcakes, use a new plastic disposable pastry bag (see page 19) or a heavy-duty resealable plastic bag with a corner snipped off. Used pastry bags may contain oil residues that will affect the meringue quality.

1. Separate eggs. Allow egg yolks, egg whites, and butter to stand at room temperature for 30 minutes. Meanwhile, line fifteen 2½-inch muffin cups with paper bake cups. In a small bowl stir together flour, baking powder, and salt. In another small bowl whisk together milk and ¼ cup lemon curd until nearly smooth. Set aside.

2. Preheat oven to 350°F. In a large mixing bowl beat butter with an electric mixer on medium to high speed for 30 seconds. Add ¾ cup granulated sugar. Beat on medium to high speed for 1 minute. Add egg yolks and vanilla. Beat until combined. Alternately add flour mixture and milk mixture to butter mixture, beating on low speed after each addition just until combined.

3. Spoon batter into prepared muffin cups, filling each about two-thirds full. Use the back of a spoon to smooth out batter in cups.

4. Bake about 15 minutes or until golden and tops spring back when lightly touched.

5. Meanwhile, place 2 tablespoons lemon curd in a small heavy resealable plastic bag. Snip off a small piece from one corner of bag. Set aside. Wash beaters thoroughly. For meringue, in a clean large mixing bowl combine egg whites and cream of tartar. Beat on medium speed until soft peaks form (tips curl). Gradually add ⅔ cup granulated sugar, 1 tablespoon at a time, beating on high speed until stiff peaks form (tips stand straight).

6. Remove cupcakes from oven. Pipe a small amount of lemon curd onto the center of each cupcake. Pipe or spoon meringue onto tops of cupcakes (see tip, left).

7. Bake about 7 minutes more or until meringue is lightly browned. Cool cupcakes in muffin cups on wire racks for 5 minutes. Remove cupcakes from muffin cups. Cool for 30 to 45 minutes before serving or cover loosely and chill in the refrigerator for up to 4 hours. Dust with powdered sugar before serving.

Per cupcake: 229 cal., 8 g total fat (5 g sat. fat), 80 mg chol., 148 mg sodium, 36 g carb., 1 g dietary fiber, 26 g sugar, 3 g protein.

Snickerdoodle Cookie Cups

Prep: 35 minutes **Chill:** 1 hour **Bake:** 15 minutes at 375°F **Cool:** 45 minutes
Makes 24 to 26 (2½-inch) cupcakes

1 cup butter, softened

1½ cups sugar

1 teaspoon baking soda

1 teaspoon cream of tartar

¼ teaspoon salt

2 eggs

1 teaspoon vanilla

3 cups all-purpose flour

1 cup almond toffee bits

½ cup chopped pecans, toasted

¼ cup sugar

1 teaspoon ground cinnamon

1 teaspoon freshly grated nutmeg or ½ teaspoon ground nutmeg

1 recipe Spiced Buttercream Frosting

  Crushed almond toffee bits (optional)

1. In a large mixing bowl beat butter with an electric mixer on medium to high speed for 30 seconds. Add 1½ cups sugar, baking soda, cream of tartar, and salt. Beat until combined, scraping sides of bowl occasionally. Add eggs, one at a time, beating after each addition just until combined. Beat in vanilla. Beat in as much of the flour as you can with the mixer. Using a wooden spoon, stir in any remaining flour, 1 cup toffee bits, and pecans. Cover and chill about 1 hour or until dough is easy to handle.

2. Preheat oven to 375°F. Line twenty-four to twenty-six 2½-inch muffin cups with paper bake cups or grease and lightly flour muffin cups. In a small bowl combine ¼ cup sugar, cinnamon, and nutmeg.

3. Use a rounded 2-tablespoon scoop to measure dough. Shape into balls. Roll balls in sugar mixture to coat. Press each ball lightly into a prepared muffin cup, making tops of all cookie cups even.

4. Bake for 15 to 18 minutes or until tops are lightly browned and edges are just firm (centers will dip slightly). Cool in muffin cups on wire racks for 5 minutes. Remove cookie cups from muffin cups. Cool completely on wire racks.

5. Spoon Spiced Buttercream Frosting into a pastry bag fitted with a large star tip. Pipe frosting onto tops of cookie cups into tall swirls. If desired, sprinkle with crushed toffee bits.

Spiced Buttercream Frosting

Allow ⅔ cup butter to stand at room temperature for 30 minutes. In a large mixing bowl beat butter with an electric mixer on medium speed until smooth. Add 2 cups powdered sugar, beating well. Beat in ¼ cup milk, 1 teaspoon vanilla, ¼ teaspoon ground cinnamon, and ¼ teaspoon freshly grated nutmeg or pinch ground nutmeg. Gradually beat in an additional 6 cups powdered sugar. Beat in 2 to 4 teaspoons milk until frosting reaches spreading consistency.

Make-Ahead Directions:

Place frosted cupcakes in a single layer in airtight containers; seal. Store in the refrigerator for up to 3 days. Or freeze for up to 3 months.

Per cupcake: 454 cal., 18 g total fat (10 g sat. fat), 56 mg chol., 238 mg sodium, 72 g carb., 1 g dietary fiber, 59 g sugar, 3 g protein.

Sticky Pecan Upside-Down Baby Cakes

Prep: 20 minutes **Bake:** 25 minutes at 350°F **Cool:** 5 minutes
Makes 12 (3½-inch) baby cakes

Nonstick spray for baking
⅔ cup packed brown sugar
½ cup butter
⅓ cup honey
1½ cups coarsely chopped pecans
1 teaspoon finely shredded orange peel
2½ cups all-purpose flour
1 teaspoon baking powder
½ teaspoon baking soda
½ teaspoon salt
3 eggs
2 cups granulated sugar
1 cup vegetable oil
1 8-ounce carton sour cream
2 teaspoons vanilla

1. Line a large baking sheet with foil. Lightly coat twelve 3½-inch (jumbo) muffin cups with nonstick spray for baking. Set aside.

2. Preheat oven to 350°F. In a medium saucepan combine brown sugar, butter, and honey. Cook and stir over medium heat about 2 minutes or until smooth. Remove from heat. Stir in pecans and orange peel. Set aside.

3. In a medium bowl stir together flour, baking powder, baking soda, and salt. Set aside.

4. In a large mixing bowl beat eggs and granulated sugar with an electric mixer on medium to high speed about 3 minutes or until thick and lemon-color. Add oil, sour cream, and vanilla. Beat until combined. Gradually add flour mixture, beating on low speed until smooth.

5. Place 2 tablespoons of the pecan mixture in the bottom of each prepared muffin cup. Spoon a heaping ⅓ cup of the batter into each cup. Place muffin cups on prepared baking sheet.

6. Bake for 25 to 30 minutes or until a wooden toothpick inserted in the centers comes out clean. Cool cupcakes in muffin cups on wire racks for 5 minutes. Using a sharp knife or narrow metal spatula, loosen edges of cupcakes from sides of muffin cups. Invert cupcakes onto wire racks. Spoon any pecan mixture remaining in the muffin cups onto cupcakes. Serve warm or cool.

Per baby cake: 679 cal., 41 g total fat (10 g sat. fat), 77 mg chol., 285 mg sodium, 76 g carb., 2 g dietary fiber, 55 g sugar, 6 g protein.

Jelly-Filled Doughnut Cupcakes

Prep: 35 minutes **Stand:** 30 minutes **Bake:** 15 minutes at 350°F **Cool:** 45 minutes
Makes 18 (2½-inch) cupcakes

½	cup butter
2	eggs
2⅓	cups all-purpose flour
2½	teaspoons baking powder
½	teaspoon baking soda
½	teaspoon salt
½	cup granulated sugar
½	cup packed brown sugar
1½	teaspoons vanilla
1	cup milk
1	cup raspberry, strawberry, or cherry jelly; lemon curd; and/or orange marmalade
¼	cup powdered sugar

1. Allow butter and eggs to stand at room temperature for 30 minutes. Meanwhile, line eighteen 2½-inch muffin cups with paper bake cups or waxed paper. In a medium bowl stir together flour, baking powder, baking soda, and salt. Set aside.

2. Preheat oven to 350°F. In a large mixing bowl beat butter with an electric mixer on medium to high speed for 30 seconds. Add granulated sugar, brown sugar, and vanilla. Beat until combined, scraping sides of bowl occasionally. Add eggs, one at a time, beating well after each addition. Alternately add flour mixture and milk to butter mixture, beating on low speed after each addition just until combined.

3. Spoon batter into prepared muffin cups, filling each about two-thirds full. Use the back of a spoon to smooth batter.

4. Bake for 15 to 18 minutes or until a toothpick inserted in centers comes out clean. Cool cupcakes in muffin cups on wire racks for 5 minutes. Remove cupcakes from muffin cups. Cool completely on wire racks.

5. Spoon jelly, lemon curd, and/or marmalade into pastry bag(s) fitted with small round tip(s). Insert tip into the top of each cupcake and squeeze the jelly, lemon curd, and/or marmalade into cupcake until some is visible on top. Dust cupcakes with powdered sugar.

Make-Ahead Directions:
Store cupcakes in a single layer in an airtight container in the refrigerator for up to 3 days.

Per cupcake: 221 cal., 6 g total fat (4 g sat. fat), 38 mg chol., 207 mg sodium, 40 g carb., 1 g dietary fiber, 24 g sugar, 3 g protein.

Cinnamon Roll Cupcakes

Prep: 45 minutes **Stand:** 30 minutes **Bake:** 18 minutes at 350°F **Cool:** 45 minutes

Makes 26 (2½-inch) cupcakes

⅔ cup butter

2 eggs

2½ cups all-purpose flour

2½ teaspoons baking powder

½ teaspoon salt

¾ cup packed brown sugar

⅓ cup finely chopped pecans

2 teaspoons ground cinnamon

1¾ cups granulated sugar

1½ teaspoons vanilla

1¼ cups milk

1 recipe Creamy Butter Frosting

1. Allow butter and eggs to stand at room temperature for 30 minutes. Meanwhile, line twenty-six 2½-inch muffin cups with paper bake cups. In a medium bowl stir together flour, baking powder, and salt. In a small bowl stir together brown sugar, pecans, and cinnamon. Set aside.

2. Preheat oven to 350°F. In a large mixing bowl beat butter with an electric mixer on medium to high speed for 30 seconds. Gradually add granulated sugar, about ¼ cup at a time, beating on medium speed until combined, scraping sides of bowl occasionally. Beat on medium speed about 2 minutes more or until light and fluffy. Add eggs, one at a time, beating well after each addition. Beat in vanilla. Alternately add flour mixture and milk to butter mixture, beating on low speed after each addition just until combined (batter may look curdled).

3. Spoon about 1 tablespoon of the batter into each prepared muffin cup. Sprinkle about 1 teaspoon of the brown sugar mixture over batter in cups. Spoon remaining batter evenly over brown sugar mixture in cups. Sprinkle with the remaining brown sugar mixture.

4. Bake for 18 to 20 minutes or until a toothpick inserted in centers comes out clean. Cool cupcakes in muffin cups on wire racks for 10 minutes. Remove cupcakes from muffin cups. Cool completely on wire racks.

5. Spread Creamy Butter Frosting onto tops of cupcakes. Store in the refrigerator.

Creamy Butter Frosting

Allow 1 cup butter to stand at room temperature for 30 minutes. In a large mixing bowl beat butter with an electric mixer on medium to high speed for 30 seconds. Beat in 1 teaspoon vanilla and pinch salt. Gradually add 4 cups powdered sugar, beating well. Beat in ¼ cup whipping cream. Beat in an additional 4 cups powdered sugar. Beat in 2 to 3 tablespoons whipping cream until frosting is light and fluffy and reaches spreading consistency.

Make-Ahead Directions:

Store frosted cupcakes in a single layer in an airtight container in the refrigerator for up to 2 days.

Per cupcake: 403 cal., 15 g total fat (9 g sat. fat), 53 mg chol., 183 mg sodium, 67 g carb., 1 g dietary fiber, 57 g sugar, 2 g protein.

Honey Bun Cupcakes:

Prepare and bake cupcakes as directed through step 4, except cool cupcakes in muffin cups on wire racks for only 10 minutes. Meanwhile, in a medium bowl stir together 2 cups powdered sugar and 2 tablespoons honey. Stir in 2 to 3 tablespoons milk, 2 teaspoons at a time, until mixture reaches glazing consistency. Using a wooden toothpick, poke holes into tops of warm cupcakes. Spoon glaze over cupcakes, spreading evenly. Serve warm.

Per cupcake: 226 cal., 6 g total fat (3 g sat. fat), 30 mg chol., 126 mg sodium, 41 g carb., 1 g dietary fiber, 45 g sugar, 2 g protein

Blueberry Muffin Cupcakes

Prep: 40 minutes **Stand:** 30 minutes **Bake:** 15 minutes at 350°F **Cool:** 45 minutes

Makes 24 (2½-inch) cupcakes

1 cup butter

4 eggs

1⅓ cups all-purpose flour

½ cup cornmeal

2 tablespoons cornstarch

2 teaspoons baking powder

¼ teaspoon salt

1 cup sugar

2 teaspoons vanilla

1½ cups fresh blueberries

1 recipe Streusel Topping

1 recipe Vanilla Icing (optional)

1. Allow butter and eggs to stand at room temperature for 30 minutes. Meanwhile, line twenty-four 2½-inch muffin cups with paper bake cups. In a medium bowl stir together flour, cornmeal, cornstarch, baking powder, and salt. Set aside.

2. Preheat oven to 350°F. In a large mixing bowl beat butter with an electric mixer on medium to high speed for 30 seconds. Gradually add sugar, about ¼ cup at a time, beating on medium speed until combined. Scrape sides of bowl; beat about 5 minutes or until light and fluffy. Beat in vanilla. Add eggs, one at a time, beating on low to medium speed for 1 minute after each addition and scraping sides of bowl frequently. Add flour mixture, stirring just until combined.

3. Spoon batter into prepared muffin cups, filling each two-thirds to three-fourths full. Sprinkle blueberries over batter in muffin cups. Sprinkle with Streusel Topping.

4. Bake for 15 to 18 minutes or until a toothpick inserted in centers comes out clean (avoid berries when inserting toothpick). Cool cupcakes in muffin cups on wire racks for 10 minutes. Remove cupcakes from muffin cups. Cool completely on wire racks. If desired, drizzle cupcakes with Vanilla Icing.

Streusel Topping

In a medium bowl combine 1 cup all-purpose flour, ⅓ cup packed brown sugar, ½ teaspoon ground cinnamon, and ⅛ teaspoon salt. With a pastry blender, cut in ¼ cup butter until mixture resembles coarse crumbs.

Vanilla Icing

Allow 1 tablespoon butter to stand at room temperature for 30 minutes. In a medium bowl combine butter, 1½ cups powdered sugar, and ½ teaspoon vanilla. Stir in 1 to 2 tablespoons milk to make icing drizzling consistency.

Make-Ahead Directions:

Place uniced cupcakes in a single layer in an airtight container; seal. Store at room temperature for up to 2 days. Or freeze for up to 1 month. Thaw cupcakes at room temperature before icing.

Per cupcake: 239 cal., 11 g total fat (7 g sat. fat), 62 mg chol., 152 mg sodium, 33 g carb., 1 g dietary fiber, 20 g sugar, 3 g protein.

Mix and Match Berries

Customize these cupcakes by mixing and matching your favorite berries. Swap all or part of the 1½ cups blueberries with raspberries, blackberries, and/or chopped strawberries.

Chai Breakfast Cupcakes

Prep: 25 minutes **Stand:** 30 minutes **Bake:** 15 minutes at 350°F **Cool:** 45 minutes

Makes 24 (2½-inch) cupcakes

½ cup butter

2 eggs

1½ cups all-purpose flour

½ cup whole wheat flour

1½ teaspoons baking powder

½ teaspoon baking soda

½ teaspoon ground ginger

¼ teaspoon salt

1¼ cups milk

4 chai tea bags

1½ cups sugar

½ teaspoon vanilla

¾ cup maple-flavor granola or granola with dried fruit

1 recipe Chai Cream Cheese Icing (optional)

1. Allow butter and eggs to stand at room temperature for 30 minutes. Meanwhile, line twenty-four 2½-inch muffin cups with paper bake cups. In a medium bowl stir together all-purpose flour, whole wheat flour, baking powder, baking soda, ginger, and salt. Set aside. In a small saucepan heat milk just until simmering. Remove from heat. Add tea bags; steep for 5 minutes. Remove tea bags, pressing bags to release excess tea back into saucepan. Cool.

2. Preheat oven to 350°F. In a large mixing bowl beat butter with an electric mixer on medium to high speed about 1 minute or until fluffy. Add sugar and vanilla. Beat until combined, scraping sides of bowl occasionally. Add eggs, one at a time, beating well after each addition. Alternately add flour mixture and milk mixture to butter mixture, beating on low speed after each addition just until combined.

3. Spoon batter into prepared muffin cups, filling each about two-thirds full. Use the back of a spoon to smooth out batter in cups. Sprinkle with granola.

4. Bake for 15 to 20 minutes or until a wooden toothpick inserted in centers comes out clean. Cool cupcakes in muffin cups on wire racks for 5 minutes. Remove cupcakes from muffin cups. Cool completely on wire racks. If desired, drizzle with Chai Cream Cheese Icing.

Chai Cream Cheese Icing

Allow one 3-ounce package cream cheese and 2 tablespoons butter to stand at room temperature for 30 minutes. In a large mixing bowl beat cream cheese, butter, and 1 teaspoon vanilla with an electric mixer on medium to high speed until light and fluffy. Gradually beat in 1¼ cups powdered sugar. Beat in enough cooled, strong brewed chai tea, 1 teaspoon at a time, to make icing drizzling consistency.

Make-Ahead Directions:

Place uniced cupcakes in a single layer in an airtight container; seal. Freeze for up to 1 month. Thaw at room temperature before icing.

Per cupcake: 181 cal., 6 g total fat (3 g sat. fat), 35 mg chol., 138 mg sodium, 29 g carb., 1 g dietary fiber, 17 g sugar, 3 g protein.

Peanut Butter
Cupcakes,
page 74

Filled and Stuffed Cupcakes

Could they be the eighth wonder of the world? One bite will make a believer out of anyone. Rich, decadent cupcakes are made even more lavish with baked-in creamy centers, fabulous fillings, and fluffy layers of goodness. For these sweet cakes, the marvel is all in the middle and waiting to be revealed.

Buttercakes with Sour Cream Frosting

Prep: 45 minutes **Stand:** 30 minutes **Bake:** 15 minutes at 350°F **Cool:** 45 minutes

Makes 24 (2½-inch) cupcakes

1 cup butter

3 eggs

2 cups all-purpose flour

2 teaspoons baking powder

½ teaspoon baking soda

¼ teaspoon salt

1⅓ cups sugar

2 teaspoons vanilla

⅔ cup buttermilk or sour milk (see tip, page 11)

½ cup raspberry or strawberry jam

1 recipe Sour Cream Frosting

Pastel-color sprinkles, nonpareils, or small candies (optional)

1. Allow butter and eggs to stand at room temperature for 30 minutes. Meanwhile, line twenty-four 2½-inch muffin cups with paper bake cups. In a medium bowl stir together flour, baking powder, baking soda, and salt. Set aside.

2. Preheat oven to 350°F. In a large mixing bowl beat butter with an electric mixer on medium to high speed for 30 seconds. Add sugar. Beat until light and fluffy, scraping sides of bowl occasionally. Add eggs, one at a time, beating well after each addition. Beat in vanilla. Alternately add flour mixture and buttermilk to butter mixture, beating on low speed after each addition just until combined.

3. Spoon batter into prepared muffin cups, filling each about two-thirds full. Bake for 15 to 18 minutes or until a wooden toothpick inserted in centers comes out clean. Cool cupcakes in muffin cups on wire racks for 5 minutes. Remove cupcakes from muffin cups. Cool completely on wire racks.

4. Using the handle of a wooden spoon, make an indentation in the center of each cupcake. Spoon jam into a pastry bag fitted with a small round tip. Pipe a scant teaspoon of jam into each indentation. Spoon Sour Cream Frosting into another pastry bag fitted with an open star tip. Pipe five large rosettes around the top edge of each cupcake. Pipe one rosette in the center of each cupcake, making sure it touches the other five rosettes. If desired, decorate with sprinkles. Chill until ready to serve.

Sour Cream Frosting

Allow ½ cup butter to stand at room temperature for 30 minutes. In a large mixing bowl beat butter with an electric mixer on medium to high speed for 30 seconds. Beat in one 8-ounce carton sour cream and 1 teaspoon vanilla. Gradually add 2 pounds powdered sugar (about 8 cups), beating well. Beat in 1 to 3 teaspoons milk until frosting reaches piping consistency.

Per cupcake: 397 cal., 15 g total fat (9 g sat. fat), 65 mg chol., 195 mg sodium, 63 g carb., 1 g dietary fiber, 53 g sugar, 4 g protein.

Chocolate Cupcake Ice Cream Sandwiches

Prep: 15 minutes Freeze: 1 hour

Makes 6 cupcakes

6 2½-inch Chocolate Cupcakes (see recipe, page 10)

2 cups chocolate chip ice cream

1 10-ounce jar maraschino cherries (about 20 cherries)

⅓ cup chopped toasted pecans

⅓ cup cherry preserves

1 recipe Sweetened Whipped Cream (see recipe, page 70)

1. Remove paper liners from cupcakes, if present. Cut cupcakes horizontally in half. Place cupcakes on a waxed paper–lined tray or baking sheet. Cover with waxed paper; freeze for 1 hour.

2. Meanwhile, in a chilled large bowl stir ice cream with a wooden spoon to soften. Drain maraschino cherries, reserving six of the cherries for garnish. Coarsely chop the remaining cherries. Stir chopped cherries and pecans into softened ice cream. Cover and freeze for 1 hour.

3. For each serving, place a cupcake bottom, cut side up, in a dessert dish. Top with about ⅓ cup of the ice cream mixture. Spread the cut side of a cupcake top with a scant 1 tablespoon cherry preserves. Replace cupcake top onto ice cream mixture. Pipe or spoon Sweetened Whipped Cream onto cupcake top. Garnish with a reserved maraschino cherry.

Per cupcake: 524 cal., 26 g total fat (10 g sat. fat), 91 mg chol., 330 mg sodium, 69 g carb., 2 g dietary fiber, 46 g sugar, 6 g protein.

Mocha-Filled Banana Cupcakes

Prep: 40 minutes **Stand:** 30 minutes **Bake:** 18 minutes at 350°F **Cool:** 45 minutes

Makes 24 to 30 (2½-inch) cupcakes

1 8-ounce package cream cheese

3 eggs

Nonstick cooking spray

2¼ cups all-purpose flour

1½ cups sugar

1½ teaspoons baking powder

1 teaspoon baking soda

½ teaspoon salt

¼ cup sugar

1½ teaspoons instant espresso powder

Pinch salt

2 ounces semisweet chocolate, melted and cooled

1 cup mashed ripe bananas (2 to 3 bananas)

¾ cup buttermilk or sour milk (see tip, page 11)

½ cup shortening

1 teaspoon vanilla

1 recipe Banana Butter Frosting

Banana slices or dried banana chips (optional)

Unsweetened cocoa powder

1. Allow cream cheese and eggs to stand at room temperature for 30 minutes. Lightly coat twenty-four to thirty 2½-inch muffin cups (see Mini Cupcakes, page 65) with cooking spray. In a large mixing bowl combine flour, 1½ cups sugar, baking powder, baking soda, and ½ teaspoon salt. Set aside.

2. Preheat oven to 350°F. In a medium bowl beat cream cheese and ¼ cup sugar with an electric mixer on medium to high speed until combined. Beat in one of the eggs, espresso powder, and pinch salt. Stir in melted chocolate.

3. Add mashed bananas, buttermilk, shortening, and vanilla to flour mixture. Beat on low speed until combined. Add the remaining 2 eggs, beating on medium speed until combined (batter may climb beaters).

4. Spoon 1 rounded tablespoon of the banana mixture into each prepared muffin cup. Drop 1 rounded teaspoon of the cream cheese mixture over banana mixture in each muffin cup. Spoon remaining banana mixture over cream cheese mixture in muffin cups, filling each two-thirds to three-fourths full.

5. Bake for 18 to 20 minutes or until a wooden toothpick inserted in centers of cupcakes comes out clean. Cool cupcakes in muffin cups on wire racks for 5 minutes. Remove cupcakes from muffin cups. Cool completely on wire racks.

6. Spoon Banana Butter Frosting into a pastry bag fitted with an open star tip. Pipe a swirl of frosting onto the tops of cupcakes. If desired, top each cupcake with a banana slice. Dust with cocoa powder.

Banana Butter Frosting

Allow ½ cup butter to stand at room temperature for 30 minutes. In a medium mixing bowl beat butter with an electric mixer on medium speed until smooth. Beat in ½ cup mashed ripe banana. Gradually add 3 cups powdered sugar, beating well. Beat in 1 tablespoon milk and 2 teaspoons vanilla. Gradually beat in an additional 3½ to 4 cups powdered sugar until frosting reaches piping consistency.

Make-Ahead Directions:

Store the unfrosted cupcakes in a single layer in an airtight freezer container in the freezer for up to 1 month. Thaw the cupcakes at room temperature before frosting.

Per cupcake: 364 cal., 13 g total fat (6 g sat. fat), 47 mg chol., 205 mg sodium, 61 g carb., 1 g dietary fiber, 50 g sugar, 3 g protein.

Mini Cupcakes:

Lightly coat seventy-two 1¾-inch muffin cups with cooking spray. Spoon 1 rounded teaspoon of the banana mixture into each prepared muffin cup. Drop 1 level teaspoon of the cream cheese mixture over banana mixture in each muffin cup. Scoop 1 spoonful of the remaining banana mixture over cream cheese mixture in each muffin cup (cream cheese mixture will not be completely covered). Bake for 12 to 14 minutes or until a toothpick inserted near centers of cupcakes comes out clean. Cool cupcakes in muffin cups on wire racks for 5 minutes. Remove from muffin cups. Cool completely on wire racks. Frost as directed. Makes 72 (1¾-inch) cupcakes.

Per mini cupcake: 121 cal., 4 g total fat (2g sat. fat), 16 mg chol., 68 mg sodium, 20 g carb., 17 g sugar, 1 g protein.

Ginger-Pear Muffin Cakes

Prep: 25 minutes **Bake:** 15 minutes at 350°F **Cool:** 45 minutes

Makes 12 (2½-inch) cupcakes

Nonstick spray for baking

1½ cups all-purpose flour

1 teaspoon baking powder

1 teaspoon ground ginger

1 teaspoon ground cinnamon

½ teaspoon baking soda

¼ teaspoon salt

⅔ cup mild-flavor molasses

¼ cup packed brown sugar

¼ cup butter, melted

1 egg

½ cup boiling water

2 small pears, cored, stemmed (if desired), and each cut into 6 wedges

3 ounces dark chocolate or bittersweet chocolate, cut into pieces

Turbinado (raw) sugar (optional)

1. Preheat oven to 350°F. Lightly coat twelve 2½-inch muffin cups with spray for baking. Set aside.

2. In a large bowl stir together flour, baking powder, ginger, cinnamon, baking soda, and salt. In a medium bowl combine molasses, brown sugar, melted butter, and egg. Pour egg mixture into flour mixture; stir until combined. Stir in the boiling water. Divide batter among prepared muffin cups. Insert a pear wedge into the batter in each muffin cup.

3. Bake for 15 to 18 minutes or until a wooden toothpick inserted in centers comes out clean. Place pieces of chopped chocolate onto tops of cupcakes. Cool cupcakes in muffin cups on wire racks for 10 minutes. Remove cupcakes from muffin cups. If desired, sprinkle with turbinado sugar. Cool completely on wire racks.

Per cupcake: 221 cal., 7 g total fat (4 g sat. fat), 29 mg chol., 163 mg sodium, 39 g carb., 2 g dietary fiber, 21 g sugar, 1 g protein.

Ginger-Pear Muffin Cakes How-To

1. Insert a pear wedge into the batter in each cup. You can leave the stem on one of the pear wedges for decorative appeal, or remove it before placing in the cup.

2. Immediately after baking, place pieces of chopped chocolate on tops of cupcakes, allowing them to melt as cupcakes cool.

Cherry Baby Cakes

Prep: 40 minutes **Bake:** 12 minutes at 350°F **Cool:** 45 minutes

Makes 60 (1¾-inch) cupcakes

1⅓ cups all-purpose flour

⅔ cup sugar

2 teaspoons baking powder

¼ teaspoon salt

⅔ cup milk

¼ cup butter, softened

1 egg

1 teaspoon vanilla

⅔ cup cherry marmalade or cherry preserves, large pieces snipped if necessary

60 maraschino cherries with stems, drained

1 recipe Powdered Sugar Icing

1. Preheat oven to 350°F. Line sixty 1¾-inch muffin cups with paper bake cups.*

2. In a large mixing bowl combine flour, sugar, baking powder, and salt. Add milk, butter, egg, and vanilla. Beat with an electric mixer on low speed until combined. Beat on medium speed for 1 minute more. Spoon 1 teaspoon of the batter into the bottom of each prepared muffin cup. Add ½ teaspoon of the cherry marmalade to each muffin cup. Top each muffin cup with another ½ teaspoon of the batter.

3. Bake about 12 minutes or until a wooden toothpick inserted in centers comes out clean. Cool cupcakes in muffin cups on wire racks for 5 minutes. Remove cupcakes from muffin cups. Cool completely on wire racks.

4. Pat maraschino cherries dry with paper towels. Frost each cupcake with about ½ teaspoon of the Powdered Sugar Icing. Dip half of each cherry into the remaining icing; place on top of cupcakes.

Powdered Sugar Icing

In a medium bowl stir together 2½ cups powdered sugar, 2 tablespoons milk, and ½ teaspoon vanilla. Stir in enough additional milk, 1 teaspoon at a time, to make icing drizzling consistency.

*Test Kitchen Tip:

If you don't have 1¾-inch muffin cups, line sixteen 2½-inch muffin cups with paper bake cups. Prepare batter as directed. Spoon 1 tablespoon of the batter into each prepared muffin cup. Add 1 teaspoon of the marmalade and another 1 tablespoon of the batter (you will need only ⅓ cup marmalade). Bake about 15 minutes or until a wooden toothpick inserted in centers comes out clean. Frost with Powdered Sugar Icing. Add a cherry as directed (you will need only 16 cherries).

Make-Ahead Directions:

Place uniced cupcakes in a single layer in airtight containers; seal. Store in the freezer for up to 3 months. Thaw cupcakes at room temperature before icing.

Per cupcake: 63 cal., 1 g total fat (1 g sat. fat), 6 mg chol., 36 mg sodium, 13 g carb., 0 g dietary fiber, 7 g sugar, 0 g protein.

Banana Split Cupcakes

Prep: 30 minutes **Stand:** 30 minutes **Bake:** 18 minutes at 350°F **Cool:** 45 minutes

Makes 24 (2½-inch) cupcakes

¾ cup butter

3 eggs

2 cups all-purpose flour

1½ teaspoons baking powder

¾ teaspoon salt

¼ teaspoon baking soda

½ cup mashed ripe banana (1 large)

⅓ cup milk

¼ cup sour cream

1 teaspoon vanilla

1 cup sugar

1 recipe Sweetened Whipped Cream

2 pints ice cream (any flavor)

Chocolate-flavor syrup

Maraschino cherries with stems and/or chopped nuts

1. Allow butter and eggs to stand at room temperature for 30 minutes. Meanwhile, line twenty-four 2½-inch muffin cups with paper bake cups. In a medium bowl stir together flour, baking powder, salt, and baking soda. In a small bowl combine mashed banana, milk, sour cream, and vanilla. Set aside.

2. Preheat oven to 350°F. In a large mixing bowl beat butter with an electric mixer on medium to high speed for 30 seconds. Gradually add sugar, about ¼ cup at a time, beating on medium speed until light and fluffy, scraping sides of bowl occasionally. Add eggs, one at a time, beating well after each addition. Alternately add flour mixture and banana mixture to butter mixture, beating on low speed after each addition just until combined.

3. Spoon batter into prepared muffin cups, filling each one-half to two-thirds full. Use the back of a spoon to smooth out batter in muffin cups.

4. Bake for 18 to 20 minutes or until a toothpick inserted in centers comes out clean. Cool cupcakes in muffin cups on wire racks for 5 minutes. Remove cupcakes from muffin cups. Cool completely on wire racks.

5. Just before serving, spoon some of the Sweetened Whipped Cream into a pastry bag fitted with a large star tip. Insert tip into tops of cupcakes. Squeeze about 1 tablespoon of the whipped cream into the center of each cupcake.

6. For each serving, top a cupcake with a small scoop of ice cream. Drizzle with syrup. Pipe some of the remaining Sweetened Whipped Cream on top of ice cream. Top with maraschino cherries and/or nuts. Serve immediately.

Sweetened Whipped Cream

In a chilled small mixing bowl beat 1 cup whipping cream, 2 tablespoons sugar, and ½ teaspoon vanilla or almond extract with the chilled beaters of an electric mixer on medium to high speed just until stiff peaks form (tips stand straight). Do not overbeat.

Per cupcake: 245 cal., 13 g total fat (8 g sat. fat), 67 mg chol., 179 mg sodium, 28 g carb., 1 g dietary fiber, 19 g sugar, 3 g protein.

Chocolate-Peppermint Cupcakes

Prep: 50 minutes **Stand:** 30 minutes **Bake:** 20 minutes at 350°F **Cool:** 45 minutes
Makes 12 (2½-inch) cupcakes

2 eggs
Nonstick cooking spray
1¼ cups all-purpose flour
¼ cup unsweetened cocoa powder
1 teaspoon baking powder
½ teaspoon salt
¼ teaspoon baking soda
¼ cup shortening
½ cup sugar
1 teaspoon vanilla
⅔ cup cold water
⅓ cup sugar
⅓ cup miniature semisweet chocolate pieces
1 recipe Creamy Peppermint Frosting
Crushed peppermint candies
Small candy canes and/or red nonpareils

1. Separate eggs. Allow egg yolks and egg whites to stand at room temperature for 30 minutes. Meanwhile, lightly coat twelve 2½-inch muffin cups with cooking spray. In a medium bowl combine flour, cocoa powder, baking powder, salt, and baking soda. Set aside.

2. Preheat oven to 350°F. In a very large mixing bowl beat shortening with an electric mixer on medium to high speed for 30 seconds. Add the ½ cup sugar and the vanilla. Beat until combined, scraping sides of bowl occasionally. Add egg yolks, one at a time, beating well after each addition. Alternately add flour mixture and the cold water to shortening mixture, beating on low speed after each addition just until combined.

3. Thoroughly wash beaters. In a large mixing bowl beat egg whites on medium speed until soft peaks form (tips curl). Gradually add the ⅓ cup sugar, 1 tablespoon at a time, beating on high speed until stiff peaks form (tips stand straight). Fold one-fourth of the beaten egg whites into chocolate batter to lighten. Gently fold in the remaining beaten egg whites. Gently fold in chocolate pieces.

4. Spoon batter into prepared muffin cups, filling each about two-thirds full.

5. Bake for 20 to 22 minutes or until a toothpick inserted in centers comes out clean. Cool cupcakes in muffin cups on wire racks for 5 minutes. Remove cupcakes from muffin cups. Cool completely on wire racks.

6. Up to 4 hours before serving, use a serrated knife to cut cupcakes horizontally in half. Spoon about 1 tablespoon of the Creamy Peppermint Frosting onto cut side of each cupcake bottom. Replace cupcake tops, pressing gently to spread frosting to edges.

7. Place ¼ cup crushed peppermint candies on a sheet of waxed paper. Roll sides of cupcakes in crushed candies to coat the exposed frosting. Pipe or spread the remaining frosting onto tops of cupcakes. If desired, sprinkle tops of cupcakes with additional crushed peppermint candies.

Creamy Peppermint Frosting

Allow ½ cup butter to stand at room temperature for 30 minutes. In a large mixing bowl beat butter, one 7-ounce jar marshmallow crème, and 1 teaspoon peppermint extract with an electric mixer on medium speed until smooth. Gradually add 2 cups powdered sugar, beating well. Beat in 2 tablespoons milk. Gradually beat in an additional 2 cups powdered sugar. If necessary, beat in additional milk, 1 teaspoon at a time, until frosting reaches spreading consistency.

Per cupcake: 474 cal., 15 g total fat (7 g sat. fat), 56 mg chol., 236 mg sodium, 84 g carb., 1 g dietary fiber, 66 g sugar, 3 g protein.

Peanut Butter Cupcakes

Prep: 45 minutes **Bake:** 18 minutes at 350°F **Cool:** 45 minutes

Makes 24 (2½-inch) cupcakes

1⅓ cups all-purpose flour

⅔ cup finely crushed graham crackers

1 tablespoon baking powder

1 cup creamy peanut butter

⅓ cup shortening

1⅓ cups sugar

2 eggs

1 teaspoon vanilla

1 cup milk

24 bite-size chocolate-covered peanut butter cups, unwrapped

Raspberry or strawberry jam

Bite-size chocolate-covered peanut butter cups, unwrapped and quartered (optional)

1. Preheat oven to 350°F. Line twenty-four 2½-inch muffin cups with paper bake cups. In a medium bowl stir together flour, crushed graham crackers, and baking powder. Set aside.

2. In a very large mixing bowl beat peanut butter and shortening with an electric mixer on medium speed until combined. Gradually add sugar, beating on medium speed until well mixed. Beat in eggs and vanilla. Alternately add flour mixture and milk to peanut butter mixture, beating on low speed after each addition just until combined.

3. Spoon 1 rounded tablespoon of the batter into the bottom of each prepared muffin cup. Add 1 of the whole peanut butter cups to each muffin cup. Spoon the remaining batter into muffin cups to cover peanut butter cups.

4. Bake about 18 minutes or until a wooden toothpick inserted near edges comes out clean (cupcakes may have a slight indentation). Cool cupcakes in muffin cups on wire racks for 5 minutes. Remove cupcakes from muffin cups. Cool completely on wire racks. Spoon a small amount of jam on top of each cupcake. If desired, garnish each with a quartered peanut butter cup.

Per cupcake: 295 cal., 15 g total fat (5 g sat. fat), 21 mg chol., 139 mg sodium, 38 g carb., 2 g dietary fiber, 28 g sugar, 6 g protein.

Pumpkin Cupcakes with Spiced Mascarpone Cream Filling

Prep: 25 minutes **Bake:** 15 minutes at 350°F **Cool:** 45 minutes
Makes 12 (2½-inch) cupcakes

1 cup all-purpose flour
¾ teaspoon baking powder
¾ teaspoon baking soda
¾ teaspoon ground cinnamon
¼ teaspoon salt
⅛ teaspoon ground nutmeg
⅛ teaspoon ground cloves
2 eggs, lightly beaten
⅔ cup canned pumpkin
⅓ cup granulated sugar
⅓ cup packed brown sugar
⅓ cup vegetable oil
⅓ cup golden raisins
¼ cup chopped walnuts
1 recipe Spiced Mascarpone Cream Filling
¼ cup crystallized ginger, finely chopped

1. Preheat oven to 350°F. Grease and flour twelve 2½-inch muffin cups.
2. In a medium bowl stir together flour, baking powder, baking soda, cinnamon, salt, nutmeg, and cloves. In a large bowl combine eggs, pumpkin, granulated sugar, brown sugar, and oil; whisk until smooth. Add flour mixture to pumpkin mixture, one-third at a time, stirring after each addition just until combined. Stir in raisins and walnuts.
3. Spoon batter into prepared muffin cups, filling each about two-thirds full.
4. Bake for 15 to 18 minutes or until a wooden toothpick inserted in the centers comes out clean. Cool cupcakes in muffin cups on a wire rack for 5 minutes. Remove cupcakes from muffin cups. Cool completely on wire racks.
5. Cut each cupcake horizontally in half. Spread some of the Spiced Mascarpone Cream Filling onto cut side of each cupcake bottom. Replace cupcake tops. Sprinkle with crystallized ginger.

Spiced Mascarpone Cream Filling

Allow ½ cup mascarpone cheese and 6 tablespoons butter to stand at room temperature for 30 minutes. In a large mixing bowl beat mascarpone cheese, butter, ¼ teaspoon ground cinnamon, and ¼ teaspoon ground ginger with an electric mixer on medium to high speed until light and fluffy. Gradually add 2 cups powdered sugar, beating well. If necessary, beat in 1 tablespoon milk, 1 teaspoon at a time, until filling reaches spreading consistency.

Per cupcake: 353 cal., 19 g total fat (7 g sat. fat), 63 mg chol., 213 mg sodium, 45 g carb., 1 g dietary fiber, 31 g sugar, 5 g protein.

Icing Primer

To frost cupcakes quickly and efficiently, first make sure the frosting is at room temperature. If you're using homemade frosting that has been refrigerated, you will need to let it stand at room temperature until it is soft and spreadable. Use a thin flat spatula (see page 19) to scoop a generous portion of frosting onto the top of a cupcake. Use gentle side-to-side strokes with the spatula to push frosting across the top of the cupcake. If the tops of cupcakes are crumbly or if you're using a light-color frosting on chocolate cupcakes, you can place some of the frosting into a separate bowl. Use this frosting to apply a thin layer of frosting to each cupcake to act as a crumb coat; let frosting layer dry. Apply a thicker layer of frosting as directed.

Tiny Chocolate-Cherry Bombs

Prep: 35 minutes **Bake:** 18 minutes at 350°F **Cool:** 45 minutes
Makes 55 (1¾-inch) cupcakes

2 10-ounce jars maraschino cherries with stems
1¼ cups all-purpose flour
1 cup granulated sugar
½ cup unsweetened cocoa powder
½ teaspoon baking soda
½ teaspoon baking powder
¼ teaspoon salt
⅔ cup milk
⅓ cup butter, melted and cooled, or canola oil
2 tablespoons kirsch, other cherry brandy, brandy, cherry juice, or milk
1½ teaspoons vanilla
1 egg
1 cup powdered sugar

1. Preheat oven to 350°F. Line fifty-five 1¾-inch muffin cups with silver or red foil bake cups. Drain cherries, reserving 2 tablespoons of the juice. Set aside.

2. In a large mixing bowl combine flour, granulated sugar, cocoa powder, baking soda, baking powder, and salt. Add milk, melted butter, kirsch, and vanilla. Beat with an electric mixer on low speed just until combined. Beat on medium speed for 2 minutes more. Add egg. Beat for 2 minutes more.

3. Spoon 1 tablespoon of the batter into each prepared muffin cup. Push a cherry into batter in each cup, keeping stem end up.*

4. Bake for 18 to 20 minutes or until tops spring back when lightly touched. Cool cupcakes in muffin cups on wire racks for 10 minutes. Remove cupcakes from muffin cups. Cool completely on wire racks.

5. In a medium bowl combine powdered sugar and 1 tablespoon of the reserved cherry juice. Add enough additional reserved cherry juice, 1 teaspoon at a time, to make icing drizzling consistency. Drizzle over cupcakes. Let stand until set.

*Test Kitchen Tip:
If you run out of cherries, just add an extra tablespoon of batter to the muffin cups for plain chocolate bombs.

Per cupcake: 66 cal., 1 g total fat (1 g sat. fat), 7 mg chol., 36 mg sodium, 13 g carb., 1 g dietary fiber, 10 g sugar, 1 g protein.

Lemon Dreams

Prep: 45 minutes **Stand:** 30 minutes **Bake:** 15 minutes at 350°F **Cool:** 45 minutes
Makes 20 to 24 (2½-inch) cupcakes

¾ cup butter

3 eggs

2 cups all-purpose flour

1½ teaspoons baking powder

½ teaspoon baking soda

½ teaspoon salt

1½ cups sugar

1 cup buttermilk or sour milk (see tip, page 11)

2 teaspoons finely shredded lemon peel

1 cup lemon curd

1 recipe Lemon Cream Frosting

Finely shredded lemon peel (optional)

1. Allow butter and eggs to stand at room temperature for 30 minutes. Meanwhile, line twenty to twenty-four 2½-inch muffin cups with paper bake cups. In a medium bowl stir together flour, baking powder, baking soda, and salt. Set aside.

2. Preheat oven to 350°F. In a large mixing bowl beat butter with an electric mixer on medium to high speed for 30 seconds. Gradually add sugar, beating until combined. Add eggs, one at a time, beating well after each addition. Alternately add flour mixture and buttermilk to butter mixture, beating on low speed after each addition just until combined. Stir in the 2 teaspoons lemon peel. Spoon batter into prepared muffin cups, filling each about two-thirds full. Use the back of a spoon to smooth out batter in cups.

3. Bake for 15 to 18 minutes or until a wooden toothpick inserted near centers comes out clean. Cool cupcakes in muffin cups on wire racks for 5 minutes. Remove cupcakes from muffin cups. Cool completely on wire racks. If desired, remove paper liners from cupcakes.

4. Spoon lemon curd into a pastry bag fitted with a large round or open star tip. Insert tip into tops of cupcakes. Squeeze some of the lemon curd into center of each cupcake. If desired, spoon Lemon Cream Frosting into pastry bag fitted with a large round tip. Generously spread or pipe onto tops of cupcakes. If desired, garnish with additional lemon peel.

Lemon Cream Frosting

Allow 6 ounces cream cheese and ⅓ cup butter to stand at room temperature for 30 minutes. In a large mixing bowl combine cream cheese, butter, and ¼ cup lemon curd. Beat with an electric mixer on medium to high speed until smooth. Gradually add 3 cups powdered sugar, beating well. Beat in 1 tablespoon milk. Gradually beat in an additional 3 cups powdered sugar. If necessary, beat in enough additional milk, 1 teaspoon at a time, until frosting reaches spreading consistency.

Per cupcake: 443 cal., 15 g total fat (9 g sat. fat), 79 mg chol., 272 mg sodium, 77 g carb., 2 g dietary fiber, 64 g sugar, 3 g protein.

Pineapple-Carrot Cupcakes

Prep: 35 minutes **Stand:** 30 minutes **Bake:** 15 minutes at 350°F **Cool:** 45 minutes

Makes 24 (2½-inch) cupcakes

4 eggs

1 3-ounce package cream cheese

2 cups all-purpose flour

2 cups sugar

2 teaspoons baking powder

1 teaspoon salt

1 teaspoon ground cinnamon

½ teaspoon baking soda

2 tablespoons sugar

1 egg yolk

Pinch salt

¼ cup canned crushed pineapple, well drained*

3 cups finely shredded carrots (6 medium)**

¾ cup vegetable oil

1 teaspoon vanilla

1 recipe Cream Cheese Frosting (see recipe, page 14)

½ cup finely chopped toasted walnuts

Ground cinnamon (optional)

1. Allow the 4 eggs and the cream cheese to stand at room temperature for 30 minutes. Meanwhile, grease and lightly flour twenty-four 2½-inch muffin cups or line with paper bake cups. In a large bowl stir together flour, the 2 cups sugar, the baking powder, the 1 teaspoon salt, the 1 teaspoon cinnamon, and the baking soda. Set aside.

2. For filling, in a medium mixing bowl beat cream cheese and the 2 tablespoons sugar with an electric mixer on medium to high speed until combined. Beat in the egg yolk and the pinch salt. Fold in pineapple.

3. Preheat oven to 350°F. In another bowl stir together the 4 eggs, the carrots, oil, and vanilla. Add egg mixture to flour mixture. Stir until combined.

4. Spoon about 1 tablespoon of the batter into the bottom of each prepared muffin cup. Drop about 1 rounded teaspoon of the filling in to each muffin cup. Spoon remaining batter over filling in muffin cups.

5. Bake for 15 to 18 minutes or until a toothpick inserted in centers of cupcakes comes out clean. Cool cupcakes in muffin cups on wire racks for 5 minutes. Remove cupcakes from muffin cups. Cool completely on wire racks.

6. Spread Cream Cheese Frosting onto tops of cupcakes. Roll edges of frosting in toasted walnuts. If desired, sprinkle tops with additional cinnamon. Store in the refrigerator.

*Test Kitchen Tip:
Place the pineapple in a fine-mesh sieve placed over a bowl. Press pineapple with the back of a wooden spoon to release any juice.

**Test Kitchen Tip:
Make sure to finely shred the carrots or the pieces may sink during baking.

Make-Ahead Directions:
Place unfrosted cupcakes in a single layer in an airtight container; seal. Store in the refrigerator for up to 3 days.

Per cupcake: 390 cal., 18 g total fat (6 g sat. fat), 60 mg chol., 241 mg sodium, 56 g carb., 1 g dietary fiber, 47 g sugar, 3 g protein.

Edging Elegance

To create the lovely edge of walnuts around the outside of these cupcakes, smooth frosting all the way to the outer edges of each cupcake top. Place the chopped nuts on a small plate or in a shallow bowl. Before the frosting sets up, hold a cupcake by the base and roll the outside edge of frosting in the nuts, turning the cupcake as you go. (Press down gently if you want to create a smooth, nut-coated edge.) You can add more chopped nuts to the plate if necessary. For other cupcake recipes, use colored sugars, crushed cookies, jimmies, or finely chopped candies in place of the nuts.

Chocolate-Coconut Cupcakes

Prep: 40 minutes **Bake:** 18 minutes at 350°F **Cool:** 45 minutes
Makes 26 (2½-inch) cupcakes

1 cup powdered sugar
1 cup flaked coconut
⅓ cup sweetened condensed milk
¼ cup chopped almonds, toasted
3 cups all-purpose flour
2¼ cups granulated sugar
1½ teaspoons baking powder
1 teaspoon salt
3 eggs, lightly beaten
1½ cups milk
½ cup vegetable oil
½ cup butter, melted and cooled
2 teaspoons almond extract
1½ teaspoons vanilla
1 teaspoon coconut extract
1 recipe Ganache (see recipe, page 15)
  Flaked coconut
26 whole almonds, toasted

1. Line twenty-six 2½-inch muffin cups with paper bake cups. For filling, in a small bowl combine powdered sugar, the 1 cup coconut, sweetened condensed milk, and the chopped almonds, stirring until well mixed. Set aside.

2. Preheat oven to 350°F. In a very large mixing bowl stir together flour, granulated sugar, baking powder, and salt. In a medium bowl combine eggs, milk, oil, melted butter, almond extract, vanilla, and coconut extract.

3. Add egg mixture all at once to flour mixture. Beat with an electric mixer on medium to high speed for 2 minutes, scraping sides of bowl occasionally.

4. Spoon batter into prepared muffin cups, filling each about two-thirds full. Spoon about 1 rounded teaspoon of the filling on top of the batter in each cup.

5. Bake for 18 to 20 minutes or until a wooden toothpick inserted in centers comes out clean. Cool cupcakes in muffin cups on wire racks for 10 minutes. Remove cupcakes from muffin cups. Cool completely on wire racks.

6. Gently spread Ganache onto tops of cupcakes. Sprinkle cupcakes with additional coconut. Top each cupcake with a whole almond. Let stand until Ganache is set.

Make-Ahead Directions:
Place iced cupcakes in a single layer in an airtight container; seal. Store at room temperature for up to 3 days.

Per cupcake: 367 cal., 20 g total fat (10 g sat. fat), 49 mg chol., 171 mg sodium, 46 g carb., 2 g dietary fiber, 32 g sugar, 5 g protein.

Cherry-Almond Vanilla Cupcakes

Prep: 45 minutes **Stand:** 30 minutes **Bake:** 15 minutes at 350°F **Cool:** 45 minutes
Makes 24 (2½-inch) cupcakes

½ cup butter

4 egg whites

2 cups all-purpose flour

1 teaspoon baking powder

½ teaspoon salt

¼ teaspoon baking soda

¾ cup buttermilk or sour milk (see tip, page 11)

⅓ cup maraschino cherry juice

1½ cups sugar

1 teaspoon vanilla

½ teaspoon almond extract

12 maraschino cherries, halved

1 recipe Cherry-Almond Butter Frosting

Maraschino cherries with stems (optional)

1. Allow butter and egg whites to stand at room temperature for 30 minutes. Meanwhile, line twenty-four 2½-inch muffin cups with paper bake cups or coat with nonstick cooking spray. In a medium bowl stir together flour, baking powder, salt, and baking soda. In a 2-cup glass measuring cup combine buttermilk and cherry juice. Set aside.

2. Preheat oven to 350°F. In a large mixing bowl beat butter with an electric mixer on medium to high speed for 30 seconds. Add sugar, vanilla, and almond extract. Beat until combined. Add egg whites, one at a time, beating well after each addition. Alternately add flour mixture and buttermilk mixture to butter mixture, beating on low speed after each addition just until combined.

3. Spoon batter into prepared muffin cups, filling each about two-thirds full. Use the back of a spoon to smooth out batter in cups. Press a cherry half into batter in each cup.

4. Bake for 15 to 18 minutes or until tops spring back when lightly touched. Cool cupcakes in muffin cups on wire racks for 5 minutes. Remove cupcakes from muffin cups. Cool completely on wire racks.

5. Spoon Cherry-Almond Butter Frosting into a pastry bag fitted with a large star tip. Pipe frosting onto tops of cupcakes. If desired, top with cherries with stems.

Cherry-Almond Butter Frosting

In a large mixing bowl beat ½ cup butter, softened, with an electric mixer on medium speed until smooth. Gradually add 1 cup powdered sugar, beating well. Slowly beat in 3 tablespoons maraschino cherry juice or milk* and ½ teaspoon almond extract. Gradually beat in an additional 3 cups powdered sugar. If necessary, beat in additional maraschino cherry juice or milk, 1 teaspoon at a time, until frosting reaches piping consistency.

*Test Kitchen Tip:
If you use milk, tint the frosting pink with food coloring.

Per cupcake: 262 cal., 8 g total fat (5 g sat. fat), 21 mg chol., 151 mg sodium, 47 g carb., 0 g dietary fiber, 37 g sugar, 2 g protein.

Piña Colada Cakes

Prep: 30 minutes **Stand:** 30 minutes **Bake:** 18 minutes at 350°F **Cool:** 45 minutes
Makes 24 (2½-inch) cupcakes

⅓ cup butter

2 eggs

2 cups all-purpose flour

¾ teaspoon baking powder

½ teaspoon baking soda

½ teaspoon salt

1¼ cups sugar

1 teaspoon vanilla

½ cup sour cream

½ cup milk

6 soft macaroon cookies, crumbled (1 cup)

¼ cup chopped macadamia nuts

1 cup pineapple preserves

1 recipe Coconut Frosting
   Toasted flaked coconut

1. Allow butter and eggs to stand at room temperature for 30 minutes. Meanwhile, line twenty-four 2½-inch muffin cups with paper bake cups. In a medium bowl stir together flour, baking powder, baking soda, and salt. Set aside.

2. Preheat oven to 350°F. In a large mixing bowl beat butter with an electric mixer on medium to high speed for 30 seconds. Add sugar and vanilla. Beat until combined. Add eggs, one at a time, beating well after each addition. In a small bowl combine sour cream and milk. Alternately add flour mixture and sour cream mixture to butter mixture, beating on low speed after each addition just until combined. Stir in crumbled cookies and macadamia nuts. Spoon batter into prepared muffin cups.

3. Bake for 18 to 20 minutes or until a wooden toothpick inserted near centers comes out clean. Cool cupcakes in muffin cups on wire racks for 5 minutes. Remove cupcakes from muffin cups. Cool completely on wire racks. If desired, remove paper liners from cupcakes.

4. Spoon pineapple preserves into a pastry bag fitted with a large round or open star tip. Insert tip into tops of cupcakes. Squeeze some of the preserves into the center of each cupcake. If necessary, use the tip of a paring knife to make a slit in the top of cupcakes to make it easier to insert tip into cupcakes.

5. Generously spread Coconut Frosting over tops of cupcakes. Sprinkle with toasted coconut.

Coconut Frosting

In a large mixing bowl prepare one 7.25-ounce package fluffy white frosting mix according to package directions. Beat in 1 teaspoon coconut extract. Gradually add 4 cups powdered sugar, beating well.

Per cupcake: 319 cal., 8 g total fat (5 g sat. fat), 27 mg chol., 165 mg sodium, 61 g carb., 1 g dietary fiber, 48 g sugar, 3 g protein.

Cannoli Cupcakes

Prep: 45 minutes **Stand:** 30 minutes **Bake:** 15 minutes at 350°F **Cool:** 45 minutes

Makes 24 (2½-inch) cupcakes

½ cup butter

4 egg whites

2 cups all-purpose flour

1 teaspoon baking powder

½ teaspoon salt

¼ teaspoon baking soda

1½ cups sugar

1 teaspoon vanilla

1 cup buttermilk or sour milk (see tip, page 11)

¾ cup miniature semisweet chocolate pieces

1 recipe Ricotta Frosting

½ cup chopped pistachio nuts

2 tablespoons grated chocolate

1. Allow butter and egg whites to stand at room temperature for 30 minutes. Meanwhile, line twenty-four 2½-inch muffin cups with paper bake cups. In a medium bowl stir together flour, baking powder, salt, and baking soda. Set aside.

2. Preheat oven to 350°F. In a large mixing bowl beat butter with an electric mixer on medium to high speed for 30 seconds. Add sugar and vanilla. Beat until combined. Add egg whites, one at a time, beating well after each addition. Alternately add flour mixture and buttermilk to butter mixture, beating on low speed after each addition just until combined (batter may look curdled). Fold in chocolate pieces.

3. Spoon batter into prepared muffin cups, filling each about two-thirds full. Use the back of a spoon to smooth out batter in cups.

4. Bake for 15 to 18 minutes or until a wooden toothpick inserted in centers comes out clean. Cool cupcakes in muffin cups on wire racks for 10 minutes. Remove cupcakes from muffin cups. Cool completely on wire racks.

5. Just before serving, spoon Ricotta Frosting into a pastry bag fitted with a large round tip. Insert tip into tops of cupcake. Squeeze some of the frosting into the center of each cupcake. Generously pipe remaining frosting onto tops of cupcakes. Sprinkle with pistachio nuts and grated chocolate. Store in the refrigerator.

Ricotta Frosting

Allow 1 cup butter to stand at room temperature for 30 minutes. In a large mixing bowl beat butter with an electric mixer on medium to high speed for 30 seconds. Beat in 1 teaspoon vanilla and pinch salt. Gradually add 4 cups powdered sugar, beating well. Beat in ⅓ cup ricotta cheese. Beat in an additional 4 cups powdered sugar. Beat in 2 tablespoons milk until frosting is light and fluffy and reaches piping consistency.

Make-Ahead Directions:

Store frosted cupcakes in a single layer in an airtight container in the refrigerator for up to 2 days.

Per cupcake: 420 cal., 16 g total fat (9 g sat. fat), 33 mg chol., 184 mg sodium, 68 g carb., 1 g dietary fiber, 57 g sugar, 4 g protein.

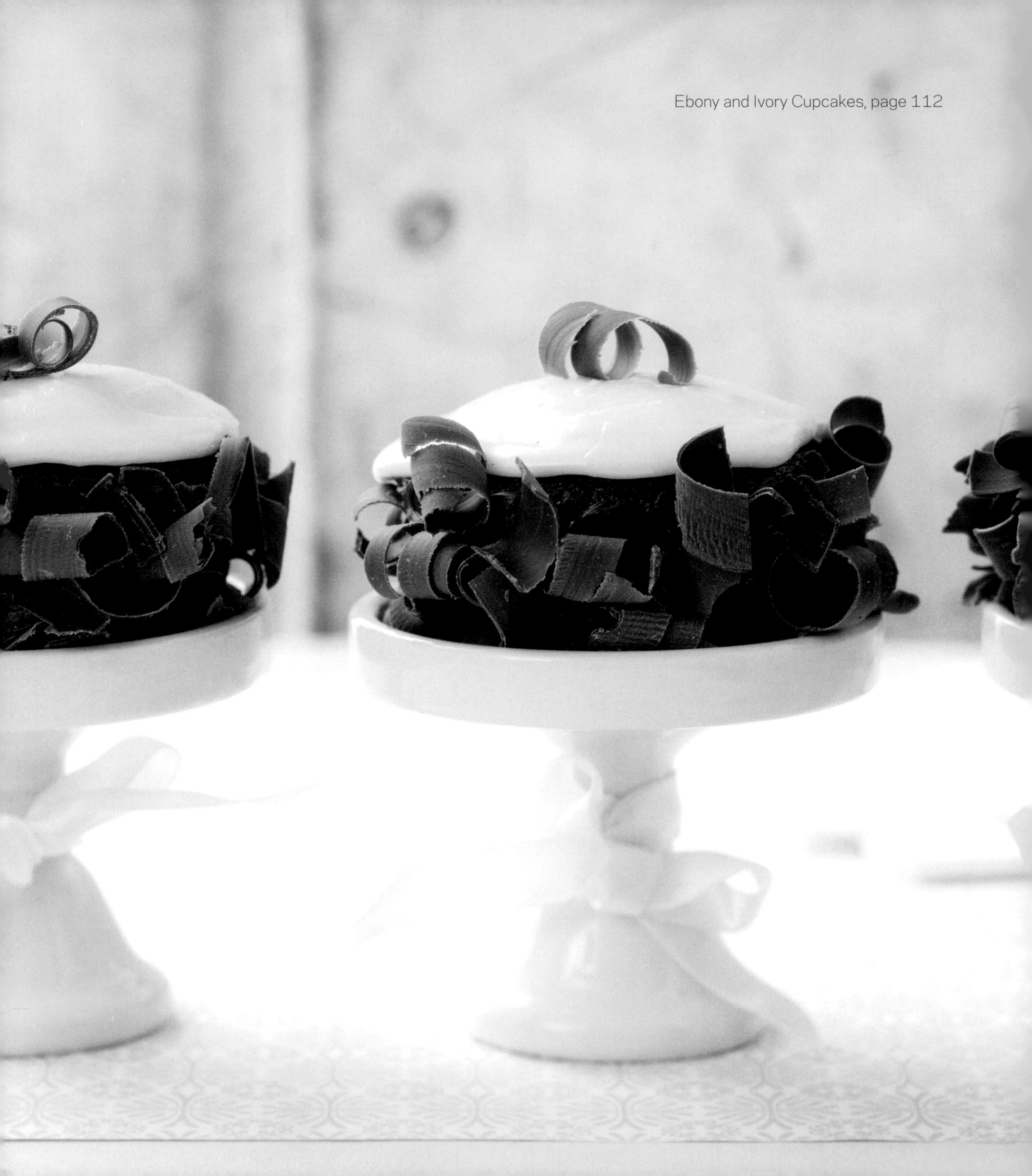

Ebony and Ivory Cupcakes, page 112

Chocolate Cupcakes

Deep, luscious chocolate is a reward after a long day's work, a treasure to enjoy with a hot bubble bath, or a dessert to share for a special birthday. Each bite wraps us in blanket of warmth and love, urging us to come back for just one more nibble. These sweets are all that and more, turning chocolate into soft, tender baby cakes beckoning with brilliant swirls of icing and decorations. Go ahead—give in to temptation.

German Chocolate Cupcakes

Prep: 25 minutes **Freeze:** 4 hours **Stand:** 30 minutes **Bake:** 25 minutes at 350°F **Cool:** 45 minutes

Makes 12 (2½-inch) cupcakes

1 recipe Chocolate-Pecan Ice Cream "Frosting"

½ cup butter

2 eggs

2 ounces sweet baking chocolate

¼ cup water

1 cup all-purpose flour

½ teaspoon baking soda

¼ teaspoon salt

½ cup sugar

½ teaspoon vanilla

½ cup buttermilk or sour milk (see tip, page 11)

Caramel-flavor ice cream topping

⅔ cup toasted shaved coconut*

Pecan halves, toasted (optional)

1. Prepare Chocolate-Pecan Ice Cream "Frosting." Cover and freeze for at least 4 hours.

2. Allow butter and eggs to stand at room temperature for 30 minutes. Meanwhile, in a small saucepan combine chocolate and the water. Cook and stir over low heat until chocolate is melted; cool about 10 minutes. Line twelve 2½-inch muffin cups with paper bake cups. In a small bowl stir together flour, baking soda, and salt. Set aside.

3. Preheat oven to 350°F. In a large mixing bowl beat butter with an electric mixer on medium to high speed for 30 seconds. Add sugar, beating on medium to high speed for 1 minute, scraping sides of bowl. Add eggs and vanilla. Beat on low speed until combined. Beat in chocolate mixture. Alternately add flour mixture and buttermilk to butter mixture, beating on low speed after each addition just until combined.

4. Spoon batter into prepared muffin cups, filling each about two-thirds full. Use the back of a spoon to smooth out batter in cups.

5. Bake about 25 minutes or until a wooden toothpick inserted in centers comes out clean. Cool cupcakes in muffin cups on wire racks for 5 minutes. Remove cupcakes from muffin cups. Cool completely on wire racks.

6. Before serving, heat caramel topping until warm. Remove cupcakes from paper liners; place cupcakes on dessert plates or in shallow bowls. Top each cupcake with one round of Chocolate-Pecan Ice Cream "Frosting." Top with toasted coconut and, if desired, pecan halves. Drizzle with warm caramel topping. Serve immediately.

Chocolate-Pecan Ice Cream "Frosting"

Line a baking sheet with waxed paper. Cut ½ gallon chocolate ice cream into sheets about 2 inches thick. Use a cookie cutter to cut ice cream rounds just larger than the cupcakes. Place on prepared baking sheet. Press ¾ to 1 cup broken pecans, toasted, into ice cream, letting them protrude from the ice cream. Cover and freeze for 4 to 24 hours.

*Test Kitchen Tip:

Use a vegetable peeler to shave strips of coconut from a halved, peeled coconut. Place in a shallow baking pan. Bake in a 350°F oven about 10 minutes or until edges are lightly browned, stirring occasionally. You may also use purchased raw chip coconut, but only bake for 2 to 3 minutes.

Per cupcake: 411 cal., 25 g total fat (12 g sat. fat), 80 mg chol., 261 mg sodium, 43 g carb., 2 g dietary fiber, 28 g sugar, 6 g protein.

Chocolate Hugs and Kisses Cupcakes

Prep: 40 minutes **Stand:** 30 minutes **Bake:** 18 minutes at 350°F **Cool:** 45 minutes
Makes 16 (2½-inch) cupcakes

⅓ cup unsalted butter

2 eggs

¾ cup all-purpose flour

⅓ cup unsweetened cocoa powder

1 teaspoon baking powder

½ teaspoon baking soda

½ teaspoon ground cinnamon

¼ teaspoon salt

¾ cup sugar

1 teaspoon vanilla

½ cup sour cream

1 recipe Cherry Frosting or Chocolate Frosting

1 recipe Hugs and Kisses Cookies

1. Allow butter and eggs to stand at room temperature for 30 minutes. Meanwhile, line sixteen 2½-inch muffin cups with paper bake cups. In a medium bowl stir together flour, cocoa powder, baking powder, baking soda, cinnamon, and salt. Set aside.

2. Preheat the oven to 350°F. In a large mixing bowl beat butter with an electric mixer on medium to high speed for 30 seconds. Add sugar. Beat until light and fluffy. Beat in eggs and vanilla until smooth. Beat in sour cream and the flour mixture.

3. Spoon 2 slightly rounded tablespoons of the batter into each prepared muffin cup. Bake about 18 minutes or until tops spring back when lightly touched. Cool cupcakes in muffin cups on wire racks for 10 minutes. Remove cupcakes from muffin cups. Cool completely on wire racks.

4. Spread Cherry Frosting or Chocolate Frosting onto tops of cupcakes (you will have some frosting left over). Top with Hugs and Kisses Cookies.

Cherry Frosting

In a chilled large mixing bowl combine 1½ cups powdered sugar, one 8-ounce container sour cream, 1 cup whipping cream (do not use ultra-pasteurized whipping cream), and 2 tablespoons maraschino cherry juice. Beat with the chilled beaters of an electric mixer on medium to high speed for 3 to 5 minutes or until fluffy.

Chocolate Frosting

Prepare Cherry Frosting as directed, except omit cherry juice and beat in ¼ cup unsweetened cocoa powder.

Hugs and Kisses Cookies

Preheat oven to 375°F. Knead ⅓ cup all-purpose flour into half of a 16.5-ounce package refrigerated sugar cookie dough. On a lightly floured surface, roll dough until ¼ inch thick. Using 1½-inch X- and O-shape cookie cutters, cut 16 cookies for cupcakes (cut remaining dough into desired shapes). Bake 1½-inch cookies about 6 minutes or until edges are lightly browned (larger cookies will bake 7 to 8 minutes). Transfer to a wire rack. Cool completely. Frost with Cherry Frosting or Chocolate Frosting and sprinkle with red sugar.

Per cupcake: 246 cal., 15 g total fat (9 g sat. fat), 88 mg chol., 125 mg sodium, 28 g carb., 1 g dietary fiber, 21 g sugar, 3 g protein.

Marbled Chocolate Cupcakes

Prep: 45 minutes **Stand:** 30 minutes **Bake:** 15 minutes at 350°F **Cool:** 45 minutes
Makes 20 (2½-inch) cupcakes

⅓ cup butter

2 eggs

1¼ cups all-purpose flour

¼ cup unsweetened cocoa powder

½ teaspoon baking powder

¼ teaspoon baking soda

¼ teaspoon salt

¼ teaspoon ground cinnamon

1 cup sugar

2 ounces semisweet chocolate, bittersweet chocolate, or milk chocolate, melted and cooled

1½ teaspoons vanilla

¾ cup milk

⅓ cup seedless red raspberry or blackberry preserves

1 recipe Chocolate Ganache

1 recipe Decorating Icing

1. Allow butter and eggs to stand at room temperature for 30 minutes. Meanwhile, line twenty 2½-inch muffin cups with foil bake cups. In a medium bowl stir together flour, cocoa powder, baking powder, baking soda, salt, and cinnamon. Set aside.

2. Preheat oven to 350°F. In a large mixing bowl beat butter with an electric mixer on medium to high speed for 30 seconds. Add sugar. Beat until combined. Add eggs, one at a time, beating well after each addition. Beat in melted chocolate and vanilla. Alternately add flour mixture and milk to chocolate mixture, beating on low speed after each addition until combined.

3. Spoon batter into prepared muffin cups, filling each nearly two-thirds full. Bake for 15 to 18 minutes or until a wooden toothpick inserted near centers comes out clean. Cool cupcakes in muffin cups on wire racks for 10 minutes. Remove cupcakes from muffin cups. Cool completely on wire racks.

4. Remove paper liners from cupcakes. Place cupcakes 2 inches apart on wire racks set over waxed paper. Spread a scant 1 teaspoon of the preserves over each cupcake.

5. Slowly drizzle a small amount of Chocolate Ganache over each cupcake, allowing it to spread and cover preserves and entire surface of the cupcake. If necessary, spread ganache gently so it covers the preserves completely. Spoon Decorating Icing into a pastry bag fitted with a small round tip (or spoon icing into a heavy resealable plastic bag; snip off a small piece from one corner of bag). Pipe large dots onto each cupcake. Drag a toothpick through icing dots to create swirls and designs.

Chocolate Ganache

In a small saucepan bring ½ cup whipping cream just to boiling over medium-high heat. Remove from heat. Add 7 ounces chopped semisweet chocolate, bittersweet chocolate, or milk chocolate (do not stir). Let stand for 5 minutes. Stir until smooth. Cool for 15 minutes.

Decorating Icing

Place 1½ cups powdered sugar in a small bowl. Add 4 to 7 teaspoons milk, 1 teaspoon at a time, to make icing piping consistency. If desired, stir in a few drops desired color of food coloring.

Per cupcake: 247 cal., 10 g total fat (6 g sat. fat), 38 mg chol., 89 mg sodium, 37 g carb., 1 g dietary fiber, 29 g sugar, 3 g protein.

Dark Chocolate–Raspberry Cakes

Prep: 45 minutes **Stand:** 30 minutes **Bake:** 18 minutes at 350°F **Cool:** 45 minutes **Chill:** 40 minutes
Makes 24 (2½-inch) cupcakes

½ cup butter
2 eggs
  Nonstick cooking spray
1⅔ cups all-purpose flour
½ cup unsweetened Dutch-process cocoa powder or unsweetened cocoa powder
1 teaspoon baking soda
½ teaspoon baking powder
½ teaspoon salt
⅔ cup granulated sugar
⅔ cup packed brown sugar
1½ teaspoons vanilla
1 cup buttermilk or sour milk (see tip, page 11)
2 cups fresh raspberries
1 recipe Chocolate Truffle Icing
  Fresh raspberries (optional)

1. Allow butter and eggs to stand at room temperature for 30 minutes. Meanwhile, lightly coat twenty-four 2½-inch muffin cups with cooking spray. In a medium bowl stir together flour, cocoa powder, baking soda, baking powder, and salt. In a small bowl combine granulated sugar and brown sugar. Set aside.

2. Preheat oven to 350°F. In a large mixing bowl beat butter with an electric mixer on medium to high speed for 30 seconds. Gradually add sugar mixture, about ¼ cup at a time, beating on medium speed until combined. Scrape sides of bowl occasionally; beat on medium speed about 5 minutes or until light and fluffy. Add eggs, one at a time, beating well after each addition. Beat in vanilla.

3. Alternately add flour mixture and buttermilk to butter mixture, beating on low speed after each addition just until combined. Beat on medium to high speed for 20 seconds more.

4. Divide half of the batter among prepared muffin cups. Divide the 2 cups raspberries among muffin cups, adding 3 or 4 berries to the center of each cup. Spoon the remaining batter over berries in muffin cups.

5. Bake for 18 to 20 minutes or until a wooden toothpick inserted near centers comes out clean. Cool cupcakes in muffin cups on wire racks for 5 minutes. Remove cupcakes from muffin cups. Cool completely on wire racks.

6. To glaze cupcakes, invert one cupcake at a time onto a slotted spoon. Hold the cupcake over the bowl of Chocolate Truffle Icing and spoon icing over cupcake, allowing excess to drip down sides. Place glazed cupcakes on a wire rack set on a parchment-lined baking sheet. Chill about 20 minutes or until icing is set. If desired, garnish cupcakes with additional raspberries.

Chocolate Truffle Icing

In a medium heavy saucepan combine 1 cup whipping cream and 2 tablespoons light-color corn syrup. Cook and stir over medium-low heat just until mixture is simmering. Remove from heat. Stir in 1⅓ cups semisweet chocolate pieces and ¾ teaspoon vanilla; whisk until chocolate is melted. Transfer to a large bowl. Cover and chill about 20 minutes or until icing reaches a thick, pourable consistency, stirring occasionally.

Per cupcake: 219 cal., 11 g total fat (7 g sat. fat), 40 mg chol., 168 mg sodium, 29 g carb., 2 g dietary fiber, 18 g sugar, 3 g protein.

Chocolate, Caramel, and Pecan Cupcakes

Prep: 20 minutes **Stand:** 30 minutes **Bake:** 16 minutes at 350°F **Cool:** 45 minutes
Makes 24 to 26 (2½-inch) cupcakes

¾   cup butter

3   eggs

2   cups all-purpose flour

¾   cup unsweetened cocoa powder

1   teaspoon baking powder

½   teaspoon salt

2   cups sugar

2   teaspoons vanilla

1½   cups milk

12   or 13 chocolate turtle candies, such as DeMets brand, cut in half

1   recipe Ganache (see recipe, page 15)

⅓   to ½ cup coarsely chopped pecans, toasted

Caramel-flavor ice cream topping (optional)

1. Allow butter and eggs to stand at room temperature for 30 minutes. Meanwhile, line twenty-four to twenty-six 2½-inch muffin cups with paper bake cups. In a medium bowl stir together flour, cocoa powder, baking powder, and salt. Set aside.

2. Preheat oven to 350°F. In a large mixing bowl beat butter with an electric mixer on medium to high speed for 30 seconds. Gradually add sugar, beating on medium speed until well mixed. Scrape sides of bowl; beat on medium speed for 2 minutes more. Add eggs, one at a time, beating well after each addition. Beat in vanilla. Alternately add flour mixture and milk to butter mixture, beating on low speed after each addition just until combined.

3. Spoon batter into prepared muffin cups, filling each about three-fourths full. Place a candy half on top of batter in each cup.

4. Bake for 16 to 18 minutes or until tops spring back when lightly touched. Cool cupcakes in muffin cups on wire racks for 5 minutes. Remove cupcakes from muffin cups. Cool completely on wire racks.

5. To serve, remove paper liners from cupcakes. Spread Ganache over tops of cupcakes. Sprinkle with pecans. If desired, drizzle with caramel ice cream topping.

Per cupcake: 339 cal., 19 g total fat (10 g sat. fat), 59 mg chol., 163 mg sodium, 41 g carb., 2 g dietary fiber, 25 g sugar, 5 g protein.

Triple-Chocolate Cupcakes

Prep: 1 hour **Stand:** 30 minutes **Bake:** 15 minutes at 350°F **Cool:** 45 minutes
Makes 12 (2½-inch) cupcakes

3 eggs
6 ounces bittersweet chocolate, chopped
½ cup butter, cut into pieces
3 tablespoons crème de cacao
½ cup all-purpose flour
½ teaspoon baking powder
¼ teaspoon salt
½ cup sugar
1 teaspoon vanilla
1 recipe Dark Chocolate Butter Frosting
    Chopped bittersweet chocolate

1. Separate eggs. Allow egg yolks and whites to stand at room temperature for 30 minutes. Meanwhile, in a medium saucepan combine the 6 ounces chocolate and the butter. Cook and stir over medium heat until melted. Remove from heat. Stir in crème de cacao; cool.

2. Grease and flour twelve 2½-inch muffin cups or line with paper bake cups or parchment paper. In a small bowl stir together flour, baking powder, and salt. Set aside.

3. Preheat oven to 350°F. In a large mixing bowl beat egg yolks and sugar with an electric mixer on high speed about 3 minutes or until thick and lemon-colored. Beat in chocolate mixture and vanilla. Add flour mixture, beating just until combined. Set aside.

4. Wash beaters thoroughly. In a medium bowl beat egg whites on medium to high speed just until stiff peaks form (tips stand straight). Stir a small amount of the beaten egg whites into chocolate mixture to lighten. Fold in the remaining beaten egg whites.

5. Spoon batter into the prepared muffin cups, filling each about two-thirds full.

6. Bake for 15 to 18 minutes or until tops spring back when lightly touched. Cool cupcakes in muffin cups on wire racks for 5 minutes. Remove cupcakes from muffin cups. Cool completely on wire racks.

7. Spoon Dark Chocolate Butter Frosting into a pastry bag fitted with a medium star tip. Pipe long stars of frosting onto tops of cupcakes. Sprinkle with additional chopped chocolate.

Dark Chocolate Butter Frosting

Allow 6 tablespoons butter to stand at room temperature for 30 minutes. In a large mixing bowl beat butter with an electric mixer on medium speed until smooth. Gradually add 1 cup powdered sugar, beating well. Beat in 2 ounces dark chocolate, melted and cooled; 2 tablespoons milk, and 1 tablespoon crème de cacao. Gradually beat in an additional 3 cups powdered sugar. Beat in an additional 1 to 2 tablespoons milk until frosting reaches piping consistency.

Per cupcake: 473 cal., 23 g total fat (14 g sat. fat), 90 mg chol., 180 mg sodium, 67 g carb., 2 g dietary fiber, 58 g sugar, 5 g protein.

Black Forest Cupcakes

Prep: 1 hour 45 minutes Stand: 30 minutes Bake: 18 minutes at 350°F Cool: 45 minutes

Makes 25 (2½-inch) cupcakes

⅔ cup butter

2 eggs

2¼ cups all-purpose flour

1 teaspoon baking powder

¾ teaspoon baking soda

¼ teaspoon salt

1¾ cups sugar

3 ounces unsweetened chocolate, melted and cooled

1 teaspoon vanilla

1 cup water

¼ cup kirsch, other cherry brandy, or water

1 recipe Tart Cherry Filling (see recipe opposite) or one 21-ounce can cherry pie filling

1 recipe Cocoa Butter Frosting (see recipe opposite) (optional)

Grated semisweet chocolate (optional)

1 recipe Sweetened Whipped Cream (see recipe opposite)

25 maraschino cherries with stems

1. Allow butter and eggs to stand at room temperature for 30 minutes. Meanwhile, line twenty-five 2½-inch muffin cups with paper bake cups. In a medium bowl stir together flour, baking powder, baking soda, and salt. Set aside.

2. Preheat oven to 350°F. In a large mixing bowl beat butter with an electric mixer on medium to high speed for 30 seconds. Gradually add sugar, about ¼ cup at a time, beating on medium speed until light and fluffy. Add eggs, one at a time, beating well after each addition. Beat in melted chocolate and vanilla. Alternately add flour mixture and the water to butter mixture, beating on low speed after each addition just until combined. Stir in kirsch.

3. Spoon batter into prepared muffin cups, filling each one-half to two-thirds full. Use the back of a spoon to smooth out batter in cups.

4. Bake for 18 to 22 minutes or until a wooden toothpick inserted in centers comes out clean. Cool cupcakes in muffin cups on wire racks for 10 minutes. Remove cupcakes from muffin cups. Cool completely on wire racks.

5. Using a spoon, scoop out a 1-inch-deep indentation from the center of each cupcake, leaving a ½-inch rim around the edge. Spoon about 1 tablespoon of the Tart Cherry Filling into the center of each cupcake. Cover and chill until serving time.

6. Just before serving, if desired, pipe Cocoa Butter Frosting onto the center of each cupcake. If desired, sprinkle with grated chocolate. Spoon Sweetened Whipped Cream into a large pastry bag fitted with an open star tip. Pipe a star onto each cupcake and top with a cherry.

Make-Ahead Directions:

Prepare Black Forest Cupcakes as directed. Cover and chill for up to 24 hours. Let stand at room temperature for 30 minutes before serving.

Per cupcake: 269 cal., 13 g total fat (8 g sat. fat), 50 mg chol., 119 mg sodium, 36 g carb., 1 g dietary fiber, 25 g sugar, 3 g protein.

Vary the Berry

If cherries aren't your top flavor choice for the Black Forest Cupcakes, use water in place of the kirsch and substitute a 21-ounce can of your favorite pie filling for the Tart Cherry Filling. Yummy possibilities include raspberry, strawberry, or blackberry pie filling.

Tart Cherry Filling

In a medium saucepan stir together ¾ cup sugar and 3 tablespoons cornstarch. Stir in ⅓ cup water. Add 3 cups fresh or frozen pitted tart red cherries. Cook and stir over medium heat until thickened and bubbly. Cook and stir for 2 minutes more. Remove from heat. Stir in 4 teaspoons kirsch or cherry brandy. Cover surface with plastic wrap; cool.

Cocoa Butter Frosting

Allow ⅓ cup butter to stand at room temperature for 30 minutes. In a large mixing bowl beat butter with an electric mixer on medium speed until smooth. Gradually add 1 cup powdered sugar, 2 tablespoons unsweetened cocoa powder, and 1 ounce unsweetened chocolate, melted, beating well. Beat in 2 tablespoons milk and 1 teaspoon vanilla. Slowly beat in an additional 3¼ cups powdered sugar. Beat in additional milk until frosting reaches piping or spreading consistency.

Sweetened Whipped Cream

In a chilled medium mixing bowl combine 1½ cups whipping cream, 2 tablespoons sugar, and 1½ teaspoons vanilla. Beat with the chilled beaters of an electric mixer on medium speed until soft peaks form (tips curl). Do not overbeat.

Double Chocolate Muffin Cupcakes

Prep: 15 minutes **Cool:** 10 minutes **Bake:** 18 minutes at 375°F

Makes 12 cupcakes

1¼ cups all-purpose flour

½ cup granulated sugar

⅓ cup packed brown sugar

¼ cup unsweetened cocoa powder

2 teaspoons baking powder

¼ teaspoon baking soda

¼ teaspoon salt

1 cup miniature semisweet chocolate pieces

½ cup vegetable oil

½ cup milk

1 egg

1. Preheat oven to 375°F. Line twelve 2½-inch muffin cups with paper bake cups; set aside. In a medium bowl combine flour, granulated sugar, brown sugar, cocoa powder, baking powder, baking soda, and salt. Stir in chocolate pieces. Make a well in center of flour mixture; set aside.

2. In a small bowl whisk together the oil, milk, and egg. Add oil mixture all at once to the flour mixture. Stir just until moistened. Spoon batter into prepared muffin cups, filling each two-thirds full. Bake for 18 to 20 minutes or until edges are firm (tops will be slightly rounded). Cool in muffin cups on a wire rack for 5 minutes. Remove from muffin cups; serve warm.

Per cupcake: 295 cal., 15 g total fat (4 g sat. fat), 19 mg chol., 148 mg sodium, 38 g carb., 2 g dietary fiber, 25 g sugar, 3 g protein.

Cream-Filled Fudgy Cupcakes

Prep: 20 minutes **Bake:** at 350°F per package directions **Cool:** 45 minutes
Makes 30 (2½-inch) cupcakes

1   8-ounce package cream cheese, softened

⅓   cup sugar

1   egg
    Pinch salt

1   cup semisweet chocolate pieces (6 ounces)

1   package 2-layer-size chocolate cake mix

2½   to 3 cups Butter Frosting (see recipe, page 14) or canned vanilla frosting

2½   to 3 cups Milk Chocolate Butter Frosting (see recipe, page 14) or canned chocolate frosting

1. In a medium mixing bowl beat cream cheese and sugar with an electric mixer on medium to high speed until combined. Beat in egg and salt. Stir in chocolate pieces. Set aside.

2. Preheat oven to 350°F. Line thirty 2½-inch muffin cups with paper bake cups. Prepare cake mix according to package directions. Spoon batter into prepared muffin cups, filling each about one-half full. Drop 1 rounded teaspoon of the cream cheese mixture into each muffin cup.

3. Bake according to package directions for cupcakes. Cool cupcakes in muffin cups on wire racks for 5 minutes. Remove cupcakes from muffin cups. Cool completely on wire racks.

4. Spoon Butter Frosting into a pastry bag fitted with a star tip. Spoon Milk Chocolate Butter Frosting in to another pastry bag fitted with a star tip. Pipe stars of frosting onto top of each cupcake, alternating colors.

Per cupcake: 161 cal., 9 g total fat (4 g sat. fat), 29 mg chol., 141 mg sodium, 20 g carb., 1 g dietary fiber, 13 g sugar, 2 g protein.

Ebony and Ivory Cupcakes

Prep: 30 minutes **Bake:** 20 minutes at 350°F **Cool:** 45 minutes
Makes 12 (2½-inch) cupcakes

- 1 cup all-purpose flour
- 1 cup sugar
- ½ teaspoon baking soda
- ¼ teaspoon salt
- ½ cup butter
- ½ cup water
- ¼ cup unsweetened cocoa powder
- 1 egg
- ¼ cup buttermilk or sour milk (see tip, page 11)
- 1½ teaspoons vanilla
- Canned chocolate frosting
- Chocolate shavings
- 1 recipe Powdered Sugar Glaze

1. Preheat oven to 350°F. Line twelve 2½-inch muffin cups with paper or foil bake cups. In a medium mixing bowl stir together flour, sugar, baking soda, and salt. Set aside.

2. In a small saucepan combine butter, the water, and cocoa powder. Bring just to boiling, stirring constantly. Remove from heat. Add cocoa powder mixture to flour mixture. Beat with an electric mixer on low speed just until combined. Add egg, buttermilk, and vanilla. Beat on low speed for 1 minute more. (Batter will be thin.)

3. Spoon batter into prepared muffin cups, filling each about one-half full. Bake for 20 to 22 minutes or until a wooden toothpick inserted in centers comes out clean.

4. Cool cupcakes in muffin cups on wire racks for 5 minutes. Remove cupcakes from muffin cups. Cool completely on wire racks.

5. Remove paper or foil liners from cupcakes. Frost the sides of each cupcake with chocolate frosting; roll in chocolate shavings to coat. Immediately pour some of the Powdered Sugar Glaze over each cupcake. Using a narrow metal spatula, spread glaze over cupcake surface just enough to cover. If desired, top with additional chocolate shavings.

Powdered Sugar Glaze

In a medium bowl combine 3 cups powdered sugar, 2 tablespoons milk, and 1 teaspoon vanilla. Stir in enough additional milk, 1 teaspoon at a time, until glaze reaches spreading consistency. (The consistency should be thicker than whipping cream, but runny.)

Per cupcake: 287 cal., 9 g total fat (5 g sat. fat), 38 mg chol., 168 mg sodium, 51 g carb., 0 g dietary fiber, 42 g sugar, 2 g protein.

Peanut Butter–Chocolate Twist Cupcakes

Prep: 45 minutes **Stand:** 30 minutes **Bake:** 15 minutes at 375°F **Cool:** 45 minutes

Makes 34 to 36 (2½-inch) cupcakes

½ cup butter

3 eggs

2½ cups all-purpose flour

2½ teaspoons baking powder

½ teaspoon salt

⅓ cup creamy peanut butter

1 cup packed brown sugar

¾ cup granulated sugar

1½ teaspoons vanilla

1 cup milk

4 ounces milk chocolate, melted

1 recipe Peanut Butter Frosting

1 recipe Chocolate Frosting

Shaved milk chocolate and/or bite-size chocolate-covered peanut butter cups, halved

1. Allow butter and eggs to stand at room temperature for 30 minutes. Meanwhile, line thirty-four to thirty-six 2½-inch muffin cups with paper bake cups. In a medium bowl combine flour, baking powder, and salt. Set aside.

2. Preheat oven to 375°F. In a large mixing bowl beat butter with an electric mixer on medium to high speed for 30 seconds. Add peanut butter. Beat until combined. Gradually add brown sugar and granulated sugar, about ¼ cup at a time, beating on medium speed until combined. Scrape sides of bowl; beat on medium speed about 2 minutes more or until fluffy. Add eggs, one at a time, beating well after each addition. Beat in vanilla. Alternately add flour mixture and milk to butter mixture, beating on low speed after each addition just until combined.

3. Transfer half of the batter to a separate mixing bowl; add melted chocolate. Beat on low speed just until combined.

4. Fill prepared muffin cups by alternating spoonfuls of peanut butter batter and chocolate batter, filling each cup about two-thirds full. Use a butter knife or skewer to swirl batter in each cup.

5. Bake for 15 to 18 minutes or until a toothpick inserted in centers comes out clean. Cool cupcakes in muffin cups on wire racks for 5 minutes. Remove cupcakes from muffin cups. Cool completely on wire racks.

6. Spoon Peanut Butter Frosting and Chocolate Frosting side by side into a pastry bag fitted with a large round or star tip. Pipe frostings in swirls onto tops of cupcakes. Top with shaved chocolate and/or peanut butter cup halves.

Peanut Butter Frosting

Allow one 8-ounce package cream cheese to stand at room temperature for 30 minutes. In a large mixing bowl beat cream cheese, ½ cup creamy peanut butter, and 2 teaspoons vanilla with an electric mixer on medium speed until light and fluffy. Gradually beat in 6 cups powdered sugar. Beat in enough milk, 1 teaspoon at a time, until frosting reaches piping consistency. Divide frosting into two portions. Set one portion aside for Chocolate Frosting (see recipe, below).

Chocolate Frosting

In a medium bowl combine the one portion Peanut Butter Frosting and 4 ounces milk chocolate, melted and cooled. Beat with an electric mixer on medium speed until combined. If necessary, beat in enough powdered sugar or milk until frosting reaches piping consistency.

Per cupcake: 293 cal., 11 g total fat (5 g sat. fat), 36 mg chol., 149 mg sodium, 45 g carb., 1 g dietary fiber, 37 g sugar, 4 g protein.

Salted Caramel and Bourbon Chocolate Cupcakes

Prep: 50 minutes **Stand:** 30 minutes **Bake:** 18 minutes at 325°F **Cool:** 45 minutes

Makes 32 to 34 (2½-inch) cupcakes

1 cup butter

3 eggs

2 cups all-purpose flour

1 teaspoon baking soda

½ teaspoon salt

1½ cups water

⅓ cup bourbon

3 ounces unsweetened chocolate, chopped

2 ounces bittersweet chocolate, chopped

2 cups sugar

1½ teaspoons vanilla

1 recipe Fudge Frosting

1 recipe Salted Caramel

Sea salt, such as fleur de sel

1 Allow butter and eggs to stand at room temperature for 30 minutes. Meanwhile, line thirty-two to thirty-four 2½-inch muffin cups with paper bake cups. In a medium bowl stir together flour, baking soda, and the ½ teaspoon salt. In a 2-cup glass measuring cup combine the water and bourbon. Set aside.

2. In a small microwave-safe bowl microwave unsweetened chocolate and bittersweet chocolate on 100% power (high) for 1 minute; stir. Microwave for 30 seconds more; stir until chocolate is smooth. Cool slightly.

3. Preheat oven to 325°F. In a large mixing bowl beat butter with an electric mixer on medium to high speed for 30 seconds. Gradually add sugar, about ¼ cup at a time, beating on medium speed until combined and scraping sides of bowl occasionally. Add eggs, one at a time, beating well after each addition. Beat in melted chocolate and vanilla. Alternately add flour mixture and bourbon mixture to chocolate mixture, beating on low speed after each addition just until combined.

4. Spoon batter into prepared muffin cups, filling each about three-fourths full. Use the back of a spoon to smooth out batter in cups.

5. Bake about 18 minutes or until a wooden toothpick inserted in centers comes out clean. Tops of cupcakes may sink slightly, but this will provide a nest for the Salted Caramel filling. (If desired, scoop out some of each cupcake top with a spoon to make more of an indentation for the filling.) Cool cupcakes in muffin cups on wire racks for 5 minutes. Remove cupcakes from muffin cups. Cool completely on wire racks.

6. Spoon Fudge Frosting into a pastry bag fitted with a star tip. Pipe a border of frosting around edge of each cupcake. Spoon about 1 teaspoon of the Salted Caramel into the center of each cupcake. Sprinkle the caramel lightly with sea salt.

Fudge Frosting

In a large saucepan combine 6 ounces chopped bittersweet chocolate and 2 tablespoons butter. Cook and stir over low heat until melted; cool for 5 minutes. Stir in ½ cup sour cream. Gradually add 2½ cups powdered sugar, beating with an electric mixer on medium speed until combined.

Salted Caramel

In a small saucepan combine 2 tablespoons whipping cream and 1 tablespoon bourbon. Heat over medium-low heat until steaming but not boiling. Stir in 24 vanilla caramels, unwrapped, and ¼ teaspoon sea salt (such as fleur de sel). Heat until melted, stirring constantly.

Per cupcake: 266 cal., 12 g total fat (8 g sat. fat), 40 mg chol., 212 mg sodium, 37 g carb., 1 g dietary fiber, 28 g sugar, 2 g protein.

Special Salt

The bland, slightly bitter taste of regular table salt just won't cut it in the Salted Caramel. Go for fleur de sel ("flower of salt" in French) at a gourmet food store or online. Or, if you can't find fleur de sel, most grocery stores carry a basic sea salt.

Peaches and Cream Cupcakes,
page 128

Cake Mix Fix-Ups

There's a reason why cake mixes are so popular—they make homemade goodness easy enough to whip up any night of the week. Plus, with a few flavor tweaks, a plain-Jane yellow or chocolate cake mix can become something magnificently different and unique. These cute cupcakes take cake mix to a whole new level of fabulousness, complete with drizzles, drops, sprinkles, and decorations. Enjoy the simplicity!

Lazy-Daisy Cupcakes

Prep: 40 minutes **Bake:** 12 minutes at 350°F per batch **Cool:** 45 minutes
Makes 84 (1¾-inch) cupcakes or 24 (2½-inch) cupcakes

1 16-ounce package pound cake mix
1 egg
1 16-ounce can creamy white frosting
   Sugar
   Small gumdrops
   Small oval or round candies

1. Preheat oven to 350°F. Line desired number of 1¾-inch muffin cups* with paper bake cups. Prepare cake mix according to package directions, except add additional egg. Spoon batter into prepared muffin cups, filling each about two-thirds full (about 1 tablespoon in each).

2. Bake about 12 minutes or until a wooden toothpick inserted in centers comes out clean. Cool cupcakes in muffin cups on wire racks for 5 minutes. Remove cupcakes from muffin cups. Cool completely on wire racks. Repeat with the remaining batter.

3. Spread frosting onto tops of cupcakes. On a work surface sprinkled with sugar, use a rolling pin or your hands to flatten a gumdrop. Using kitchen scissors, snip the flattened gumdrop into pieces to resemble flower petals. Place petals on frosted cupcake with a small candy in the center to resemble a flower. Repeat to decorate all of the cupcakes.

*Test Kitchen Tip:
The batter should make 84 mini cupcakes. If you prefer, make twenty-four 2½-inch cupcakes instead or make some mini cupcakes and some regular-size cupcakes.

Per cupcake: 68 cal., 2 g total fat (1 g sat. fat), 7 mg chol., 33 mg sodium, 13 g carb., 0 g dietary fiber, 9 g sugar, 0 g protein.

Icing on the Cake
Everyone loves options, so here are more ideas for adding flavor to cupcake tops.

O To spruce up the flavor of canned frosting, try stirring in ¼ cup miniature semisweet chocolate pieces; 2 tablespoons chopped drained maraschino cherries; or 2 teaspoons grated citrus peel. Or add peppermint, almond, or other extract to taste.

O After frosting cupcakes, sprinkle with finely chopped hard candy, candy bars, honey-roasted peanuts, or broken peanut brittle.

Caramel-Gingerbread Cupcakes

Prep: 30 minutes **Freeze:** 4 to 24 hours **Bake:** 15 minutes at 350°F **Cool:** 45 minutes
Makes 12 (2½-inch) cupcakes

½ gallon vanilla ice cream

2 to 3 teaspoons grated fresh ginger or ½ to 1 teaspoon ground ginger

½ to ¾ cup almond toffee bits

1 14.5-ounce package gingerbread mix

1¼ cups lukewarm water

1 egg

1 12-ounce jar caramel-flavor ice cream topping*

6 gingersnaps, broken

1. Line a 3-quart rectangular baking dish with plastic wrap or foil; set aside. In a chilled medium bowl stir ice cream with a wooden spoon until softened. Stir in ginger. Spread ice cream mixture in the prepared dish. Sprinkle with toffee bits, pressing lightly into ice cream. Cover and freeze for 4 to 24 hours.

2. Preheat oven to 350°F. Line twelve 2½-inch muffin cups with paper bake cups or lightly grease muffin cups. Prepare gingerbread mix according to package directions using the lukewarm water and egg. Spoon batter into prepared muffin cups about filling three-fourths full. Use the back of a spoon to smooth out batter in cups.

3. Bake for 15 to 18 minutes or until a wooden toothpick inserted in centers comes out clean. Cool cupcakes in muffin cups on wire racks for 5 minutes. Remove cupcakes from muffin cups. Cool completely on wire racks.

4. Before serving, in a small saucepan heat caramel topping over medium-low heat until warm, stirring occasionally. Remove from heat; cover and keep warm.

5. Remove paper liners from cupcakes. Slice cupcakes horizontally in half. Place cupcakes on dessert plates or in shallow bowls; set aside. Using the edges of the plastic wrap or foil, lift ice cream out of dish. Cut out twelve 2-inch squares of ice cream. (Save the leftover ice cream to eat later.) Place ice cream squares on cut sides of cupcake bottoms. Replace cupcake tops, cut side down. Drizzle with warm caramel topping and sprinkle with gingersnap pieces. Serve immediately.

*Test Kitchen Tip:
To make an orange-caramel sauce, add ½ cup orange marmalade to the caramel topping before heating.

Per cupcake: 585 cal., 28 g total fat (13 g sat. fat), 111 mg chol., 370 mg sodium, 78 g carb., 1 g dietary fiber, 21 g sugar, 6 g protein.

PB and Jelly Cupcakes

Prep: 40 minutes **Stand:** 30 minutes **Bake:** 20 minutes at 350°F **Cool:** 45 minutes

Makes 24 (2½-inch) cupcakes

¼ cup butter

3 eggs

1 cup creamy peanut butter

1 8-ounce package sour cream

¾ cup water

1 package 2-layer-size golden butter cake mix

1 recipe Strawberry Cream Cheese Frosting

1. Allow butter and eggs to stand at room temperature for 30 minutes. Meanwhile, line twenty-four 2½-inch muffin cups with paper bake cups.

2. Preheat oven to 350°F. In a large mixing bowl beat butter, peanut butter, and sour cream with an electric mixer on medium to high speed until smooth. Add eggs and the water. Beat until combined. Add cake mix. Beat until combined.

3. Spoon ¼ cup of the batter into each prepared muffin cup. Use the back of a spoon to smooth out batter in cups.

4. Bake for 20 to 25 minutes or until the tops spring back when lightly touched. Cool cupcakes in muffin pans on wire racks for 5 minutes. Remove cupcakes from muffin cups. Cool completely on wire racks.

5. Spoon Strawberry Cream Cheese Frosting into a pastry bag fitted with a large star tip. Pipe frosting onto tops of cupcakes. Serve immediately or store in an airtight container in the refrigerator for up to 2 days.

Strawberry Cream Cheese Frosting

Allow one 8-ounce package cream cheese and ½ cup butter to stand at room temperature for 30 minutes. In a large mixing bowl beat cream cheese and butter with an electric mixer on medium to high speed until light and fluffy. Gradually add 6 cups powdered sugar, beating until smooth. Gently fold in ¼ cup seedless strawberry preserves, leaving streaks of preserves in frosting.

Per cupcake: 384 cal., 19 g total fat (9 g sat. fat), 54 mg chol., 293 mg sodium, 53 g carb., 1 g dietary fiber, 43 g sugar, 5 g protein.

Velvety Red Cupcakes with Coconut Filling

Prep: 1 hour **Chill:** 1 hour **Bake:** 20 minutes at 350°F **Cool:** 45 minutes

Makes 30 (2½-inch) cupcakes

1   8-ounce package cream cheese, softened

⅓   cup sugar

1   egg

1   teaspoon vanilla

½   teaspoon coconut extract (optional)

⅛   teaspoon salt

1½   cups flaked coconut

1   package 2-layer-size red velvet cake mix

1   recipe Vanilla Butter Cream Frosting

1. For filling, in a large mixing bowl beat cream cheese and sugar with an electric mixer on medium speed until light and fluffy. Beat in egg, vanilla, coconut extract (if desired), and salt. Stir in coconut. Cover and chill for at least 1 hour or until stiff.

2. Preheat oven to 350°F. Line thirty 2½-inch muffin cups with paper bake cups.

3. Prepare cake mix according to package directions. Spoon 2 tablespoons of the batter into each prepared muffin cup. Drop 1 tablespoon of the filling in each muffin cup. Top each muffin cup with another 1 tablespoon of the batter. Use a small spoon to smooth batter over filling to cover.

4. Bake about 20 minutes or until a wooden toothpick inserted near centers comes out clean. Cool cupcakes in muffin cups on wire racks for 5 minutes. Remove cupcakes from muffin cups. Cool completely on wire racks.

5. If desired, spoon Vanilla Butter Cream Frosting into a pastry bag fitted with a large round tip. Generously spread or pipe frosting onto tops of cupcakes.

Vanilla Butter Cream Frosting

Allow ½ cup butter to stand at room temperature for 30 minutes. In a large mixing bowl beat butter with an electric mixer on medium to high speed for 30 seconds. Add 1 cup powdered sugar, beating well. Slowly beat in 6 tablespoons half-and-half, light cream, or whole milk; 1½ teaspoons vanilla; and ½ teaspoon coconut extract (if desired). Gradually beat in an additional 3½ cups powdered sugar. If necessary, beat in 1 tablespoon half-and-half, light cream, or milk; 1 teaspoon at a time; until frosting reaches spreading consistency.

Per cupcake: 255 cal., 13 g total fat (7 g sat. fat), 47 mg chol., 220 mg sodium, 34 g carb., 1 g dietary fiber, 27 g sugar, 3 g protein.

Peaches and Cream Cupcakes

Prep: 25 minutes **Bake:** 18 minutes at 350°F **Cool:** 45 minutes
Makes 24 (2½-inch) cupcakes

1 package 2-layer-size white cake mix

2 eggs

1 6-ounce carton peach yogurt

⅔ cup peach nectar

½ cup vegetable oil

1 medium peach, pitted and finely chopped, or 1 cup frozen unsweetened peach slices, thawed, well drained, and finely chopped

1 recipe Peach Buttercream Frosting

Colored or coarse sugar (optional)

1. Preheat oven to 350°F. Line twenty-four 2½-inch muffin cups with paper bake cups; set aside.

2. In a large bowl beat cake mix, eggs, yogurt, peach nectar, and oil with an electric mixer on low speed until combined. Beat on medium speed for 2 minutes more. Fold in peaches. Spoon batter into prepared muffin cups, filling each about three-fourths full.

3. Bake for 18 to 22 minutes or until tops spring back when lightly touched. Cool cupcakes in muffin cups on wire racks for 5 minutes. Remove cupcakes from muffin cups. Cool completely on wire racks.

4. Spoon Peach Buttercream Frosting into a pastry bag fitted with a small closed star tip. Pipe frosting onto tops of cupcakes. If desired, lightly sprinkle cupcakes with colored sugar.

Peach Buttercream Frosting

Allow ⅓ cup butter to stand at room temperature for 30 minutes. In a large mixing bowl beat butter with an electric mixer on medium to high speed until smooth. Add 1 cup powdered sugar, beating well. Beat in 3 tablespoons peach nectar. Gradually beat in an additional 3 cups powdered sugar. Beat in enough additional peach nectar until frosting reaches spreading consistency.

Per cupcake: 254 cal., 10 g total fat (3 g sat. fat), 25 mg chol., 174 mg sodium, 40 g carb., 0 g dietary fiber, 2 g protein.

Chill It

If you don't have enough muffin cups or if all of the cupcakes do not fit in the oven at once, store the remaining batter in the refrigerator while the first batch bakes.

Mini Snowball Cakes

Prep: 40 minutes **Bake:** 10 minutes at 350°F **Cool:** 45 minutes
Makes 36 (1¾-inch) cupcakes

1 package 1-layer-size white cake mix
½ cup canned eggnog
1 egg
1 teaspoon vanilla
⅛ teaspoon ground nutmeg
1 recipe Eggnog Frosting
1 cup shredded coconut, toasted (if desired)

1. Preheat oven to 350°F. Line thirty-six 1¾-inch muffin cups with paper bake cups.

2. In a medium mixing bowl beat cake mix, eggnog, egg, vanilla, and nutmeg with an electric mixer on low speed just until combined. Beat on medium speed for 2 minutes more, scraping sides of bowl frequently. Spoon batter into prepared muffin cups, filling each about two-thirds full (about 1 rounded teaspoon in each).

3. Bake for 10 to 12 minutes or until a wooden toothpick inserted near centers comes out clean. Cool cupcakes in muffin cups on wire racks for 5 minutes. Remove cupcakes from muffin cups. Cool completely on wire racks.

4. Remove paper liners from cupcakes. Using a small metal spatula, lightly spread Eggnog Frosting on tops and sides of cupcakes.* Immediately roll frosted tops in coconut. If desired, place cupcakes in decorative candy or cupcake paper cups.

Eggnog Frosting

Allow half of an 8-ounce package cream cheese and 3 tablespoons butter to stand at room temperature for 30 minutes. In a medium mixing bowl beat cream cheese and butter with an electric mixer on medium speed until light and fluffy. Beat in 1 cup powdered sugar and ½ teaspoon vanilla until smooth. Gradually beat in 1 to 2 tablespoons canned eggnog until frosting reaches dipping consistency.

*Test Kitchen Tip:

For an easier way to decorate, simply dip the tops of cupcakes in frosting before dipping in coconut.

Per cupcake: 75 cal., 4 g total fat (2 g sat. fat), 11 mg chol., 68 mg sodium, 10 g carb., 0 g dietary fiber, 4 g sugar, 1 g protein.

Lemon-Spice Cupcakes

Prep: 25 minutes **Bake:** at 350°F per package directions **Cool:** 45 minutes
Makes 24 (2½-inch) cupcakes

1   package 2-layer-size lemon cake mix
1   16-ounce can cream cheese frosting
1   teaspoon apple pie spice
    Crushed lemon drop candies

1. Preheat oven to 350°F. Line twenty-four 2½-inch muffin cups with foil or paper bake cups. Prepare and bake cake mix according to package directions for cupcakes. Cool cupcakes in muffin cups on wire racks for 5 minutes. Remove cupcakes from muffin cups. Cool completely on wire racks.

2. For spice frosting, in a medium bowl stir together cream cheese frosting and apple pie spice. Spoon frosting into a pastry bag fitted with a large round tip. Pipe frosting onto tops of cupcakes. If desired, sprinkle with crushed candies.

Per cupcake: 196 cal., 8 g total fat (2 g sat. fat), 28 mg chol., 183 mg sodium, 30 g carb., 0 g dietary fiber, 21 g sugar, 2 g protein.

Brownie Surprise Cupcakes

Prep: 15 minutes **Bake:** 22 minutes at 350°F **Cool:** 45 minutes
Makes 15 (2½-inch) cupcakes

1 21-ounce package fudge brownie mix

15 miniature chocolate-coated caramel-topped nougat bars with peanuts or dark chocolate-covered mint creams

    Canned vanilla frosting

15 well-drained maraschino cherries with stems (optional)

1. Preheat oven to 350°F. Line fifteen 2½-inch muffin cups with paper bake cups.

2. Prepare brownie mix according to package directions. Spoon 1 tablespoon of the batter into the bottom of each prepared muffin cup. Place a nougat bar in each muffin cup. Top each muffin cup with the remaining batter.

3. Bake for 22 minutes. Cool cupcakes in muffin cups on wire racks for 5 minutes. Remove cupcakes from muffin cups. Cool completely on wire racks (cupcakes might dip slightly in centers).

4. If desired, remove paper liners from cupcakes. Spread vanilla frosting onto tops of cupcakes. If desired, garnish each cupcake with a cherry.

Per cupcake: 397 cal., 18 g total fat (4 g sat. fat), 29 mg chol., 215 mg sodium, 59 g carb., 1 g dietary fiber, 43 g sugar, 3 g protein.

Ginger-Peach Ice Cream Cupcakes

Prep: 40 minutes **Bake:** at 350°F per package directions **Cool:** 45 minutes **Chill:** 30 minutes
Freeze: 1 to 2 hours **Stand:** 5 minutes **Makes** 24 (2½-inch) cupcakes

1   package 2-layer-size spice cake mix
1   quart vanilla ice cream
1   large ripe peach, peeled and finely chopped
1   teaspoon grated fresh ginger
⅔   cup packed brown sugar
¼   cup powdered sugar
2   tablespoons cornstarch
1   8-ounce package cream cheese, softened
¼   cup butter, softened
½   teaspoon vanilla

1. Preheat oven to 350°F. Line twenty-four 2½-inch muffin cups with paper bake cups. Prepare and bake cake mix according to package directions for cupcakes. Cool cupcakes in muffin cups on wire racks for 5 minutes. Remove cupcakes from muffin cups. Cool completely on wire racks.

2. Remove paper liners from cupcakes. Cut cupcakes horizontally in half. Line muffin cups with fresh paper bake cups. Place bottoms of cupcakes in the prepared muffin cups.

3. In a chilled large bowl stir ice cream with a wooden spoon until softened. Stir in peach and ginger. Drop spoonfuls of ice cream mixture onto bottoms of cupcakes. Replace tops of cupcakes; press together lightly. Place cupcakes in freezer while preparing icing.

4. For icing, in a small bowl combine brown sugar, powdered sugar, and cornstarch. Set aside. In a large mixing bowl beat cream cheese and butter with an electric mixer on medium to high speed until light and fluffy, scraping sides of bowl occasionally. Add brown sugar mixture and vanilla. Beat until smooth. Cover and chill for 30 minutes.

5. Remove cupcakes from freezer. Spoon icing into a pastry bag fitted with a ½-inch plain round tip. Pipe icing onto tops of cupcakes. Freeze for 1 to 2 hours or until firm. Let stand at room temperature for 5 to 10 minutes before serving.

Per cupcake: 258 cal., 13 g total fat (6 g sat. fat), 54 mg chol., 210 mg sodium, 33 g carb., 0 g dietary fiber, 24 g sugar, 3 g protein.

Chocolate-Orange Cupcakes

Prep: 30 minutes **Bake:** 18 minutes at 350°F **Cool:** 45 minutes

Makes 24 (2½-inch) cupcakes

2 oranges

1 8-ounce package reduced-fat cream cheese (Neufchâtel), softened

¼ cup sugar

4 eggs

1 package 2-layer-size devil's food cake mix

½ cup vegetable oil

1 recipe Butter Cream Frosting

Orange fruit jelly candy wedges (optional)

Melted chocolate (optional)

1. Preheat oven to 350°F. Line twenty-four 2½-inch muffin cups with paper bake cups. Finely shred peel from the oranges. Set aside. Squeeze juice from oranges; add enough water to juice to equal 1 cup total liquid. Set aside.

2. In a medium mixing bowl beat cream cheese and sugar with an electric mixer on medium to high speed until combined. Beat in one of the eggs; stir in 1 tablespoon of the shredded orange peel. Set aside.

3. In a large mixing bowl beat cake mix, oil, orange juice mixture, and the remaining 3 eggs on low speed about 30 seconds or until moistened. Beat on medium speed for 2 minutes more, scraping sides of bowl occasionally. Spoon batter into prepared muffin cups, filling each about three-fourths full. Drop 1 slightly rounded teaspoon of the cream cheese mixture into each muffin cup.

4. Bake for 18 to 22 minutes or until tops spring back when lightly touched. Cool cupcakes in muffin cups on wire racks for 10 minutes. Remove cupcakes from muffin cups. Cool completely on wire racks.

5. Spread Butter Cream Frosting onto tops of cupcakes. If desired, dip orange candy wedges into melted chocolate; let stand on waxed paper until chocolate is set. Top each cupcake with a chocolate-dipped orange candy.

Butter Cream Frosting

Allow ¾ cup butter to stand at room temperature for 30 minutes. In a medium mixing bowl beat butter with an electric mixer on medium speed until smooth. Add 1 cup powdered sugar, beating well. Beat in 1 tablespoon half-and-half, light cream, or milk and the remaining orange peel from cupcakes. Beat in an additional 1½ cups powdered sugar. If necessary, beat in enough additional half-and-half, light cream, or milk until frosting reaches spreading consistency.

Per cupcake: 275 cal., 15 g total fat (6 g sat. fat), 58 mg chol., 256 mg sodium, 34 g carb., 1 g dietary fiber, 3 g protein.

Easy Topped Cupcakes

Prep: 30 minutes **Freeze:** 4 hours **Bake:** at 350°F per package directions **Cool:** 45 minutes
Makes 12 (2½-inch) cupcakes

12 scoops butter pecan ice cream

1 package 2-layer-size desired-flavor cake mix

1 recipe Sweetened Whipped Cream

¾ cup caramel-flavor ice cream topping

¾ cup chopped toasted pecans

1. Line a large baking sheet with waxed paper. Using a 2- to 3-inch-diameter ice cream scoop, drop 12 scoops of ice cream onto prepared baking sheet. Cover and freeze for 4 hours.

2. Preheat oven to 350°F. Line twenty-four 2½-inch muffin cups with paper bake cups or lightly grease muffin cups; set aside. Prepare and bake cake mix according to package directions for cupcakes. Cool cupcakes in muffin cups on wire racks for 5 minutes. Remove cupcakes from muffin cups. Cool completely on wire racks.

3. Remove paper bake cups, if using, from 12 of the cupcakes. (Store the remaining cupcakes for another use.) Place the 12 cupcakes in shallow bowls or on dessert plates.* Spoon Sweetened Whipped Cream into a pastry bag fitted with a large star tip. Working quickly, place a scoop of ice cream on each cupcake. Spoon 1 tablespoon of the caramel topping over each ice cream scoop, allowing topping to drip down. Pipe Sweetened Whipped Cream over caramel topping. Sprinkle with pecans. Serve immediately.

Sweetened Whipped Cream
In a chilled small mixing bowl beat ½ cup whipping cream, 1½ teaspoons sugar, and ½ teaspoon vanilla with the chilled beaters of an electric mixer on medium speed until soft peaks form (tips curl). Do not overbeat.

*Test Kitchen Tip:
Assemble only as many desserts as you are going to serve at one time. Store unfrosted cupcakes in an airtight container at room temperature for up to 3 days or freeze for up to 3 months. Thaw frozen cupcakes before serving.

Make-Ahead Directions:
Prepare as directed in step 1, except cover and freeze for up to 3 days. Continue as directed.

Per cupcake: 356 cal., 19 g total fat (7 g sat. fat), 58 mg chol., 320 mg sodium, 45 g carb., 1 g dietary fiber, 30 g sugar, 3 g protein.

Banana Split Easy Topped Cupcakes:

Prepare as directed, except substitute strawberry ice cream for the butter pecan ice cream. Omit caramel topping and pecans. Serve as directed, except top ice cream with ¾ cup chocolate fudge ice cream topping, 1 cup chopped bananas, Sweetened Whipped Cream, and ¾ cup chopped dry-roasted peanuts.

Per cupcake: 373 cal., 19 g total fat (7 g sat. fat), 55 mg chol., 204 mg sodium, 47 g carb., 2 g dietary fiber, 28 g sugar, 5 g protein.

Lemon-Coconut Cupcakes

Prep: 40 minutes Bake: at 350°F per package directions Cool: 45 minutes
Makes 24 (2½-inch) cupcakes

1 package 2-layer-size white cake mix

1 cup lemon curd or cranberry curd

⅔ cup butter, softened

7 cups powdered sugar

½ cup unsweetened coconut milk or milk

Unsweetened coconut milk, milk, or powdered sugar (optional)

Shredded or flaked coconut

1. Preheat oven to 350°F. Lightly grease twenty-four 2½-inch muffin cups. Prepare and bake cake mix according to package directions for cupcakes. Cool cupcakes in muffin cups on wire racks for 5 minutes. Remove cupcakes from muffin cups. Cool completely on wire racks.

2. Using a serrated knife, cut each cupcake horizontally in half. Spread about 2 teaspoons of the lemon curd on cupcake bottoms. Replace cupcake tops.

3. For frosting, in a medium mixing bowl beat butter with an electric mixer on medium to high speed until fluffy. Add 1 cup of the powdered sugar, beating well. Gradually beat in the ½ cup coconut milk. Gradually beat in the remaining 6 cups powdered sugar. If necessary, beat in enough additional coconut milk, milk, or powdered sugar until frosting reaches spreading consistency.

4. Generously spread frosting onto tops of cupcakes. Sprinkle with coconut, pressing gently to coat.

Make-Ahead Directions:
Place frosted cupcakes in a single layer in airtight containers; seal. Store in the refrigerator for up to 3 days.

Per cupcake: 556 cal., 20 g total fat (10 g sat. fat), 24 mg chol., 321 mg sodium, 93 g carb., 2 g dietary fiber, 5 g protein.

Chocolate Cupcakes with a Kick

Prep: 35 minutes **Bake:** 18 minutes at 350°F **Cool:** 45 minutes
Makes 24 (2½-inch) cupcakes

1 package 2-layer-size chocolate or devil's food cake mix

1¼ cups sour cream

3 eggs

⅓ cup vegetable oil

2 tablespoons instant coffee crystals

½ to 1 teaspoon ground chipotle chile pepper

1 11.5-ounce package semisweet chocolate chunks

2 teaspoons all-purpose flour

1 recipe Vanilla Cream Cheese Frosting

2 ounces semisweet chocolate, chopped

¼ cup whipping cream

1. Preheat oven to 350°F. Line twenty-four 2½-inch muffin cups with paper bake cups. In a large mixing bowl beat cake mix, sour cream, eggs, oil, coffee crystals, and ground chile pepper with an electric mixer on low speed until combined. Beat on medium to high speed for 2 minutes more (batter will be thick).

2. In a medium bowl toss chocolate chunks with flour. Fold into batter. Divide batter among prepared muffin cups, filling about two-thirds full. Bake for 18 to 22 minutes or until tops spring back when lightly touched. Cool cupcakes in muffin cups on wire racks for 5 minutes. Remove cupcakes from muffin cups. Cool completely on wire racks. Spread Vanilla Cream Cheese Frosting onto tops of cupcakes.

3. For chocolate drizzle, place chopped chocolate in a small bowl. In a small saucepan heat whipping cream just until boiling. Pour hot cream over chopped chocolate (do not stir). Let stand for 5 minutes. Stir until smooth. Pour chocolate mixture into a small heavy resealable plastic bag. Snip off a small piece from one corner of bag. Drizzle chocolate mixture over frosted cupcakes.

Vanilla Cream Cheese Frosting

Allow one 8-ounce package cream cheese and ½ cup butter to stand at room temperature for 30 minutes. In a medium mixing bowl beat cream cheese and butter with an electric mixer on medium to high speed for 30 seconds. Beat in ½ teaspoon vanilla. Gradually add 2 to 2½ cups powdered sugar, beating until frosting reaches spreading consistency.

Per cupcake: 335 cal., 21 g total fat (10 g sat. fat), 55 mg chol., 251 mg sodium, 37 g carb., 2 g dietary fiber, 27 g sugar, 4 g protein.

Chai Cupcakes

Prep: 20 minutes **Bake:** 16 minutes at 350°F **Cool:** 45 minutes
Makes 24 (2½-inch) cupcakes

1 package 2-layer-size white cake mix

1¼ cups half-and-half or light cream

½ cup vegetable oil

2 eggs

1½ teaspoons Chai Spice Seasoning (page 238)

1 recipe Butter Frosting or canned vanilla frosting

1. Preheat oven to 350°F. Line twenty-four 2½-inch muffin cups with paper bake cups.

2. In a large mixing bowl beat cake mix, half-and-half, oil, eggs, and the 1½ teaspoons spice seasoning with an electric mixer on medium speed for 2 minutes. Spoon batter into prepared muffin cups, filling each about two-thirds full. Use the back of a spoon to smooth out batter in cups.

3. Bake for 16 to 18 minutes or until a wooden toothpick inserted near centers comes out clean. Cool cupcakes in muffin cups on wire racks for 5 minutes. Remove cupcakes from muffin cups. Cool completely on wire racks.

4. Spread Butter Frosting onto tops of cupcakes. Sprinkle with additional spice blend.

Butter Frosting

Allow ½ cup butter to stand at room temperature for 30 minutes. In a large mixing bowl beat butter with an electric mixer on medium speed until smooth. Gradually add 2 cups powdered sugar, beating well. Beat in 3 tablespoons milk and 1½ teaspoons vanilla. Gradually beat in an additional 4 cups powdered sugar. If necessary, beat in 1 tablespoon milk, 1 teaspoon at a time, until frosting reaches spreading consistency.

*Test Kitchen Tip:

If desired, substitute 1 teaspoon pumpkin pie spice or apple pie spice and ½ teaspoon ground cardamom for the 1½ teaspoons chai spice blend. Sprinkle frosted cupcakes with additional pumpkin pie spice or apple pie spice.

Per cupcake: 305 cal., 12 g total fat (5 g sat. fat), 33 mg chol., 184 mg sodium, 48 g carb., 0 g dietary fiber, 39 g sugar, 2 g protein.

Hazelnut Crème Brûlée Cupcakes
and Caramel-Nut Frappé
(pages 156 and 157)

Celebration Cupcakes

We all know that a good cupcake is like a hug for the heart. But when you add your gal pals and an array of exquisite cakes to the equation, you get something even more spectacular—a reason for a party in any season. Wedding showers, baby showers, and girly cocktail gatherings glimmer and gleam with the addition of themed and/or flavored cakes to bump up the "special" of any occasion.

Black-and-White Irish Cream Cupcakes

Prep: 40 minutes **Stand:** 1 hour 30 minutes **Bake:** 20 minutes at 350°F **Cool:** 45 minutes

Makes 28 (2½-inch) cupcakes

½ cup butter

4 egg whites

2 cups all-purpose flour

1 teaspoon baking powder

½ teaspoon baking soda

½ teaspoon salt

1¾ cups sugar

3 tablespoons Irish cream liqueur

1 teaspoon vanilla

1¼ cups buttermilk or sour milk (see tip, page 11)

3 ounces bittersweet chocolate, melted and cooled

1 recipe Irish Cream Ganache

1 recipe Irish Cream Icing

Coffee beans, chopped (optional)

1. Allow butter and egg whites to stand at room temperature for 30 minutes. Meanwhile, line twenty-eight 2½-inch muffin cups with paper bake cups. In a medium bowl stir together flour, baking powder, baking soda, and salt. Set aside.

2. Preheat oven to 350°F. In a large mixing bowl beat butter with an electric mixer on medium to high speed for 30 seconds. Add sugar, liqueur, and vanilla. Beat until combined, scraping sides of bowl occasionally. Add egg whites, one at a time, beating well after each addition. Alternately add flour mixture and buttermilk to butter mixture, beating on low speed after each addition just until combined.

3. Transfer 2½ cups batter (about half) to a medium bowl; stir in melted chocolate. Fill each prepared muffin cup about two-thirds full, spooning chocolate batter into one side of cup and white batter into other side of cup.

4. Bake about 20 minutes or until tops spring back when lightly touched. Cool cupcakes in muffin cups on wire racks for 5 minutes. Remove cupcakes from muffin cups. Cool completely on wire racks.

5. Spread Irish Cream Ganache onto tops of cupcakes. Let stand at room temperature about 1 hour (or chill in the refrigerator about 15 minutes) or until ganache is set. Spoon Irish Cream Icing onto centers of cupcakes. If desired, sprinkle icing with chopped coffee beans. Let stand until icing is set.

Irish Cream Ganache

In a small saucepan bring ½ cup whipping cream just to boiling over medium-high heat. Remove from heat. Add 6 ounces chopped bittersweet chocolate (do not stir). Let stand for 5 minutes. Stir in 1 tablespoon Irish cream liqueur until smooth. Cool about 15 minutes or until slightly thickened.

Irish Cream Icing

In a small bowl stir together 1 cup powdered sugar, 1 tablespoon Irish cream liqueur, and ¼ teaspoon vanilla.

Per cupcake: 203 cal., 9 g total fat (6 g sat. fat), 16 mg chol., 124 mg sodium, 30 g carb., 1 g dietary fiber, 21 g sugar, 3 g protein.

Irish Cream Float

In a small saucepan heat and stir 1 ounce bittersweet chopped chocolate over low heat until melted. Cool slightly. Pipe or brush stripes of melted chocolate onto the insides of four 8-ounce glasses. Chill in the refrigerator about 15 minutes or until chocolate is set. To serve, spoon alternating scoops of chocolate and vanilla ice cream into each glass. In a small pitcher or 4-cup glass measuring cup stir together 1½ cups milk and ¼ cup Irish Cream liqueur; slowly stir in ½ cup carbonated water. Pour into glasses over ice cream. Serve immediately. Makes 4 servings.

After-Dinner Almond Coffee

In a small mug stir together ½ cup hot brewed espresso, 1 tablespoon packed brown sugar, and 1 tablespoon amaretto. Top with 1 tablespoon whipped cream; stir slightly. Makes 1 serving.

Marbled Almond Cupcakes

Prep: 40 minutes **Stand:** 30 minutes **Bake:** 15 minutes at 350°F **Cool:** 45 minutes
Makes 20 (2½-inch) cupcakes

- 4 egg whites
- 2 cups all-purpose flour
- 1 teaspoon baking powder
- ½ teaspoon baking soda
- ½ teaspoon salt
- ½ cup shortening
- 1¾ cups sugar
- 3 tablespoons amaretto
- 1 teaspoon vanilla
- 1 cup buttermilk or sour milk (see tip, page 11)
- 2 tablespoons unsweetened cocoa powder
- 1 to 2 tablespoons amaretto
- 1 recipe Marbled Almond Frosting

1. Allow egg whites to stand at room temperature for 30 minutes. Meanwhile, line twenty 2½-inch muffin cups with paper bake cups. In a medium bowl stir together flour, baking powder, baking soda, and salt. Set aside.

2. Preheat oven to 350°F. In a large mixing bowl beat shortening with an electric mixer on medium to high speed for 30 seconds. Add sugar, the 3 tablespoons amaretto, and the vanilla. Beat until combined, scraping sides of bowl occasionally. Add egg whites, one at a time, beating well after each addition. Alternately add flour mixture and buttermilk to shortening mixture, beating on low speed after each addition just until combined.

3. Transfer 1¼ cups of the batter to a small bowl; stir in cocoa powder. Spoon white batter into prepared muffin cups, filling each about one-third full. Spoon about 1 tablespoon chocolate batter into each muffin cup. Top with the remaining white batter; swirl gently to marble.

4. Bake for 15 to 18 minutes or until tops spring back when lightly touched. Cool cupcakes in muffin cups on wire racks for 5 minutes. Remove cupcakes from muffin cups. Prick tops of warm cupcakes with a fork. Brush tops with the 1 to 2 tablespoons amaretto. Cool completely on wire racks.

5. Spoon white and chocolate Marbled Almond Frosting side by side in to a large pastry bag fitted with a large star tip. (Or spoon frostings side by side in to a corner of a heavy resealable plastic bag. Snip off a ¼-inch piece from the corner of bag.) Pipe frosting onto tops of cupcakes.

Marbled Almond Frosting

In a large mixing bowl beat 1 cup shortening and 2 tablespoons amaretto with an electric mixer on medium speed until smooth. Gradually add 2½ cups powdered sugar, beating well. Beat in 2 tablespoons milk. Gradually beat in an additional 1½ cups powdered sugar. Beat in additional milk (1 to 2 tablespoons) until frosting reaches piping consistency. Transfer half of the frosting to a medium bowl; stir in 3 tablespoons unsweetened cocoa powder.

Per cupcake: 364 cal., 15 g total fat (4 g sat. fat), 1 mg chol., 133 mg sodium, 54 g carb., 1 g dietary fiber, 42 g sugar, 3 g protein.

Spiked Raspberry-Lemonade Cupcakes

Prep: 40 minutes **Stand:** 30 minutes **Bake:** 15 minutes at 350°F **Cool:** 45 minutes

Makes 18 (2½-inch) cupcakes

¾ cup butter

3 eggs

1¾ cups all-purpose flour

1 teaspoon baking powder

¼ teaspoon baking soda

¼ teaspoon salt

1½ cups sugar

2 teaspoons finely shredded lemon peel

2 tablespoons lemon juice

2 tablespoons raspberry liqueur or milk

⅔ cup buttermilk or sour milk (see tip, page 11)

Red food coloring

1 recipe Creamy Raspberry Frosting

Lemon slices (optional)

Fresh raspberries (optional)

1. Allow butter and eggs to stand at room temperature for 30 minutes. Meanwhile, line eighteen 2½-inch muffin cups with paper bake cups. In a medium bowl stir together flour, baking powder, baking soda, and salt. Set aside.

2. Preheat oven to 350°F. In a large mixing bowl beat butter with an electric mixer on medium to high speed for 30 seconds. Add sugar, lemon peel, lemon juice, and liqueur. Beat until combined, scraping sides of bowl occasionally. Add eggs, one at a time, beating well after each addition. Alternately add flour mixture and buttermilk to butter mixture, beating on low speed after each addition just until combined. Tint batter pink with a few drops of red food coloring.

3. Spoon batter into prepared muffin cups, filling each about three-fourths full. Use the back of a spoon to smooth out batter in cups.

4. Bake for 15 to 18 minutes or until a toothpick inserted in centers comes out clean. Cool cupcakes in muffin cups on wire racks for 5 minutes. Remove cupcakes from muffin cups. Cool completely on wire racks.

5. Spread Creamy Raspberry Frosting onto tops of cupcakes. If desired, garnish with lemon slices and/or raspberries.

Creamy Raspberry Frosting

Allow ¾ cup butter to stand at room temperature for 30 minutes. In a large mixing bowl beat butter with an electric mixer on medium speed until smooth. Gradually add 2 cups powdered sugar, beating well. Beat in 3 tablespoons milk, 3 tablespoons raspberry liqueur, and 5 drops red food coloring. Gradually beat in an additional 5 to 5½ cups powdered sugar until frosting reaches spreading consistency.

Per cupcake: 455 cal., 16 g total fat (10 g sat. fat), 77 mg chol., 202 mg sodium, 75 g carb., 0 g dietary fiber, 63 g sugar, 3 g protein.

Raspberry Sipper

In a glass stir together ⅓ cup lemonade, ⅓ cup Prosecco, and 2 tablespoons raspberry liqueur. If desired, add ice cubes and garnish with lemon slice and/or raspberries. Serve immediately. Makes 1 serving.

Hazelnut Crème Brûlée Cupcakes

Prep: 45 minutes **Stand:** 30 minutes **Bake:** 15 minutes at 350°F **Cool:** 45 minutes

Makes 24 (2½-inch) cupcakes

¾ cup butter

3 eggs

2½ cups all-purpose flour

2 teaspoons baking powder

½ teaspoon salt

1¾ cups sugar

2 tablespoons hazelnut liqueur

2 teaspoons vanilla

1 cup milk

½ cup finely chopped toasted hazelnuts (filberts)

1 recipe Vanilla-Hazelnut Buttercream

1 recipe Caramelized Sugar Drizzle

Freshly grated nutmeg or ground nutmeg (optional)

1. Allow butter and eggs to stand at room temperature for 30 minutes. Meanwhile, line twenty-four 2½-inch muffin cups with paper bake cups. In a medium bowl stir together flour, baking powder, and salt. Set aside.

2. Preheat oven to 350°F. In a large mixing bowl beat butter with an electric mixer on medium to high speed for 30 seconds. Gradually add sugar, about ¼ cup at a time, beating on medium speed until combined. Scrape sides of bowl; beat for 2 minutes more. Add eggs, one at a time, beating well after each addition. Beat in liqueur and vanilla. Alternately add flour mixture and milk to butter mixture, beating on low speed after each addition just until combined. Fold in nuts.

3. Spoon batter into prepared muffin cups, filling each about three-fourths full. Use the back of a spoon to smooth out batter in cups.

4. Bake for 15 to 18 minutes or until tops spring back when lightly touched. Cool cupcakes in muffin cups on wire racks for 5 minutes. Remove cupcakes from muffin cups. Cool completely on wire racks.

5. Spread or pipe Vanilla-Hazelnut Buttercream onto tops of cupcakes. Quickly drizzle with Caramelized Sugar Drizzle. If desired, lightly sprinkle cupcakes with nutmeg.

Per cupcake: 306 cal., 11 g total fat (6 g sat. fat), 49 mg chol., 152 mg sodium, 49 g carb., 1 g dietary fiber, 38 g sugar, 3 g protein.

Vanilla-Hazelnut Buttercream

Allow ⅓ cup butter to stand at room temperature for 30 minutes. In a large mixing bowl beat butter with an electric mixer on medium speed until smooth. Gradually add 1 cup powdered sugar, beating well. Beat in 2 tablespoons milk, 1 tablespoon hazelnut liqueur, and 1 teaspoon vanilla. Gradually beat in an additional 3 cups powdered sugar. Beat in an additional 3 to 4 teaspoons milk until buttercream reaches spreading consistency.

Caramelized Sugar Drizzle

In a large skillet cook ⅓ cup sugar over medium-high heat until sugar starts to melt, shaking skillet occasionally. Do not stir. When sugar starts to melt, reduce heat to low and cook about 5 minutes or until all of the sugar is melted, stirring as needed with a wooden spoon. Remove from heat. Immediately drizzle sugar mixture over frosted cupcakes.

Caramel-Nut Frappé

In a blender combine 1½ cups milk, ¼ cup hazelnut liqueur, and ¼ cup caramel-flavor ice cream topping. Add 2 cups ice cubes. Cover and blend until smooth. Pour into four glasses. Top each serving with a scoop of vanilla ice cream, drizzle with additional ice cream topping, and sprinkle with hazelnuts. Makes 4 servings.

**Cinnamon-Chocolate
Coffee Cooler**
In a glass stir together ½ cup
chocolate milk, 2 tablespoons
coffee liqueur, and a dash ground
cinnamon. Add ice cubes. Serve with
a cinnamon stick. Makes 1 serving.

Spiked Hot Cocoa Cupcakes

Prep: 40 minutes **Stand:** 30 minutes **Bake:** 20 minutes at 350°F/450°F **Cool:** 45 minutes

Makes 28 (2½-inch) cupcakes

¾ cup butter

3 eggs

2¼ cups all-purpose flour

½ cup unsweetened cocoa powder

1 tablespoon instant espresso powder or instant coffee crystals

1 teaspoon baking soda

¾ teaspoon baking powder

½ teaspoon salt

1¾ cups sugar

¼ cup coffee liqueur

2 teaspoons vanilla

1¼ cups chocolate milk

1 recipe Marshmallow-Coffee Frosting

1. Allow butter and eggs to stand at room temperature for 30 minutes. Meanwhile, line twenty-eight 2½-inch muffin cups with paper bake cups or grease and flour muffin cups. In a medium bowl stir together flour, cocoa powder, espresso powder, baking soda, baking powder, and salt. Set aside.

2. Preheat oven to 350°F. In a large mixing bowl beat butter with an electric mixer on medium to high speed for 30 seconds. Gradually add sugar, about ¼ cup at a time, beating on medium speed until combined. Scrape sides of bowl; beat about 2 minutes more or until light and fluffy. Add eggs, one at a time, beating well after each addition. Beat in liqueur and vanilla. Alternately add flour mixture and chocolate milk to butter mixture, beating on low speed after each addition just until combined. Beat on medium to high speed for 20 seconds more.

3. Spoon batter into prepared muffin cups, filling each about three-fourths full. Use the back of a spoon to smooth out batter in cups.

4. Bake for 15 to 18 minutes or until tops spring back when lightly touched. Cool cupcakes in muffin cups on wire racks for 5 minutes. Remove cupcakes from muffin cups. Cool completely on wire racks.

5. Increase oven temperature to 450°F. Pipe or spread Marshmallow-Coffee Frosting onto tops of cupcakes. Place frosted cupcakes on a large baking sheet. Bake about 5 minutes or until frosting is lightly browned. Cool completely on wire racks.

Marshmallow-Coffee Frosting

In the top of a 2-quart double boiler combine 1½ cups sugar, ⅓ cup cold water, 2 egg whites, and ¼ teaspoon cream of tartar. Beat with an electric mixer on low speed for 30 seconds. Place the double boiler top over boiling water (upper pan should not touch water). Cook, beating constantly with the mixer on high speed, for 10 to 13 minutes or until an instant-read thermometer registers 160°F when inserted in mixture, stopping mixer and quickly scraping bottom and sides of pan every 5 minutes to prevent sticking. Remove pan from heat. Add 1 tablespoon coffee liqueur and 1 teaspoon vanilla. Beat about 1 minute or until frosting is fluffy and holds soft peaks (tips curl).

Per cupcake: 202 cal., 6 g total fat (4 g sat. fat), 33 mg chol., 163 mg sodium, 34 g carb., 1 g dietary fiber, 26 g sugar, 3 g protein.

Champagne Wedding Cupcakes

Prep: 1 hour **Stand:** 30 minutes **Bake:** 15 minutes at 350°F **Cool:** 45 minutes

Makes 18 to 20 mini wedding cakes

6	eggs
⅔	cup butter
1	vanilla bean, split, or 1 teaspoon vanilla
2¾	cups all-purpose flour
1	tablespoon baking powder
1	teaspoon salt
1½	cups sugar
¾	cup champagne
⅔	to ¾ cup raspberry, strawberry, or blackberry jam
1	recipe Wedding Cake Frosting (see recipe, opposite)
	Edible gold or silver glitter, luster dust, and/or pearl candy beads

1. Separate eggs. Discard four yolks. Allow remaining yolks and whites and butter to stand at room temperature for 30 minutes. Meanwhile, generously grease eighteen to twenty 2½-inch muffin cups and eighteen to twenty 1¾-inch muffin cups. If using vanilla bean, use a sharp knife to scrape seeds from vanilla bean halves; set seeds aside. In a medium bowl stir together flour, baking powder, and salt. Set aside.

2. Preheat oven to 350°F. In a large mixing bowl beat egg whites with an electric mixer on high speed until stiff peaks form (tips stand straight). Set aside.

3. In another large mixing bowl beat butter on medium to high speed for 30 seconds. Gradually add sugar, about ¼ cup at a time, beating about 2 minutes or until light and fluffy. Beat in egg yolks and vanilla seeds or vanilla extract. Alternately add flour mixture and champagne to butter mixture, beating on low speed after each addition just until combined. Fold half of the beaten egg whites into the batter to lighten. Fold in remaining beaten egg whites.

4. Spoon batter into prepared muffin cups, filling each about three-fourths full.

5. Bake about 15 minutes for 2½-inch cupcakes, 10 to 12 minutes for 1¾-inch cupcakes, or until a toothpick inserted in centers comes out clean. Cool cupcakes in muffin cups on wire racks for 5 minutes. Remove cupcakes from muffin cups. Cool completely on wire racks.

6. Spoon jam into a pastry bag fitted with a round tip. Insert tip into tops of cupcake. Squeeze about 1 teaspoon of the jam into the center of each 2½-inch cupcake and about ½ teaspoon into the center of each 1¾-inch cupcake. Stack small cupcakes on top of large cupcakes, frosting between layers with Wedding Cake Frosting.

7. Insert a long wooden skewer through centers of cupcakes to hold in place. Using a flat spatula and/or a pastry bag fitted with a star or round tip, frost and decorate cupcake stacks. Remove skewers from cupcakes; cover holes with frosting. Sprinkle with glitter, luster dust, and/or pearl candy beads as desired.

Test Kitchen Tip:

If desired, use the champagne cake mix fix-up recipe from New Year's Toast (see recipe, page 274) instead of the cupcakes above, creating eighteen to twenty 2½-inch cupcakes and eighteen to twenty 1¾-inch cupcakes.

Per mini wedding cake: 1301 cal., 63 g total fat (18 g sat. fat), 89 mg chol., 267 mg sodium, 176 g carb., 1 g dietary fiber, 156 g sugar, 4 g protein.

Wedding Cake Frosting

In a very large bowl (6- to 7-quart, or make in two batches) beat 5 cups shortening, 3 tablespoons vanilla, and 2 teaspoons almond extract with an electric mixer on medium speed for 30 seconds. Gradually add 10 cups powdered sugar, beating well. Beat in ½ cup champagne. Gradually beat in an additional 10 cups powdered sugar. Beat in an additional 2 to 4 tablespoons champagne until frosting reaches spreading or piping consistency.

Lemon Drop Cupcakes

Prep: 40 minutes **Stand:** 30 minutes **Bake:** 18 minutes at 350°F **Cool:** 45 minutes

Makes 20 (2½-inch) cupcakes

¾ cup butter

3 eggs

1¾ cups all-purpose flour

1 teaspoon baking powder

¼ teaspoon baking soda

¼ teaspoon salt

⅔ cup milk

¼ cup limoncello (Italian lemon liqueur) or milk

1½ cups sugar

1 tablespoon finely shredded lemon peel

1 recipe Lemon Frosting

½ cup lemon drop candies, finely crushed

1 recipe Glazed Lemon Slices

1. Allow butter and eggs to stand at room temperature for 30 minutes. Meanwhile, line twenty 2½-inch muffin cups with paper bake cups. In a medium bowl stir together flour, baking powder, baking soda, and salt. In a 2-cup glass measuring cup combine the ⅔ cup milk and the limoncello. Set aside.

2. Preheat oven to 350°F. In a large mixing bowl beat butter with an electric mixer on medium to high speed for 30 seconds. Add sugar and lemon peel; beat until combined. Add eggs, one at a time, beating well after each addition. Alternately add flour mixture and milk mixture to butter mixture, beating on low speed after each addition just until combined.

3. Spoon batter into prepared muffin cups, filling each about three-fourths full. Use the back of a spoon to smooth out batter in cups.

4. Bake about 18 minutes or until tops spring back when lightly touched. Cool cupcakes in muffin cups on wire racks for 5 minutes. Remove cupcakes from muffin cups. Cool completely on wire racks.

5. Up to 1 hour before serving, generously spread or pipe Lemon Frosting onto cupcakes. Sprinkle crushed candies over frosted cupcakes. Top cupcakes with Glazed Lemon Slices.

Lemon Frosting

Allow ⅓ cup butter to stand at room temperature for 30 minutes. In a large mixing bowl beat butter, ⅓ cup shortening, and 1 teaspoon vanilla with an electric mixer on medium speed for 30 seconds. Slowly add 2 cups powdered sugar, beating well. Add 2 tablespoons lemon juice. Gradually beat in an additional 2 cups powdered sugar. Beat in 1 to 2 tablespoons milk, 1 teaspoon at a time, until frosting reaches spreading consistency.

Glazed Lemon Slices

Cut 2 small lemons into ¼-inch-thick slices. Remove seeds. Roll slices in sugar to coat well. Coat a large skillet with nonstick cooking spray. Preheat skillet over medium-high heat. Arrange lemon slices in a single layer in skillet. Cook for 6 to 8 minutes or until sugar dissolves and lemon slices appear glazed (do not let them brown), turning once. Transfer to a piece of foil; cool completely. Roll cooled slices in sugar again before using. (These slices are edible, but the rind is chewy; if desired, remove slices before eating.)

Per cupcake: 350 cal., 14 g total fat (7 g sat. fat), 59 mg chol., 150 mg sodium, 53 g carb., 0 g dietary fiber, 42 g sugar, 2 g protein.

Black and White Bows

Start to Finish: 1 hour 30 minutes
Makes 24 (2½-inch) cupcakes

4 ounces vanilla candy coating, coarsely chopped

¼ cup light-color corn syrup

4 ounces dark cocoa candy melts

1 recipe Bittersweet Chocolate Ganache

12 2½-inch Chocolate Cupcakes in paper bake cups (see recipe, page 10)

1 recipe White Chocolate Ganache Frosting

12 2½-inch Simple White Cupcakes (see recipe, page 11)

Powdered sugar

1. For white clay, place vanilla candy coating in a microwave-safe dish. Microwave on 100% power (high) for 1 to 2 minutes or until melted, stirring once. Stir in 2 tablespoons of the corn syrup. Spoon onto plastic wrap. Cover and let stand for at least 1 hour or until cooled and firm. For chocolate clay, repeat with dark cocoa candy melts and the remaining 2 tablespoons corn syrup. When firm, unwrap and knead each mixture separately until smooth and pliable. Wrap each in plastic wrap; set aside.

2. Spoon Bittersweet Chocolate Ganache over Chocolate Cupcakes and White Chocolate Ganache Frosting over Simple White Cupcakes. Chill until firm.

3. Between separate sheets of waxed paper dusted with powdered sugar, roll out white clay and chocolate clay to ⅛-inch thickness. Using a pastry wheel, pizza cutter, or knife, cut clay into 1-inch-wide strips about 5 inches long. For each bow, bring ends of a strip together, making a double thickness. Turn upside down, with the seam underneath. Gently pinch in center. Trim scraps of clay into ribbon tails and center knots. Place two tails on top of each cupcake; top with a bow and a knot.

Bittersweet Chocolate Ganache

In a medium saucepan heat ½ cup whipping cream over medium heat just until boiling. Remove from heat. Add 6 ounces chopped bittersweet chocolate (do not stir). Let stand for 5 minutes. Whisk until smooth. Cool about 15 minutes or until thickened, stirring occasionally.

White Chocolate Ganache Frosting

In a small saucepan melt 2 ounces white baking chocolate with cocoa butter over low heat. Remove from heat. Stir in ¾ cup Creamy White Frosting (see recipe, page 15) or canned creamy white frosting. If necessary, stir in 1 tablespoon milk, 1 teaspoon at a time, to make frosting smooth

Per cupcake: 358 cal., 20 g total fat (12 g sat. fat), 76 mg chol., 175 mg sodium, 44 g carb., 1 g dietary fiber, 29 g sugar, 4 g protein.

One Down

To streamline the decorating process, you can use just one color for the clay and ganache instead of creating two of each. To do this, simply make twice as much of desired-color clay and ganache.

Candied Flowers

Prep: 30 minutes **Stand:** 2 hours

Makes 12 servings

- 1 cup edible flowers, such as fresh orchids, pansies, borage, and/or rose petals
- 2 tablespoons water
- 1 tablespoon refrigerated or frozen egg product, thawed
- 2 tablespoons superfine granulated sugar
- 12 2½-inch frosted cupcakes

1. Gently wash flowers in water. Place flowers on white paper towels and let air-dry or gently blot dry.

2. In a small bowl stir together the 2 tablespoons water and egg product. Using a small clean paintbrush, gently brush all sides of each flower with the egg mixture in a thin, even layer. Sprinkle each flower evenly with sugar. Shake each flower to remove excess sugar. Let dry on a wire rack for at least 2 hours.

3. Store candied flowers in an airtight container between layers of waxed paper for up to 4 weeks. Use to decorate the frosted cupcakes.

Make-Ahead Directions:

For longer storage, place candied flowers between layers of waxed paper in a freezer container. Seal, label, and freeze for up to 6 months.

Per serving: 8 cal., 0 g total fat (0 g sat. fat), 0 mg chol., 4 mg sodium, 2 g carb., 0 g dietary fiber, 2 g sugar, 0 g protein.

1. Use a small clean paintbrush to lightly coat flowers with egg mixture.

2. Dip flowers in superfine sugar, coating all sides completely.

3. Place sugar-coated flowers on a wire rack; allow flowers to dry completely (at least 2 hours) before using as decorations.

Party Time: Cupcake Exchange!

There's no reason why cookies should have all the fun—cupcakes are just as easy to swap at a good-time gal-pal dessert exchange. Try this themed celebration for an adult birthday party, bridal or baby shower, holiday celebration, or as a simple excuse to gather with the girls. Focus in on these details and your friends will feel like pampered princesses.

- ○ Pick your party's colors. Look for ribbons, centerpieces, flowers, and scrapbooking paper to match.

- ○ Design your invitations and place settings from sturdy scrapbooking paper that matches your party's colors. On the invitations, outline what the party is about and specify what guests should bring.

- ○ Suggest each guest bring one to two dozen simply designed cupcakes. (If the cupcake decorations are too elaborate, they may be hard to transport.) Good options include Cherry-Almond Vanilla Cupcakes (see recipe, page 86),

- Lemon Drop Cupcakes (see recipe, page 162), and Peanut Butter–Chocolate Twist cupcakes (see recipe, page 114).

- ○ Provide cupcake gift boxes at each place setting for guests to tote cupcakes home. Look for these boxes in the cake decorating department of hobby and crafts stores or online.

- ○ Offer guests an array of beverages such as punch, coffee, bottled water, and/or cocktails.

- ○ Set out a few savory snacks, such as salted nuts or snack mixes—they provide a nice counterpoint to the cupcakes guests will likely be nibbling and sampling.

Meringue-Topped Raspberry Cupcakes

Prep: 25 minutes **Stand:** 30 minutes **Bake:** 23 minutes at 350°F **Cool:** 5 minutes
Makes 12 (2½-inch) cupcakes

½ cup butter
1 egg
2 egg yolks
4 egg whites
1½ cups all-purpose flour
1½ teaspoons baking powder
¼ teaspoon salt
¾ cup sugar
3 tablespoons raspberry liqueur or raspberry juice blend
1½ teaspoons vanilla
½ cup milk
¼ teaspoon cream of tartar
⅔ cup sugar
12 fresh raspberries (optional)

1. Allow butter, egg, egg yolks, and egg whites to stand at room temperature for 30 minutes. Meanwhile, line twelve 2½-inch muffin cups with paper bake cups or lightly coat muffin cups with nonstick spray for baking. In a small bowl stir together flour, baking powder, and salt. Set aside.

2. Preheat oven to 350°F. In a large mixing bowl beat butter with an electric mixer on medium to high speed for 30 seconds. Add the ¾ cup sugar. Beat on medium to high speed for 1 minute. Add egg, egg yolks, liqueur, and vanilla. Beat until combined. Alternately add flour mixture and milk to butter mixture, beating on low speed after each addition just until combined.

3. Spoon batter into prepared muffin cups, filling each about three-fourths full. Use the back of a spoon to smooth out batter in cups. Bake for 15 minutes.

4. Meanwhile, wash beaters thoroughly. For meringue, in a medium bowl beat egg whites and cream of tartar on medium speed until soft peaks form (tips curl). Gradually add the ⅔ cup sugar, 1 tablespoon at a time, beating on high speed until stiff peaks form (tips stand straight).

5. Pipe or spoon meringue onto tops of cupcakes. If desired, place a raspberry on top of each cupcake, pressing into meringue. Bake for 8 to 10 minutes more or until meringue is lightly browned.

6. Cool cupcakes in muffin cups on a wire rack for 5 minutes. Remove cupcakes from muffin cups; cool slightly. Serve warm. (Or cover loosely and chill for up to 4 hours before serving.)

Per cupcake: 255 cal., 9 g total fat (5 g sat. fat), 67 mg chol., 208 mg sodium, 38 g carb., 0 g dietary fiber, 24 g sugar, 4 g protein.

Lemony Glazed Shortbread Cupcakes

Prep: 25 minutes **Bake:** 20 minutes at 300°F **Cool:** 45 minutes

Makes 24 (1¾-inch) cupcakes

- 2   cups all-purpose flour
- ¼   cup cornstarch
- 1   cup powdered sugar
- 3   tablespoons finely shredded lemon peel (3 to 4 lemons)
- ¾   cup butter, softened
- 1   tablespoon lemon juice
- ½   teaspoon salt
- ½   teaspoon vanilla
- 1   recipe Lemon Glaze

1. Preheat oven to 300°F. Line twenty-four 1¾-inch muffin cups with paper bake cups. In a medium bowl stir together flour and cornstarch. Set aside.

2. In a small bowl stir together powdered sugar and lemon peel. Using a wooden spoon, press mixture up against bowl until sugar is yellow and very fragrant. Set aside. (Pressing the lemon peel into the powdered sugar helps to release the lemon oils.)

3. In a large mixing bowl beat butter, lemon juice, salt, and vanilla with an electric mixer on medium speed until combined. Gradually add powdered sugar mixture, beating until combined. Using a wooden spoon, stir in flour mixture.

4. Press dough together to form a ball. Divide dough into 24 portions. With lightly floured fingers, press a portion of the dough evenly into bottom of each prepared muffin cup.

5. Bake for 20 to 22 minutes or until edges are very lightly browned.

6. Cool cupcakes in muffin cups on wire racks for 5 minutes. Carefully remove cupcakes from muffin cups. Immediately spoon and gently spread about ½ teaspoon of the Lemon Glaze onto tops of each warm cupcake. Cool completely on wire racks. If desired, store in the refrigerator for up to 24 hours.

Lemon Glaze

In a small bowl stir together 1½ cups powdered sugar, 2 teaspoons finely shredded lemon peel, and 1½ teaspoons lemon juice. Stir in enough milk to make icing drizzling consistency.

Make-Ahead Directions:

Place unglazed cupcakes in a single layer in airtight containers; seal. Freeze for up to 1 month. Thaw cupcakes at room temperature before glazing.

Per cupcake: 144 cal., 6 g total fat (4 g sat. fat), 15 mg chol., 100 mg sodium, 22 g carb., 0 g dietary fiber, 12 g sugar, 1 g protein.

Monogram Cupcakes

Start to Finish: 1 hour 30 minutes

Makes 24 (2½-inch) cupcakes

2   ounces vanilla candy coating

1   teaspoon shortening

1   recipe Butter Frosting (see recipe, page 14)

Desired food coloring (optional)

24   2½-inch cupcakes in paper bake cups* (any flavor)

1. Place candy coating in a microwave-safe bowl. Microwave on 100% power (high) about 1½ minutes or until melted, stirring once. Add shortening, stirring until melted. Let stand for 1 minute to cool slightly. Spoon mixture into a heavy resealable plastic bag. Snip off a very small piece from one corner of bag. Carefully pipe 1- to 1½-inch cursive letters on a sheet of foil or waxed paper for the large letters of the monogram. Pipe ¾-inch cursive letters for the small letters of the monogram, placing the letters very close together so they touch. Let stand until set.

2. If desired, tint Butter Frosting desired color(s) with food coloring.** Spoon into disposable pastry bag(s) fitted with extra-large tip(s). Pipe a very large swirl on top of each cupcake, covering the top.

3. To decorate, place a monogram on each cupcake.

*Test Kitchen Tip:
Choose silver, gold, or black paper bake cups. Or use paper bake cups that coordinate with the wedding colors.

**Test Kitchen Tip:
If desired, divide frosting and tint into colors that coordinate with the wedding colors. Frost some of the cupcakes with each color.

Per cupcake: 402 cal., 14 g total fat (9 g sat. fat), 58 mg chol., 171 mg sodium, 66 g carb., 0 g dietary fiber, 56 g sugar, 3 g protein.

Sweet Cutouts

For an alternative to the monogram designs on Monogram Cupcakes, create cutouts from the vanilla candy coating. To do this, place a sheet of waxed paper on a pan. Spread melted vanilla candy coating ¼ to ½ inch thick; let stand until just firm. If desired, use a clean artist's paintbrush to brush luster dust onto candy coating slab. Use desired 1- to 1½-inch cookie or aspic cutters (such as hearts, stars, or wedding bells) to cut out shapes. Use a thin spatula to remove shapes from waxed paper. Press shapes, upright, into frosting.

ABC Block Cupcakes

Start to Finish: 1 hour

Makes 12 large or 24 small cupcakes

2 cups Creamy White Frosting (see recipe, page 15) or canned creamy white frosting

12 large or 24 small square* cupcakes

Desired pastel-color paste food colorings

Powdered sugar

2 ounces Easy Homemade Fondant (see recipe, page 15) or white rolled fondant icing

1. Spoon ¼ cup of the Creamy White Frosting into a pastry bag fitted with a small star tip. Set aside. Place 1½ cups of the frosting in a microwave-safe bowl. Microwave on 100% power (high) about 30 seconds or just until melted. Spread melted white frosting onto tops of cupcakes. Divide remaining frosting into three portions. Tint each portion a different color with food coloring. Spoon frostings into separate pastry bags fitted with small round tips, or spoon into resealable plastic bags and snip off a small piece from one corner of each bag. Pipe colored square outlines on tops of cupcakes. Pipe white stars in corners; pipe dots in centers of stars.

2. On a surface lightly dusted with powdered sugar, divide Easy Homemade Fondant into three portions. Tint each portion a different color with food coloring. Knead each portion until evenly colored.** (Work with one portion of fondant at a time and keep fondant covered when not using.) Roll out fondant to ⅛-inch thickness.

3. Use 1½- to 2½-inch alphabet or number cookie cutters to cut out shapes. Place the letters or numbers on frosted cupcakes. If desired, use frosting in a pastry bag fitted with a small round tip to pipe outlines around the letters and numbers.

*Test Kitchen Tip:
Square muffin pans vary in size. For 12 large cupcakes, grease and flour 2½-inch square muffin cups that are 1½ inches deep. For 24 smaller cupcakes, use 2½-inch square muffin cups that are ⅞ inch deep, spooning ¼ cup batter into each. If you do not have a square muffin pan, use a 2½-inch round muffin pan lined with paper bake cups.

**Test Kitchen Tip:
If you like, wear plastic gloves to keep from discoloring your hands.

Per cupcake: 397 cal., 18 g total fat (7 g sat. fat), 43 mg chol., 133 mg sodium, 57 g carb., 0 g dietary fiber, 46 g sugar, 3 g protein.

Strawberry Cupcakes

Prep: 35 minutes **Bake:** 18 minutes at 350°F **Cool:** 45 minutes

Makes 24 (2½-inch) cupcakes

1   10-ounce package frozen halved strawberries in syrup or one 16-ounce container sliced strawberries in sugar, thawed

1   package 2-layer-size white cake mix

½   8-ounce package cream cheese

¼   cup butter

1   teaspoon vanilla

4   cups powdered sugar
    Red food coloring (optional)

24   fresh strawberries

1. Preheat oven to 350°F. Line twenty-four 2½-inch muffin cups with paper bake cups. Drain packaged strawberries, reserving syrup. Set aside 3 tablespoons of the syrup for frosting. Add enough water to the remaining syrup to measure ¾ cup total liquid. Prepare cake mix according to package directions, substituting the syrup-water mixture for the liquid called for on the package. Stir in the drained strawberries. (Batter will be thick.)

2. Spoon batter into prepared muffin cups, filling each about two-thirds full. Use the back of a spoon to smooth out batter in cups.

3. Bake about 18 minutes or until a toothpick inserted in centers comes out clean. Cool cupcakes in muffin cups on wire racks for 5 minutes. Remove cupcakes from muffin cups. Cool completely on wire racks.

4. Meanwhile, for frosting, allow cream cheese and butter to stand at room temperature for 30 minutes. In a large mixing bowl beat cream cheese, butter, vanilla, and the reserved 3 tablespoons syrup with an electric mixer on medium speed until light and fluffy. Gradually beat in powdered sugar. If desired, beat in 1 or 2 drops red food coloring. Spread or pipe frosting onto tops of cupcakes. Store frosted cupcakes in the refrigerator. Before serving, top each cupcake with a whole strawberry.

Make-Ahead Directions:

Prepare cupcakes as directed through step 3. Place unfrosted cupcakes in a single layer in an airtight container; seal. Store at room temperature for up to 3 days. Continue as directed in step 4.

Per cupcake: 248 cal., 9 g total fat (3 g sat. fat), 37 mg chol., 185 mg sodium, 41 g carb., 1 g dietary fiber, 33 g sugar, 2 g protein.

That Special Touch

Now that you have beautifully styled baby shower cupcakes, it's time to add the little extras that make the guest of honor feel like a queen. For example, tie complementary colors of thin ribbon in bows around the outside of the cupcake papers (see Strawberry Cupcakes photo, opposite). Or wrap cupcakes in two layers of paper bake cups so the outside layer doesn't become greasy. To do this, bake cupcakes in white or pastel solid-color paper cups, Before serving, place each cupcake—paper bake cup and all—into a second, more colorful bake cup. Spread out the edges slightly so the cup flares around the outside of the cupcake (see Lemon-Poppyseed Cupcakes photo, page 183).

Baby Bib Cupcakes

Start to Finish: 1 hour 30 minutes

Makes 12 (2½-inch) cupcakes

2 cups Creamy White Frosting (see recipe, page 15) or canned creamy white frosting

12 Fruit Cupcakes or other 2½-inch cupcakes in paper bake cups

Yellow, pink, and/or blue paste food colorings

Powdered sugar

8 ounces Easy Homemade Fondant (see recipe, page 15) or white rolled fondant icing

Colored sugars and/or sprinkles

1. Set aside 1 cup of the Creamy White Frosting. Spread the remaining 1 cup frosting onto Fruit Cupcakes. Tint the reserved frosting yellow, pink, or blue. (Or divide frosting and tint each portion a different color.) Spoon the tinted frosting(s) into a pastry bag(s) fitted with a small round tip(s). Set aside.

2. For bibs, on a surface lightly dusted with powdered sugar, roll out fondant to ⅛-inch thickness. Using a 2½-inch scalloped round cookie cutter, cut out 12 large circles. Using a 1-inch round cutter, cut a small circle near the top of each of the 2½-inch circles; discard small circles. Place fondant bibs about ¼ inch from the top edge of cupcakes.

3. Use tinted frosting(s) to pipe dots, ruffles, bows, and other decorations on bib edges. Decorate with colored sugars and/or sprinkles.

Fruit Cupcakes

Preheat oven to 350°F. Line twenty-four 2½-inch muffin cups with paper bake cups; set aside. Prepare one 2-layer-size package white cake mix according to package directions, except use apple juice instead of the water. Spoon batter into prepared muffin cups, filling each two-thirds to three-fourths full. Use the back of a spoon to smooth out batter in cups. Bake according to package directions for cupcakes. Cool cupcakes in muffin cups on wire racks for 5 minutes. Remove cupcakes from muffin cups. Cool completely on wire racks.

Per cupcake: 553 cal., 23 g total fat (6 g sat. fat), 56 mg chol., 327 mg sodium, 85 g carb., 1 g dietary fiber, 67 g sugar, 3 g protein.

Lamb and Ducky Cupcakes

Start to Finish: 2 hours
Makes 24 (2½-inch) cupcakes

12 2½-inch Yellow Cupcakes or Chocolate Cupcakes in paper bake cups (see recipes, page 10)

4 cups Creamy White Frosting (see recipe, page 15) or canned creamy white frosting

2½ cups shredded coconut (optional)

28 large marshmallows

12 log-shape chocolate caramel candies, such as Tootsie Rolls

48 miniature semisweet chocolate pieces

1 tube pink frosting (optional)
   Yellow food coloring

18 rich round crackers

12 2½-inch Yellow Cupcakes in paper bake cups (see recipe, page 10)

12 orange candy-coated milk chocolate pieces

1. For lamb cupcakes, spread the tops of 12 Yellow or Chocolate Cupcakes generously with some of the Creamy White Frosting and, if desired, sprinkle with some coconut. Place 1 cup of the coconut in a pie plate. Spread 16 of the marshmallows with frosting to coat. Roll coated marshmallows in coconut. Place on a waxed paper–lined baking sheet. Place in the freezer for several minutes or until frosting is set. Cut 4 of the coated marshmallows into 3 slices each; cut each slice in half for the ears. Set aside.

2. For each lamb cupcake, place one of the whole coconut-coated marshmallows in the center of a frosted cupcake. For ears, attach 2 marshmallow half-slices on each marshmallow with some of the white frosting. Cut two small pieces from one of the log-shape candies for the hooves. Form a circle with some of the remaining piece of log-shape candy to form a muzzle. If desired, use a knife to score hooves and muzzle. Attach muzzle to the front of the whole marshmallow with white frosting. Attach two miniature semisweet chocolate pieces for eyes. If desired, pipe pink frosting onto the insides of ears. Attach hooves to the bottom front of marshmallow.

3. For ducky cupcakes, tint the remaining frosting with yellow food coloring. Set aside. In a pie plate toss the remaining coconut with yellow food coloring to combine.

4. Cut each of the crackers in half. Spread all of the cracker pieces and the remaining 12 marshmallows with some of the yellow frosting; roll marshmallows and crackers in yellow coconut to coat. Place on a waxed paper–lined baking sheet. Place in the freezer for several minutes or until frosting is set.

5. Frost the 12 Yellow Cupcakes with yellow frosting. Sprinkle with some of the tinted coconut. For each duck cupcake, attach a coated marshmallow to the top of cupcake with some of the frosting. Attach two of the remaining miniature semisweet chocolate pieces to each marshmallow for eyes. Create beaks by using a knife to make a slit in each marshmallow and inserting a candy-coated chocolate piece into the slit. Press one cracker half into frosting at back for tail. Insert 2 cracker halves into frosting on sides for wings. Sprinkle remaining yellow coconut over duckies.

Per cupcake: 501 cal., 25 g total fat (12 g sat. fat), 65 mg chol., 191 mg sodium, 65 g carb., 1 g dietary fiber, 49 g sugar, 4 g protein.

1. For lambs, use a flat spatula to generously spread white frosting on cupcake tops. If desired, sprinkle cupcakes with coconut.

2. Attach a frosted, coconut-coated marshmallow on each cupcake with some frosting. Attach marshmallow pieces for ears, chocolate eyes, and candy muzzle with dabs of frosting.

3. Form remaining chocolate candies into round hooves; cut a slash into each hoof with a small, sharp knife. Attach to cupcakes with dabs of frosting.

4. For duckies, spread remaining cupcakes with yellow frosting; sprinkle with tinted coconut.

5. Top cupcake with frosted, coconut-coated marshmallow; attach candy beak and chocolate eyes with dabs of frosting.

6. Press two frosting- and coconut-coated cracker halves into frosting on sides of marshmallows for wings.

Lemon-Poppyseed Cupcakes

Prep: 35 minutes **Stand:** 40 minutes **Bake:** 10 minutes at 350°F **Cool:** 45 minutes

Makes 48 (1¾-inch) or 18 (2½-inch) cupcakes

½ cup butter
2 eggs
1¾ cups all-purpose flour
2 teaspoons poppy seeds
1½ teaspoons baking powder
½ teaspoon salt
1 cup sugar
1½ teaspoons lemon extract
½ teaspoon vanilla
⅔ cup milk
2 teaspoons finely shredded lemon peel
3 tablespoons lemon juice
1 recipe Lemon Glaze
Lemon peel strips (optional)

1. Allow butter and eggs to stand at room temperature for 30 minutes. Meanwhile, line forty-eight 1¾-inch muffin cups or eighteen 2½-inch muffin cups* with paper bake cups. In a medium bowl combine flour, poppyseeds, baking powder, and salt. Set aside.

2. Preheat oven to 350°F. In a large mixing bowl beat butter with an electric mixer on medium to high speed for 30 seconds. Add sugar, lemon extract, and vanilla. Beat about 2 minutes or until light and fluffy, scraping sides of bowl. Add eggs, one at a time, beating well after each addition. Alternately add flour mixture and milk to butter mixture, beating on low speed after each addition just until combined. Stir in shredded lemon peel and lemon juice.

3. Spoon batter into prepared muffin cups, filling each about three-fourths full. Use the back of a spoon to smooth out batter in cups.

4. Bake for 10 to 12 minutes for 1¾-inch cupcakes, 16 to 18 minutes for 2½-inch cupcakes, or until a toothpick inserted in centers comes out clean. Cool cupcakes in muffin cups on wire racks for 5 minutes. Remove cupcakes from muffin cups. Cool completely on wire racks.

5. Spread Lemon Glaze onto tops of cupcakes. If desired, top cupcakes with lemon peel strips. Let stand for 10 minutes.

Lemon Glaze

In a small bowl combine 1 cup powdered sugar and 5 teaspoons lemon juice. If necessary, stir in an additional ½ teaspoon lemon juice to reach spreading consistency. Stir in ½ teaspoon finely shredded lemon peel.

*Test Kitchen Tip:

If you like, make both sizes of cupcakes for bigger "mother" cupcakes and smaller "baby" cupcakes.

Per cupcake: 66 cal., 2 g total fat (1 g sat. fat), 14 mg chol., 54 mg sodium, 11 g carb., 0 g dietary fiber, 7 g sugar, 1 g protein.

Easy Caps and Booties Cupcakes

Start to Finish: 1 hour 30 minutes
Makes 12 (2½-inch) cupcakes

2 cups Creamy White Frosting (see recipe, page 15) or canned vanilla frosting

12 2½-inch cupcakes in paper bake cups (any flavor)

Desired colors gel paste food colorings

Small decorative candies

Pastel nonpareils (optional)

1. Set aside 1 cup of Creamy White Frosting. Spread remaining frosting onto tops of cupcakes. Set aside.

2. Divide reserved frosting among bowls; tint with desired food colorings. Spoon frostings into pastry bags fitted with couplers and very small round tips.

3. Pipe outlines of caps and booties on tops of frosted cupcakes. Switch tips on pastry bags to very small star tips. Pipe small stars to fill in the outlines of the caps and booties. If desired, add a row of small candies at bottom edges of caps and at top edges of booties. If desired, sprinkle with nonpareils.

4. For tassels on caps, use star tip to pipe spikes of frosting at the tops of caps. To pipe ties on booties, use a small round tip.

Per cupcake: 360 cal., 13 g total fat (6 g sat. fat), 46 mg chol., 137 mg sodium, 58 g carb., 0 g dietary fiber, 48 g sugar, 3 g protein.

Homeward Bound

If you have leftover cupcakes, send them home with your guests. Visit hobby and crafts stores for cupcake gift boxes.

Almond Cookie Cupcakes

Prep: 25 minutes **Bake:** 13 minutes at 325°F **Cool:** 45 minutes

Makes 36 (1¾-inch) cupcakes

1   cup packed brown sugar
⅓   cup butter
1   egg
½   teaspoon almond extract
½   teaspoon vanilla
1   cup all-purpose flour
½   teaspoon baking powder
⅛   teaspoon baking soda
½   cup chopped almonds
1   recipe Almond Glaze

1. Preheat oven to 325°F. Line thirty-six 1¾-inch muffin cups with paper bake cups.

2. In a small saucepan combine brown sugar and butter. Cook and stir over medium heat until melted and smooth. Remove from heat; cool slightly. Stir in egg, almond extract, and vanilla.

3. In a small bowl stir together flour, baking powder, and baking soda. Add flour mixture to butter mixture; stir just until combined. Stir in ⅓ cup of the chopped almonds.

4. Spoon batter into prepared muffin cups, filling each about one-half full. Sprinkle with the remaining chopped almonds.

5. Bake for 13 to 15 minutes or until tops are lightly browned. Cool cupcakes in muffin cups on wire racks for 5 minutes. Remove cupcakes from muffin cups. Cool completely on wire racks. Drizzle with Almond Glaze.

Almond Glaze

In a small bowl combine ¾ cup powdered sugar and ¼ teaspoon almond extract. Stir in 2 to 3 teaspoons milk to make glaze drizzling consistency.

Make-Ahead Directions:

Place glazed cupcakes in a single layer in airtight containers; seal. Store at room temperature for up to 3 days. Or freeze for up to 3 months.

Per cupcake: 71 cal., 3 g total fat (1 g sat. fat), 10 mg chol., 31 mg sodium, 12 g carb., 0 g dietary fiber, 8 g sugar, 1 g protein.

Lavender-Honey Cupcakes

Prep: 45 minutes **Stand:** 30 minutes **Bake:** 10 minutes at 350°F **Cool:** 45 minutes

Makes 48 (1¾-inch) or 18 (2½-inch) cupcakes

½ cup butter
2 eggs
1¾ cups all-purpose flour
2 teaspoons dried lavender
1½ teaspoons baking powder
½ teaspoon salt
1 cup sugar
¼ cup honey
1 teaspoon vanilla
⅔ cup milk
1 recipe Honey Frosting
  Dried lavender (optional)

1. Allow butter and eggs to stand at room temperature for 30 minutes. Meanwhile, line forty-eight 1¾-inch muffin cups or eighteen 2½-inch muffin cups with paper bake cups. In a medium bowl combine flour, the 2 teaspoons lavender, the baking powder, and salt. Set aside.

2. Preheat oven to 350°F. In a large mixing bowl beat butter with an electric mixer on medium to high speed for 30 seconds. Add sugar, honey, and vanilla. Beat until combined. Add eggs, one at a time, beating well after each addition. Alternately add flour mixture and milk to butter mixture, beating on low speed after each addition just until mixture is combined.

3. Spoon batter into prepared muffin cups, filling each about three-fourths full. Use the back of a spoon to smooth out batter in cups.

4. Bake for 10 to 12 minutes for 1¾-inch cupcakes, 16 to 18 minutes for 2½-inch cupcakes, or until a toothpick inserted in centers comes out clean. Cool cupcakes in muffin cups on wire racks for 10 minutes. Remove cupcakes from muffin cups. Cool completely on wire racks.

5. Pipe or spread with Honey Frosting. If desired, sprinkle cupcakes with additional lavender.

Honey Frosting

Allow 5 ounces mascarpone cheese or cream cheese (⅔ cup) and 3 tablespoons butter to stand at room temperature for 30 minutes. In a large mixing bowl beat mascarpone cheese, butter, ¼ cup honey, and ½ teaspoon vanilla with an electric mixer on medium speed until light and fluffy. Gradually add 1 cup powdered sugar, beating well. Gradually beat in an additional 2 to 2¼ cups powdered sugar until frosting reaches piping or spreading consistency.

Per cupcake: 103 cal., 4 g total fat (2 g sat. fat), 18 mg chol., 55 mg sodium, 17 g carb., 0 g dietary fiber, 13 g sugar, 1 g protein.

Weave It

To pipe a basket-weave design on cupcakes, fit a pastry bag with a medium star tip. Pipe three lines horizontally across each cupcake top. Pipe three short lines over the top of the first horizontal line from top of cupcake to top of second horizontal line. Repeat with the remaining two horizontal lines, piping in between spaces of the other lines.

Mochaccino Cupcakes, page 236

Birthdays

Let's face it: Everyone loves cupcakes. And what better time to indulge than on a day that's just for us—our birthdays! But not just any cupcake will do on party day. It has to be special, it has to be creative, and most of all, it has to reflect the guest of honor's personality and tastes. These cakes are all that and more.

Pet Shop Cupcakes

Start to Finish: 2 hours

Makes 12 (2½-inch) cupcakes

2 cups Creamy White Frosting (see recipe, page 15) or canned white frosting

Yellow food coloring

12 2½-inch cupcakes in paper bake cups (any flavor)

Large marshmallows

Pink and white tiny marshmallows

Black licorice laces

Red and blue miniature candy-coated chocolate pieces

1 cup Chocolate Butter Frosting (see recipe, page 14) or canned chocolate frosting

Log-shape chocolate-caramel candies, such as Tootsie Rolls

Pink chewy fruit-flavor square candies, such as Starburst

Pink food coloring

Miniature semisweet chocolate pieces

Heart-shape candies

Pink decorating sugar

1. For tabby cat cupcakes, tint one-third of the Creamy White Frosting with yellow food coloring. Spoon yellow frosting into a pastry bag fitted with a small star tip. Pipe yellow frosting in spikes onto 4 of the cupcakes.

2. Slice 3 large marshmallows crosswise into quarters; place two pieces, side by side, on the center of each frosted cupcake and add a pink tiny marshmallow for nose. Attach licorice whiskers with white frosting.

3. Cut the remaining marshmallow quarters into triangles; use frosting to attach marshmallow triangles to the tops of cupcakes for ears. Add red miniature candy-coated chocolate pieces for eyes and mouths.

4. For floppy-ear dog cupcakes, spread white frosting onto tops of 4 of the cupcakes. Spoon some of the Chocolate Butter Frosting into a pastry bag fitted with a round tip. Pipe chocolate patches randomly onto cupcakes (so cupcakes resemble beagles). Cut 2 large marshmallows crosswise into quarters; place two pieces, side by side, on the center of each cupcake and add a white tiny marshmallow for nose. Attach licorice whiskers with white frosting. Add blue miniature candy-coated chocolate pieces for eyes. Pipe small chocolate spots on the large and tiny marshmallows.

5. Place 4 chocolate-caramel and 4 pink chewy candies on waxed paper. Microwave on 100% power

(high) for 5 to 10 seconds or until softened. Mold the pink candies into tongue shapes, cutting off excess if necessary. When cool and firm, attach a tongue to each cupcake below nose, securing with frosting if necessary. Cut each of the 4 chocolate-caramel candies in half; mold each half into a long, oval floppy ear. When firm, attach two ears to each cupcake, securing with frosting if necessary.

6. For pink poodle cupcakes, tint the remaining white frosting with pink food coloring. Spoon pink frosting into a pastry bag fitted with a small star tip. Pipe frosting in spikes on the remaining 4 cupcakes. Cut 2 large marshmallows crosswise into quarters; place two pieces, side by side, on the center of each cupcake and add a pink tiny marshmallow for nose.

7. Place 4 pink chewy candies on waxed paper. Microwave on 100% power (high) for 5 to 10 seconds or until softened. Cut each candy in half; form each half into a long, oval ear. When firm, attach two ears to each cupcake.

8. Cut 4 white tiny marshmallows crosswise in half and arrange two pieces on each cupcake for eyes; top each with a miniature chocolate piece, using white frosting. Add a heart-shape candy to each for mouth and sprinkle the large marshmallow pieces with pink decorating sugar.

Per cupcake: 407 cal., 18 g total fat (7 g sat. fat), 44 mg chol., 139 mg sodium, 58 g carb., 0 g dietary fiber, 46 g sugar, 3 g protein.

Easy Rollers

Certain soft and chewy candies, such as Starburst, Airheads, caramels, taffy, Tootsie Rolls, and gumdrops are perfect for rolling out to flatten or molding into different shapes. Start by placing candies on a piece of waxed paper. Microwave on 100% power (high) for 5 to 10 seconds or until candies are pliable. Use a small rolling pin to roll candies flat or use your hands to mold into shapes. Gumdrops don't have to be softened before rolling; just sprinkle the work surface with granulated sugar to prevent sticking.

Pick-a-Sport Cupcakes

Start to Finish: 50 minutes

Makes 12 (2½-inch) cupcakes

2¾ cups Creamy White Frosting (see recipe, page 15) or canned creamy white frosting

Green food coloring

12 2½-inch cupcakes in paper bake cups (any flavor)

1 cup white candy coating disks

12 plain doughnut holes

Red food coloring

1. In a medium bowl tint 2 cups of the Creamy White Frosting with green food coloring to make a grass color. Spoon frosting into a pastry bag fitted with a star tip or multiopening (grass) tip. Pipe frosting onto tops of cupcakes to resemble grass.

2. For baseballs, in a small microwave-safe bowl microwave white candy coating disks on 100% power (high) for 1 minute. Stir; microwave for 30 to 60 seconds more or until melted, stirring once. Using a fork, dip the doughnut holes, one at a time, into melted candy coating, turning to coat completely. Place on waxed paper until set.

3. Tint remaining ¾ cup frosting red. Place frosting in a pastry bag fitted with a round tip. Pipe Xs onto doughnut holes to resemble the stitching on baseballs. Place a doughnut hole on each cupcake.

Per cupcake: 500 cal., 25 g total fat (10 g sat. fat), 47 mg chol., 168 mg sodium, 66 g carb., 0 g dietary fiber, 54 g sugar, 4 g protein.

Soccer Ball Cupcakes

Prepare as directed, except omit red frosting. Soften a log-shape chocolate-caramel candy in the microwave on 100% power (high) for 5 seconds. Use a rolling pin to flatten softened candy. Cut out small squares using aspic cutters; arrange squares on coated doughnut holes, using white frosting to secure.

Basketball Cupcakes

Prepare as directed, except substitute orange candy coating disks for the white candy coating disks, omit the red frosting, and use a tube of chocolate icing to pipe lines onto coated doughnut holes to resemble basketballs.

Per soccer ball or basketball cupcake: 495 calories, 24 g total fat, (10 g sat. fat), 47 mg chol., 165 mg sodium, 66 g carb., 0 g dietary fiber, 54 g sugar, 4 g protein.

1. To dip sports balls, hold doughnut holes on a fork to dip in melted candy coating. If necessar, spoon coating over balls to coat.

2. For baseballs, after coating has hardened, use a pastry bag fitted with a small round tip to pipe red baseball seams.

3. For soccer balls, use tiny aspic cutters (or a small sharp knife) to cut shapes from softened and flattened candy.

4. Attach candy cutouts to soccer balls with frosting.

Princess Cupcakes

Prep: 2 hours **Chill:** 30 minutes
Makes 12 (2½-inch) cupcakes

Flat tart taffy candies, such as Airheads

4 cups Creamy White Frosting (see recipe, page 15) or canned creamy white frosting

Pink, yellow, or purple food coloring

12 2½-inch cupcakes in paper bake cups (any flavor)

12 rolled sugar ice cream cones

Multicolor decorative sprinkles

Small decorative candies

1. Place taffy candies on waxed paper. Microwave on 100% power (high) for 5 seconds. Flatten candies and cut into ribbons. Set aside.

2. In a medium bowl combine half of the Creamy White Frosting and enough food coloring to make desired color. Stir until well mixed. Place the tinted frosting in a microwave-safe bowl. Microwave on 100% power (high) for 20 to 30 seconds or just until melted. Stir well and set aside to cool slightly.

3. Meanwhile, spread the remaining white frosting onto tops of cupcakes. Lightly cover; set aside.

4. When melted frosting is cooled but still pourable, hold each ice cream cone over the bowl and spoon melted frosting over cone to cover, allowing excess to drip into bowl. Place frosted ice cream cones, pointed ends up, on a wire rack set over waxed paper. While frosting on cones is still wet, decorate cones with sprinkles. Press one end of a taffy ribbon into the top of each cone, letting ribbon spiral down cone. Chill cones in refrigerator about 30 minutes or until firm. Spoon some of the white frosting into a pastry bag fitted with a round tip. Pipe desired designs on cones. Let cones dry completely.

5. Place cones on top of frosted cupcakes, pressing into frosting to secure. Arrange small decorative candies around bottoms of cones.

Per cupcake: 640 cal., 30 g total fat (10 g sat. fat), 43 mg chol., 166 mg sodium, 91 g carb., 1 g dietary fiber, 72 g sugar, 4 g protein.

Cupcake Rainbow

Start to Finish: 40 minutes

Makes 26 to 32 (2½-inch) cupcakes

3 to 4 cups Creamy White Frosting (see recipe, page 15) or canned creamy white frosting

Purple, blue, green, yellow, orange, and red paste food colorings

26 to 32 2½-inch cupcakes in paper bake cups (any flavor)

Purple, blue, green, yellow, orange, and red fine or coarse decorating sugars

2 cups tiny marshmallows

1. Divide Creamy White Frosting into six portions.* Tint each portion a different color with food coloring. Spoon each frosting portion into a disposable pastry bag or heavy resealable plastic bag.

2. On a very large serving platter arrange cupcakes tightly together in a rainbow shape; use 6 to 8 cupcakes for the inside row, 8 to 10 cupcakes for the middle row, and 12 to 14 cupcakes for the outside row.

3. Snip off the tip of each pastry bag or one corner of each resealable plastic bag. Pipe rows of colored frostings onto tops of cupcakes to make a large rainbow. If desired, use a narrow metal spatula to gently spread frosting to fill in gaps. Sprinkle matching sugars over colored frostings. Sprinkle marshmallows over frosting at each end of the rainbow to resemble clouds.

*Test Kitchen Tip:

The top red band of the rainbow will require the most frosting and subsequent bands of frosting will require less, so divide frosting accordingly.

Per cupcake: 328 cal., 14 g total fat (6 g sat. fat), 43 mg chol., 135 mg sodium, 47 g carb., 0 g dietary fiber, 36 g sugar, 3 g protein.

1. On a large platter or clean movable surface, tightly arrange cupcakes in the shape of a rainbow.

2. Pipe frostings into rows to create the rainbow. If desired, smooth out frosting with a spatula.

Kitty Cupcake Cones

Prep: 45 minutes **Bake:** 20 minutes at 350°F **Cool:** 45 minutes

Makes 24 kitty cupcake cones plus about 12 regular cupcakes

24 ice cream cones with flat bottoms

1 package 2-layer-size desired-flavor cake mix

1 16-ounce can white frosting

12 to 15 drops desired food coloring (optional)

Small jelly beans

Small round candies

Candy corn

Black shoestring licorice or pull-apart twist candy

1. Preheat oven to 350°F. Stand each ice cream cone in a 2½-inch muffin cup. Prepare cake mix according to package directions. Spoon 1 rounded tablespoon of the batter into each cone.* Bake for 20 to 25 minutes or until a wooden toothpick inserted in centers comes out clean. Cool completely on wire racks.

2. If desired, tint frosting with food coloring to achieve desired color. Remove cupcake cones from muffin cups. Spread frosting onto tops of cupcakes. To make kitty faces, use small jelly beans for eyes, small round candy for nose, candy corn for ears, and cut licorice strands for whiskers and mouth. Serve cupcake cones the same day they are prepared.

*Test Kitchen Tip:
Bake the remaining batter in 2½-inch muffin cups lined with paper bake cups according to package directions for cupcakes.

Per cupcake: 180 cal., 7 g total fat (2 g sat. fat), 18 mg chol., 140 mg sodium, 28 g carb., 0 g dietary fiber, 19 g sugar, 1 g protein.

Butterfly Garden

Start to Finish: 1 hour 30 minutes
Makes 12 (2½-inch) cupcakes

2 cups Butter Frosting (see recipe, page 14) or canned white frosting

Desired food colorings

12 Chocolate Chip Cookie Cupcakes or other 2½-inch cupcakes in paper bake cups

12 regular-size pretzel twists

8 ounces orange, white, red, yellow, and/or desired-color candy coating disks

Rainbow-color licorice twists

Orange, yellow, or desired-color gumdrops

Black licorice laces (optional)

Chocolate or black frosting

Orange, yellow, or desired-color jelly beans

Miniature semisweet chocolate pieces or white baking pieces

1. Tint Butter Frosting with desired food colorings. Spread frostings onto tops of Chocolate Chip Cookie Cupcakes.

2. For butterfly cupcakes, place 6 pairs of pretzels on sheets of waxed paper. Place each color of the candy coating in a microwave-safe bowl; microwave, one bowl at a time, on 100% power (high) for 30 seconds. Stir; microwave for 20 to 30 seconds more or until melted. Spoon each color into a separate pastry bag fitted with a round tip or in a heavy resealable plastic bag. Snip off a small piece from one corner of each plastic bag.

3. For pretzel wings, pipe different colors of candy coating into the spaces in the pretzels until filled, decorating each pretzel pair the same way. Let pretzel wings stand until firm (or transfer the pretzel wings on the waxed paper to a baking sheet and chill about 15 minutes or until firm).

4. Carefully peel wings from waxed paper. Insert a pair of wings into the frosting on top of each of 6 cupcakes so they stand up in a V shape. Place a piece of rainbow-color licorice between each pair of wings for the body. Add a gumdrop for head to each body. If desired, add black licorice for antennae. Pipe on eyes and nose with chocolate or black frosting.

5. For flower cupcakes, arrange two circles of jelly beans at an angle in frosting around edges of the remaining 6 cupcakes. Sprinkle miniature chocolate pieces in centers of jelly bean cupcakes.

Chocolate Chip Cookie Cupcakes

Preheat oven to 350°F. Line twenty-four 2½-inch muffin cups with paper bake cups. Prepare one package 2-layer-size yellow cake mix according to package directions, stirring ¾ cup miniature semisweet chocolate pieces into batter. Fill muffin cups; bake as directed for cupcakes. Cool cupcakes in muffin cups on wire racks for 5 minutes. Remove cupcakes from muffin cups. Cool completely on wire racks. Place extra unfrosted cupcakes in a single layer in airtight containers or resealable freezer bags; seal. Store at room temperature for up to 3 days or freeze for up to 3 months.

Per cupcake: 489 cal., 20 g total fat (11 g sat. fat), 41 mg chol., 235 mg sodium, 76 g carb., 0 g dietary fiber, 52 g sugar, 3 g protein.

1. Place desired colors of melted candy coating in resealable plastic bags. Snip a small hole in one corner of each bag.

2. Place the pretzels on pieces of waxed paper; pipe candy coating into the spaces of the pretzels, creating designs.

3. Insert two coated pretzels into frosting on each cupcake.

Baseball Glove Cupcakes

Prep: 1 hour **Bake:** at 350°F per package directions **Cool:** 45 minutes
Makes 24 (2½-inch) cupcakes

1   package 2-layer-size yellow or white cake mix

1   recipe Butter Frosting (see recipe, page 14)

    Red paste food coloring

    Brown paste food coloring

48 miniature peanut butter–filled peanut-shaped sandwich cookies, split in half and filling scraped (discard filling)

6   peanut butter–filled peanut-shape sandwich cookies, split in half and filling scraped (discard filling)

24 vanilla wafers

1. Preheat oven to 350°F. Line twenty-four 2½-inch muffin cups with paper bake cups; set aside. Prepare and bake cake mix according to package directions for cupcakes. Cool cupcakes in muffin cups on wire racks for 5 minutes. Remove cupcakes from muffin cups. Cool completely on wire racks.

2. Tint about ¼ cup of the Butter Frosting with red food coloring. Spoon frosting into a small heavy resealable plastic bag. Snip off a very small piece from one corner of bag. Set aside. Set aside about ⅔ cup of the frosting for baseball cookies.

3. Tint the remaining frosting light brown to match the color of the peanut sandwich cookies. Generously spread frosting onto tops of cupcakes. Spoon the remaining light brown frosting into a pastry bag fitted with a small round tip. Pipe frosting onto the split miniature sandwich cookies to resemble a crosshatch pattern. Press 4 of the split miniature sandwich cookies into the top edge of each cupcake for the fingers of the baseball glove. Break the split regular-size sandwich cookies in half crosswise; press one half into the top edge of each cupcake for the thumb of the baseball glove. Set cupcakes aside.

4. Spread reserved ⅔ cup white frosting on vanilla wafers. Pipe the red frosting onto frosted vanilla wafers to resemble baseball stitching. Place the decorated wafers on the baseball glove cupcakes.

Per cupcake: 405 cal., 15 g total fat (6 g sat. fat), 43 mg chol., 276 mg sodium, 68 g carb., 1 g dietary fiber, 48 g sugar, 3 g protein.

We-All-Scream-for-Ice-Cream Cake

Prep: 1 hour **Bake:** 25 minutes at 350°F **Cool:** 1 hour

Makes 24 servings (6 servings per cone cake plus 12 cupcakes)

1 package 2-layer-size desired-flavor cake mix

2 16-ounce cans creamy white frosting*

Buttercup-yellow paste food coloring

1 16-ounce can chocolate frosting*

Red food coloring

Strawberry preserves and/or chocolate ice cream topping

Chopped nuts, colored sprinkles, miniature chocolate pieces, and/or maraschino cherries

1. Preheat oven to 350°F. Grease and lightly flour one 8x8x2-inch baking pan. Line twelve 2½-inch muffin cups with foil or paper bake cups.

2. Prepare cake mix according to package directions, pouring half of the batter into prepared square pan and dividing the remaining batter among prepared muffin cups. Bake square cake for 25 to 30 minutes and cupcakes according to package directions for cupcakes, or until a wooden toothpick inserted in centers comes out clean. Cool square cake and cupcakes in pans on wire racks for 10 minutes. Remove square cake and cupcakes from pans. Cool completely on wire racks.

3. Cut the square cake into a cone shape by cutting off two triangles from each side of the cake. Place the cone shape on a large flat platter or covered cake board. Place the two smaller triangles side by side on another large flat platter or covered cake board to create a second cone shape.

4. Tint one can of the white frosting light yellow with a small amount of buttercup-yellow food coloring. Spread light yellow frosting onto both cones. In a small bowl stir together ⅓ cup of the white frosting and 1 tablespoon of the chocolate frosting. Spoon into a pastry bag fitted with a small round tip. Pipe frosting onto both cones in a diamond pattern.

5. Tint a small amount of the white frosting pink using a small amount of red food coloring. Spread pink frosting onto a few of the cupcakes. Top with a small amount of strawberry preserves and/or chocolate topping. Spread white frosting and/or chocolate frosting onto tops of the remaining cupcakes. Top with nuts, sprinkles, chocolate pieces, and/or cherries.

6. Arrange 6 cupcakes above the wide part of each cone to resemble stacks of ice cream scoops.

*Test Kitchen Tip:
You will have leftover frosting. Save for another use.

Per serving: 274 cal., 11 g total fat (2 g sat. fat), 28 mg chol., 232 mg sodium, 42 g carb., 0 g dietary fiber, 29 g sugar, 2 g protein.

Sea Turtle Cupcakes

Start to Finish: 45 minutes

Makes 12 (2½-inch) cupcakes

2 cups Creamy White Frosting (see recipe, page 15) or canned creamy white frosting

Blue and green food colorings

12 2½-inch cupcakes in paper bake cups (any flavor)

Brown sugar

3 vanilla sandwich cookies

Green gumdrops or other chewy green candies, such as Dots, halved lengthwise

Blue or green colored sugar

1 tube black icing

Black licorice laces or rainbow-color licorice twists, snipped into small pieces

1. Tint 1 cup of the Creamy White Frosting blue with food coloring. Tint the remaining frosting green with food coloring. Spoon frostings into separate resealable plastic bags. Snip off a small piece from one corner of each bag. Pipe small mounds of frosting onto tops of cupcakes, alternating colors. Use a thin metal spatula to swirl colors together. Set aside 6 of the cupcakes for plain sea cupcakes without turtles.

2. For turtle cupcakes, sprinkle brown sugar onto tops of the remaining 6 frosted cupcakes. Split sandwich cookies; discard filling. Place 1 cookie half on the center of each brown sugar–topped cupcake. Tuck 5 gumdrop halves under the edge of each cookie half for a head and 4 feet. (If necessary, flatten the gumdrop halves.) Pipe blue and green designs onto the cookies for shell plates. Sprinkle with colored sugar. Pipe blue eyes onto the turtles' heads. Use black icing to pipe pupils onto the eyes. Insert licorice pieces into frosting for tails.

Per cupcake: 411 cal., 18 g total fat (7 g sat. fat), 43 mg chol., 146 mg sodium, 59 g carb., 0 g dietary fiber, 47 g sugar, 3 g protein.

1. For swirled seawater, pipe small mounds of blue and green frostings.

2. Use a spatula to swirl frostings together.

3. Create peaks at the top to look like waves.

Beach Party Cupcakes

Start to Finish: 1 hour 30 minutes
Makes 24 (2½-inch) cupcakes

2   16-ounce cans vanilla frosting
    Blue food coloring
24 2½-inch cupcakes in paper bake cups (any flavor)
2   0.75-ounce tubs blue decorating gel
⅔   cup finely crushed vanilla wafers (16 cookies)
2   plain doughnut holes
3   or 4 assorted flavors rolled fruit leather
2   peanut butter–filled peanut-shape sandwich cookies
    Licorice laces, cut into small pieces
1   or 2 fruit-flavor ring-shape jelly candies

1. Place ¼ cup of the frosting in a small microwave-safe bowl. Set aside. Tint half of the remaining frosting with blue food coloring. Frost 12 of the cupcakes with blue frosting. Use blue gel to pipe waves onto blue-frosted cupcakes. Spread white frosting onto the tops of the remaining 12 cupcakes. Sprinkle white-frosted cupcakes generously with crushed vanilla wafers to resemble sand; set aside.

2. For beach balls, microwave the reserved ¼ cup frosting on 100% power (high) for 10 to 20 seconds or until melted. Using a fork, dip doughnut holes into melted frosting, turning to coat. Place on waxed paper; let dry. For panels on the beach balls, unroll fruit leather and cut eight 3½-inch rectangles, tapering short ends to a point. Place 4 strips on each coated doughnut hole to look like beach balls. Set aside until set.

3. For beach towels, unroll and cut the remaining fruit leather into three 2-inch rectangles. If desired, cut fringe at the short ends of rectangles. Roll up the rectangles so they resemble towels.

4. For flip-flops, separate peanut butter sandwich cookies; scrape off filling. Use filling to attach two short pieces of licorice lace on smooth side of each peanut butter cookie to look like flip-flops.

5. Arrange beach balls, beach towels, flip-flops, and ring-shape jelly candies on platter with cupcakes.

Per cupcake: 380 cal., 15 g total fat (6 g sat. fat), 43 mg chol., 235 mg sodium, 59 g carb., 0 g dietary fiber, 44 g sugar, 3 g protein.

A Day at the Zoo

Start to Finish: 1 hour

Makes 12 (2½-inch) cupcakes

- 2 cups Creamy White Frosting (see recipe, page 15) or one 16-ounce can creamy white frosting

  Black, yellow, and orange food colorings

- 1 cup Chocolate Butter Frosting (see recipe, page 14) or canned chocolate frosting

- 12 2½-inch cupcakes in paper bake cups (any flavor)

  Pink chewy fruit-flavor square candies, such as Starburst

  Miniature peanut butter sandwich cookies, such as Nutter Butter Bites

  Candy-coated milk chocolate pieces

  Miniature semisweet chocolate pieces

  Tiny marshmallows, cut in half crosswise (optional)

- 1 tube black icing

  Gummy worms

  Miniature pretzel twists

  White candy-coated licorice candy, such as Good & Plenty

  Round oat cereal

  Bite-size rich round crackers, such as Ritz Bits

  Miniature candy-coated chocolate pieces

  Miniature chocolate sandwich cookies with white filling

  Black jelly beans

  Black candy-coated sunflower kernels

1. Divide Creamy White Frosting into three portions. Tint one portion gray and one portion yellow with black and yellow food colorings; leave the remaining portion white. Spoon some of the Chocolate Butter Frosting into a pastry bag fitted with a round tip. Spoon some of the white frosting into a separate pastry bag fitted with a round tip.

2. For monkey cupcakes, frost the tops of 3 of the cupcakes with chocolate frosting. For ears, microwave a chewy fruit-flavor square candy on 100% power (high) for 7 seconds; flatten candy. Cut out small candy rounds and attach to miniature peanut butter cookies with frosting. Press ears into frosting on opposite sides of each cupcake top. Place a cookie in center of each cupcake for mouth and nose. For eyes, place 2 candy-coated milk chocolate pieces on cupcake top; pipe a white frosting dot on each and top with miniature semisweet chocolate pieces. Pipe chocolate frosting for mouth and nose.

3. For elephant cupcakes, spread gray frosting onto tops of 3 cupcakes. Pipe white frosting for eyes, or, if desired, use 1 tiny marshmallow half for each eye, and top with a dot of black icing. In a microwave-safe bowl microwave some of the gray frosting on 100% power (high) for 10 seconds or until melted. Trim gummy worms to appropriate size for trunks (if they're too long, they may be heavy and fall off). Dip gummy worms in melted gray frosting, letting excess drip off. Place on waxed paper. For ears, dip pretzels in melted gray frosting, letting excess drip off. Place on waxed paper. If desired, for pink on elephant ears, microwave and flatten chewy fruit-flavor square candy as in step 2. Using a pretzel as a guide, cut outlines from candy. Press candy outlines into frosting on back side of each pretzel. Place on waxed paper. Chill gummy worms and pretzels for about 5 minutes or until set. Arrange trunks on cupcakes. Stick white candy-coated licorice into frosting for tusks. Press ears into frosting on sides of each cupcake top.

4. For lion cupcakes, spread yellow frosting onto the tops of 3 cupcakes. Tint half of the remaining yellow frosting orange. Spread orange frosting along one side of a pastry bag fitted with a multi-opening tip. Spoon yellow frosting along the other side of the bag. Pipe frostings around edge of each cupcake for mane. Add oat cereal for ears. Pipe white frosting for eyes; add miniature semisweet chocolate pieces. Place 1 rich round cracker in center of each cupcake; attach a candy-coated chocolate piece for nose. Pipe chocolate frosting for mouth.

5. For panda cupcakes, spread white frosting onto the tops of 3 cupcakes. Split miniature chocolate sandwich cookies in half; press cookie halves into frosting for ears. Arrange jelly bean and sunflower kernels on cupcakes for nose and eyes. Pipe black icing for mouth.

Per cupcake: 490 cal., 22 g total fat (9 g sat. fat), 50 mg chol., 164 mg sodium, 72 g carb., 1 g dietary fiber, 60 g sugar, 3 g protein.

Color Wheel Cupcakes

Start to Finish: 1 hour 30 minutes
Makes 24 (2½-inch) cupcakes

1 2-layer-size package white, yellow, red velvet, or chocolate cake mix

Red, orange, yellow, green, and/or blue food colorings

2 cups Creamy White Frosting (see recipe, page 15) or canned creamy white frosting

Red, orange, yellow, green, and/or blue coarse decorating sugars

Red, orange, pink, yellow, green, and/or blue small decorative candies

1. Preheat oven to 350°F. Line twenty-four 2½-inch muffin cups with paper bake cups. Prepare cake mix according to package directions. If desired, if using white or yellow cake mix, divide batter into separate bowls and tint with desired food colorings. Bake according to package directions for cupcakes. Cool cupcakes in muffin cups on wire racks for 5 minutes. Remove cupcakes from muffin cups. Cool completely on wire racks.

2. Divide Creamy White Frosting equally among several bowls. Tint frosting in bowls with food colorings to desired colors. Set out frosting, cupcakes, sugars, and candies; allow guests to frost and decorate as desired.*

*Test Kitchen Tip:
Lay an inexpensive plastic tablecloth over your table before setting out party ingredients. At the end of the party, dispose of the tablecloth and the mess.

Per cupcake: 203 cal., 9 g total fat (2 g sat. fat), 0 mg chol., 151 mg sodium, 31 g carb., 0 g dietary fiber, 24 g sugar, 2 g protein.

Sunflower Cupcakes

Prep: 30 minutes **Stand:** 30 minutes **Bake:** 20 minutes at 350°F **Cool:** 45 minutes

Makes 12 (2½-inch) cupcakes

¼ cup butter

2 egg whites

1 cup all-purpose flour

½ teaspoon baking powder

¼ teaspoon baking soda

Pinch salt

1 cup granulated sugar

1 teaspoon vanilla

⅔ cup buttermilk or sour milk (see tip, page 11)

2 tablespoons toasted wheat germ

1 recipe Lemon Butter Frosting

Yellow colored sugar (optional)

Brown or black candy-coated sunflower kernels* or other small black candies

Green rolled fruit leather (optional)

1. Allow butter and egg whites to stand at room temperature for 30 minutes. Meanwhile, line twelve 2½-inch muffin cups with paper bake cups. In a small bowl stir together flour, baking powder, baking soda, and salt. Set aside.

2. Preheat oven to 350°F. In a large mixing bowl beat butter with an electric mixer on medium to high speed for 30 seconds. Add granulated sugar and vanilla; beat until combined. Add egg whites, one at a time, beating well after each addition.

3. Alternately add flour mixture and buttermilk to butter mixture, beating on low speed after each addition just until combined. Stir in wheat germ. Divide batter among prepared muffin cups. Use the back of a spoon to smooth out batter in cups.

4. Bake about 20 minutes or until a wooden toothpick inserted in centers comes out clean. Cool cupcakes in muffin cups on wire racks for 10 minutes. Remove cupcakes from muffin cups. Cool completely on wire racks.

5. Spoon Lemon Butter Frosting into a pastry bag fitted with a leaf or star tip. Pipe frosting onto tops of cupcakes to look like sunflower petals and, if desired, sprinkle with colored sugar. Add a cluster of candy-coated sunflower kernels to the center of each cupcake. If desired, use a small leaf-shape cookie cutter to cut leaves from green fruit leather. Arrange around cupcakes as desired.

Lemon Butter Frosting

Allow ¼ cup butter to stand at room temperature for 30 minutes. In a medium mixing bowl beat butter with an electric mixer on medium speed until smooth. Add 1 cup powdered sugar, beating well. Beat in 2 tablespoons buttermilk or milk and 1 teaspoon vanilla. Gradually beat in an additional 2 cups powdered sugar. If necessary, beat in enough additional milk until frosting reaches spreading consistency. Stir in ¼ teaspoon finely shredded lemon peel. If desired, tint with 1 or 2 drops yellow food coloring.

*Test Kitchen Tip:

Find candy-coated sunflower kernels at hobby and crafts stores or online.

Per cupcake: 313 cal., 9 g total fat (5 g sat. fat), 21 mg chol., 140 mg sodium, 55 g carb., 1 g dietary fiber, 3 g protein.

White Chocolate Liqueur Cupcakes

Prep: 30 minutes **Stand:** 30 minutes **Bake:** 20 minutes at 325°F **Cool:** 45 minutes

Makes 18 (2½-inch) cupcakes

½ cup butter

2 eggs

1½ cups all-purpose flour

½ teaspoon baking soda

¼ teaspoon salt

1 cup sugar

3 tablespoons vegetable oil

½ cup sour cream

¼ cup chocolate liqueur

1½ teaspoons vanilla

1 recipe Chocolate Liqueur Frosting

Fresh raspberries (optional)

1. Allow butter and eggs to stand at room temperature for 30 minutes. Meanwhile, line eighteen 2½-inch muffin cups with paper bake cups. In a medium bowl stir together flour, baking soda, and salt. Set aside.

2. Preheat oven to 325°F. In a large mixing bowl beat butter with an electric mixer on medium to high speed for 30 seconds. Add sugar and oil. Beat on medium speed until combined, scraping sides of bowl occasionally. Add eggs, one at a time, beating well after each addition.

3. Alternately add flour mixture and sour cream to butter mixture, beating on low speed after each addition just until combined. Stir in liqueur and vanilla.

4. Spoon batter into prepared muffin cups, filling each about three-fourths full. Use the back of a spoon to smooth out batter in cups. Bake about 20 minutes or until a wooden toothpick inserted in centers comes out clean.

5. Cool cupcakes in muffin cups on wire racks for 5 minutes. Remove cupcakes from muffin cups. Cool completely on wire racks. Spread Chocolate Liqueur Frosting onto tops of cupcakes. If desired, garnish with raspberries.

Chocolate Liqueur Frosting

Allow ½ cup butter to stand at room temperature for 30 minutes. In a large mixing bowl beat butter with an electric mixer on medium speed until smooth. Gradually add 1 cup powdered sugar, beating well. Slowly beat in ¼ cup chocolate liqueur, 2 tablespoons whipping cream, and 1½ teaspoons vanilla. Gradually beat in an additional 3 cups powdered sugar. If necessary, beat in additional whipping cream until frosting reaches spreading consistency.

Per cupcake: 342 cal., 15 g total fat (8 g sat. fat), 56 mg chol., 153 mg sodium, 48 g carb., 1 g dietary fiber, 2 g protein.

Coconut-Tangerine Snowball Cupcakes

Prep: 35 minutes **Stand:** 30 minutes **Bake:** 18 minutes at 350°F **Cool:** 45 minutes

Makes 24 (2½-inch) cupcakes

½ cup butter

3 eggs

2⅔ cups all-purpose flour

1 teaspoon baking powder

½ teaspoon baking soda

½ teaspoon salt

1⅔ cups sugar

2 teaspoons finely shredded tangerine, orange, or lemon peel

1 teaspoon vanilla

1⅓ cups buttermilk or sour milk (see tip, page 11)

⅔ cup flaked coconut, toasted

1 recipe Tangerine Creamy Frosting

Flaked coconut, toasted (optional)

1. Allow butter and eggs to stand at room temperature for 30 minutes. Meanwhile, line twenty-four 2½-inch muffin cups with paper bake cups. In a medium bowl stir together flour, baking powder, baking soda, and salt. Set aside.

2. Preheat oven to 350°F. In a large mixing bowl beat butter with an electric mixer on medium to high speed for 30 seconds. Add sugar, tangerine peel, and vanilla. Beat until combined, scraping sides of bowl occasionally. Add eggs, one at a time, beating well after each addition. Alternately add flour mixture and buttermilk to butter mixture, beating on low speed after each addition just until combined. Stir in the ⅔ cup toasted coconut.

3. Spoon batter into prepared muffin cups, filling each about two-thirds full. Use the back of a spoon to smooth out batter in cups.

4. Bake for 18 to 20 minutes or until tops are golden brown and spring back when lightly touched. Cool cupcakes in muffin cups on wire racks for 5 minutes. Remove cupcakes from muffin cups. Cool completely on wire racks.

5. Spread Tangerine Creamy Frosting onto tops of cupcakes. If desired, sprinkle with additional toasted coconut.

Tangerine Creamy Frosting
Allow one 3-ounce package cream cheese and 3 tablespoons butter to stand at room temperature for 30 minutes. In a medium mixing bowl beat cream cheese, butter, ¾ teaspoon vanilla, and ½ to ¾ teaspoon finely shredded tangerine peel with an electric mixer on medium speed until combined. Gradually add 1¾ cups powdered sugar, beating well. If necessary, beat in enough tangerine or orange juice, 1 teaspoon at a time, to make frosting spreading consistency.

Per cupcake: 229 cal., 9 g total fat (5 g sat. fat), 45 mg chol., 170 mg sodium, 36 g carb., 1 g dietary fiber, 24 g sugar, 3 g protein.

Chocolate-Rum Petits Fours

Prep: 45 minutes **Bake:** 12 minutes at 350°F **Cool:** 45 minutes

Makes 48 petits fours

Butter

Unsweetened cocoa powder

1   cup all-purpose flour

½   teaspoon baking soda

¼   teaspoon salt

2   ounces semisweet chocolate, chopped

2   tablespoons instant coffee crystals or instant espresso powder

1   tablespoon boiling water

¼   cup rum, Kahlúa, or coffee liqueur

½   cup unsalted butter, softened

1   cup sugar

1   egg

1   teaspoon vanilla

1   recipe Ganache (see recipe, page 15)

1   recipe Chocolate Butter Frosting (see recipe, page 14) or canned chocolate frosting (optional)

Chocolate-covered coffee beans, chopped (optional)

1. Preheat oven to 350°F. Butter forty-eight 1¾-inch muffin cups. Add some cocoa powder to each cup; shake and tilt pans to coat bottoms and sides of cups. Shake out any excess cocoa powder. In a medium bowl combine flour, baking soda, and salt. Set aside.

2. Place chopped chocolate in a small microwave-safe bowl. Microwave on 100% power (high) for 1 minute; stir. Microwave for 20 seconds more. Stir until smooth. Set aside to cool slightly.

3. In a 1-cup glass measuring cup dissolve coffee crystals in the boiling water; add enough cold water to measure ¾ cup total liquid. Stir in rum.

4. In a large mixing bowl beat the ½ cup butter with an electric mixer on medium to high speed for 30 seconds. Add sugar. Beat until combined. Add egg, beating well. Beat in melted chocolate and vanilla. Alternately add flour mixture and rum mixture to chocolate mixture, beginning and ending with flour mixture and beating on low speed after each addition just until combined. Spoon batter into prepared muffin cups, filling each about three-fourths full. Use the back of a spoon to smooth out batter in cups.

5. Bake about 12 minutes or until tops spring back when lightly touched. Cool cupcakes in muffin cups on wire racks for 5 minutes. Invert onto racks to remove cupcakes from cups. Cool completely on wire racks.

6. Turn cupcakes upside down on a wire rack set over a sheet of waxed paper. Holding one cupcake on the tines of a fork over the Ganache, spoon Ganache over cupcake. Place on wire rack. Repeat with remaining cupcakes. If desired, using a pastry bag fitted with a small star tip, pipe Chocolate Butter Frosting onto petits fours and garnish with chocolate-covered coffee beans.

Per petit four: 111 cal., 7 g total fat (4 g sat. fat), 19 mg chol., 38 mg sodium, 11 g carb., 0 g dietary fiber, 9 g sugar, 1 g protein.

Louisiana Praline Cupcakes

Prep: 35 minutes **Bake:** 30 minutes at 325°F/350°F **Cool:** 45 minutes

Makes 18 (2½-inch) cupcakes

1 cup butter

2 eggs

Nonstick cooking spray

1 cup coarsely chopped pecans

2 tablespoons granulated sugar

2 tablespoons dark-color corn syrup

2 cups sifted cake flour

2 teaspoons baking powder

½ teaspoon salt

⅔ cup packed brown sugar

1 teaspoon vanilla

¾ cup milk

1 recipe Praline Cream*

1. Allow butter and eggs to stand at room temperature for 30 minutes. Meanwhile, preheat oven to 325°F. Lightly coat a 9×9×2-inch baking pan with cooking spray. In a small bowl combine pecans, granulated sugar, and corn syrup. Spread in prepared baking pan. Bake for 15 minutes, stirring twice. Spread mixture on a piece of foil to cool. Break into small pieces. Increase oven temperature to 350°F.

2. Line eighteen 2½-inch muffin cups with paper bake cups. In a medium bowl stir together cake flour, baking powder, and salt. Set aside.

3. In a large mixing bowl beat butter with an electric mixer on medium to high speed for 30 seconds. Add brown sugar. Beat until combined, scraping sides of bowl occasionally. Add eggs and vanilla. Beat for 1 minute more. Alternately add flour mixture and milk to butter mixture, beating on low speed after each addition just until combined. Stir in 1 cup of the pecan mixture.

4. Divide batter among prepared muffin cups. Use the back of a spoon to smooth out batter in cups. Bake for 15 to 18 minutes or until a wooden toothpick inserted in centers comes out clean. Cool cupcakes in muffin cups on wire racks for 5 minutes. Remove cupcakes from muffin cups. Cool completely on wire racks.

5. Remove cupcakes from paper bake cups, if desired. Spoon Praline Cream into a pastry bag fitted with a large round tip. Pipe a small swirl of frosting onto tops of cupcake. Sprinkle with the remaining pecan mixture.

Praline Cream

In a small saucepan combine ¾ cup packed brown sugar, ⅓ cup butter, and 3 tablespoons milk. Bring to boiling over medium-high heat, stirring constantly to dissolve brown sugar. Reduce heat; boil gently, uncovered, for 5 minutes, stirring occasionally. Remove from heat; stir in 1 teaspoon vanilla. Pour mixture into a large mixing bowl; cool completely. Gradually add 1¼ cups powdered sugar, beating with an electric mixer on medium speed until combined. If necessary, beat in 1 to 3 teaspoons additional milk, 1 teaspoon at a time, until frosting reaches spreading consistency.

*Test Kitchen Tip:

If you want larger swirls of frosting on the tops of cupcakes, double the recipe for Praline Cream.

Per cupcake: 343 cal., 19 g total fat (9 g sat. fat), 61 mg chol., 224 mg sodium, 42 g carb., 1 g dietary fiber, 3 g protein.

Little Pumpkin Cakes

Prep: 45 minutes **Bake:** 20 minutes at 350°F **Cool:** 45 minutes
Makes 12 (2½-inch), 4 (3½-inch), or 36 (1¾-inch) cupcakes

1 cup all-purpose flour
¾ teaspoon baking powder
¾ teaspoon pumpkin pie spice
½ teaspoon salt
¼ teaspoon baking soda
2 eggs
¾ cup sugar
⅓ cup vegetable oil
½ 15-ounce can pumpkin
1 recipe Creamy White Frosting (see recipe, page 15)
1 recipe Caramelized Hazelnut Brittle or purchased nut brittle, broken into pieces (optional)

1. Grease and lightly flour twelve 2½-inch muffin cups, four 3½-inch muffin cups, or thirty-six 1¾-inch muffin cups. In a medium bowl stir together flour, baking powder, pumpkin pie spice, salt, and baking soda. Set aside.

2. Preheat oven to 350°F. In a large mixing bowl beat eggs, sugar, and oil with an electric mixer on medium speed until combined. Alternately add flour mixture and pumpkin to egg mixture, beating just until mixture is combined.

3. Spoon batter into prepared muffin cups, filling each about two-thirds full. Use the back of a spoon to smooth out batter in cups.

4. Bake until a wooden toothpick inserted in centers comes out clean. Allow 20 to 25 minutes for 2½-inch cupcakes, 25 to 30 minutes for 3½-inch cupcakes, or 12 to 15 minutes for 1¾-inch muffin cupcakes. Cool cupcakes in muffin cups on a wire rack for 5 minutes. Remove cupcakes from muffin cups. Cool completely on wire rack.

5. Spread Creamy White Frosting onto tops of cupcakes. If desired, arrange shards of Caramelized Hazelnut Brittle on tops of cupcakes.

Caramelized Hazelnut Brittle

Line a large baking sheet with foil; butter foil. Set aside. In a small saucepan melt 2 teaspoons butter over low heat. Stir in ⅓ cup chopped hazelnuts (filberts); keep hazelnuts warm over low heat. Place 1 cup sugar in a 12-inch heavy skillet; heat over medium-high heat until sugar begins to melt, shaking skillet occasionally to heat sugar evenly. Reduce heat to medium-low; cook until sugar is melted and golden, stirring only as necessary after sugar begins to melt (12 to 15 minutes). Remove from heat; quickly stir in warm hazelnuts. Immediately pour hazelnut mixture onto prepared baking sheet, allowing syrup to flow and distributing nuts evenly. Cool completely. Break candy into shards. Store in a tightly covered container in a cool, dry place for up to 1 month.

Per 2½-inch cupcake: 459 cal., 24 g total fat (5 g sat. fat), 32 mg chol., 161 mg sodium, 60 g carb., 1 g dietary fiber, 2 g protein.

How to Make Caramelized Hazelnut Brittle

1. Heat sugar in a large skillet over medium-high heat until sugar begins to melt. Reduce heat to medium-low and cook until sugar is melted and golden brown, stirring as needed once sugar melts.

2. Remove hot sugar from heat and quickly stir in toasted hazelnuts.

3. Immediately pour brittle mixture onto a greased foil-lined baking sheet, using a spoon to evenly distribute nuts.

Carrot-Zucchini Party Cupcakes

Prep: 45 minutes **Bake:** 20 minutes at 350°F **Cool:** 45 minutes
Makes 18 (2½-inch) or 56 (1¾-inch) cupcakes

1½   cups all-purpose flour
¼   cup golden raisins or dried currants
2   tablespoons finely chopped crystallized ginger
1   teaspoon baking powder
¾   teaspoon baking soda
¾   teaspoon ground cinnamon
¼   teaspoon salt
2   eggs, lightly beaten
1   cup finely shredded carrots or parsnips
1   cup finely shredded zucchini
½   cup granulated sugar
½   cup packed brown sugar
½   cup unsweetened applesauce
2   tablespoons vegetable oil
1½   teaspoons vanilla
½   cup chopped pecans, toasted
1   recipe Cream Cheese Frosting
    Chopped pecans, toasted, or chopped crystallized ginger (optional)

1. Preheat oven to 350°F. Line eighteen 2½-inch muffin cups with foil or paper bake cups or lightly grease fifty-six 1¾-inch muffin cups. In a large bowl combine flour, raisins, the 2 tablespoons crystallized ginger, the baking powder, baking soda, cinnamon, and salt. Set aside.

2. In a medium bowl combine eggs, carrots, zucchini, granulated sugar, brown sugar, applesauce, oil, and vanilla. Stir egg mixture into flour mixture until combined. Stir in the ½ cup pecans. Spoon batter into prepared muffin cups, filling each about one-half full (about 3 tablespoons each for 2½-inch cupcakes or 1 tablespoon each for 1¾-inch cupcakes).

3. Bake for 20 to 25 minutes for 2½-inch cupcakes, 15 to 18 minutes for 1¾-inch cupcakes, or until a wooden toothpick inserted in centers come out clean. Cool cupcakes in muffin cups on wire racks for 5 minutes. Remove cupcakes from muffin cups. Cool completely on wire racks.

4. Spoon Cream Cheese Frosting into a pastry bag fitted with a medium round tip. Pipe polka dots onto tops of cupcakes or decorate as desired. If desired, sprinkle with additional chopped pecans or crystallized ginger. Store in the refrigerator.

Cream Cheese Frosting

Allow one 3-ounce package cream cheese and ¼ cup butter to stand at room temperature for 30 minutes. In a medium mixing bowl beat cream cheese, butter, and 1 teaspoon vanilla with an electric mixer on medium speed until light and fluffy. Gradually beat in 2¼ to 2⅓ cups powdered sugar until frosting reaches spreading consistency.

Make-Ahead Directions:

Place frosted cupcakes in a single layer in an airtight container; seal. Store in the refrigerator for up to 3 days.

Per cupcake: 349 cal., 13 g total fat (5 g sat. fat), 54 mg chol., 243 mg sodium, 56 g carb., 2 g dietary fiber, 4 g protein.

Vanilla Bean–Coconut Cupcakes

Prep: 40 minutes **Cook:** 20 minutes **Bake:** 18 minutes at 375°F **Cool:** 45 minutes
Makes 18 (2½-inch) cupcakes

1 14-ounce can unsweetened coconut milk
¾ cup butter
3 eggs
1 vanilla bean, split lengthwise
1¾ cups all-purpose flour
¼ cup ground macadamia nuts
2¼ teaspoons baking powder
½ teaspoon salt
1⅓ cups sugar
1 recipe Vanilla-Coconut Frosting
1 cup flaked coconut, lightly toasted

1. In a medium saucepan bring coconut milk just to boiling; reduce heat. Simmer, uncovered, for 20 to 30 minutes or until milk is reduced to 1⅓ cups; cool. Meanwhile, allow butter and eggs to stand at room temperature for 30 minutes.

2. Preheat oven to 375°F. Line eighteen 2½-inch muffin cups with paper bake cups. Using the tip of a small sharp knife, scrape out seeds from vanilla bean. In a small bowl stir together flour, ground nuts, baking powder, and salt. Set aside.

3. In a large mixing bowl beat butter with an electric mixer on medium to high speed for 30 seconds. Add sugar. Beat on medium to high speed for 1 minute, scraping sides of bowl occasionally.

4. Add eggs, one at time, beating well after each addition. Stir in half of the vanilla seeds (reserve the remaining seeds for the frosting). Alternately add flour mixture and 1 cup of the reduced coconut milk (reserve the remaining coconut milk for the frosting) to butter mixture, beating on low speed after each addition just until combined.

5. Spoon batter into prepared muffin cups, filling each about three-fourths full. Use the back of a spoon to smooth out batter in cups. Bake for 18 to 20 minutes or until tops spring back when lightly touched. Cool cupcakes in muffin cups on wire racks for 5 minutes. Remove cupcakes from muffin cups. Cool completely on wire racks.

6. If desired, spoon Vanilla-Coconut Frosting into a pastry bag fitted with a large star tip. Pipe or spread Vanilla-Coconut Frosting onto tops of cupcakes. Sprinkle with toasted coconut.

Vanilla-Coconut Frosting

Allow 1 cup butter to stand at room temperature for 30 minutes. In a large mixing bowl beat butter with an electric mixer on medium to high speed for 30 seconds. Beat in the reserved reduced coconut milk from cupcakes, the reserved vanilla seeds from cupcakes, and ⅛ teaspoon salt. Gradually add 2½ cups powdered sugar, beating until fluffy.

Per cupcake: 413 cal., 26 g total fat (17 g sat. fat), 78 mg chol., 319 mg sodium, 44 g carb., 1 g dietary fiber, 33 g sugar, 3 g protein.

Island Bananas Foster Cupcakes

Prep: 35 minutes **Stand:** 30 minutes **Bake:** 20 minutes at 350°F **Cool:** 45 minutes

Makes 24 (2½-inch) cupcakes

1 cup butter

3 eggs

2 cups all-purpose flour

2 teaspoons baking powder

½ teaspoon salt

1½ cups sugar

½ teaspoon vanilla

¾ cup unsweetened coconut milk

¾ cup shredded coconut, lightly toasted

¼ cup rum or unsweetened coconut milk

1 recipe Bananas Foster Topping

Whipped cream (optional)

Shredded coconut, lightly toasted (optional)

1. Allow butter and eggs to stand at room temperature for 30 minutes. Meanwhile, line twenty-four 2½-inch muffin cups with paper bake cups. In a medium bowl stir together flour, baking powder, and salt. Set aside.

2. Preheat oven to 350°F. In a large mixing bowl beat butter with an electric mixer on medium to high speed for 30 seconds. Add sugar, about ¼ cup at a time, beating until combined. Add eggs, one at a time, beating well after each addition. Beat in vanilla. Alternately add flour mixture and coconut milk to butter mixture, beating on low speed after each addition just until combined. Fold in the ¾ cup coconut and the rum.

3. Spoon batter into prepared muffin cups, filling each about three-fourths full. Use the back of a spoon to smooth out batter in cups.

4. Bake about 20 minutes or until a wooden toothpick inserted in centers comes out clean. Cool cupcakes in muffin cups on wire racks for 5 minutes. Remove cupcakes from muffin cups. Cool completely on wire racks.

5. Spoon Bananas Foster Topping onto tops of cupcakes. If desired, spoon whipped cream into pastry bag fitted with a large star tip. Pipe whipped cream onto cupcakes and sprinkle with additional coconut.

Bananas Foster Topping

In a large skillet melt ⅓ cup butter over medium heat. Stir in ½ cup packed brown sugar, ¼ teaspoon ground cinnamon, and, if desired, ⅛ teaspoon freshly grated nutmeg. Add 3 sliced bananas; toss gently to coat. Cook and stir for 1 to 2 minutes or until bananas are heated through. Meanwhile, in a small saucepan heat ¼ cup rum over low heat just until rum almost simmers; remove from heat. If desired, use a long match to carefully ignite the rum.* Once the flame dies down, pour rum into banana mixture. Gently stir in ½ teaspoon vanilla.

*Test Kitchen Tip:
For safety, keep face and hands away from ignited rum in saucepan. (The flame is hard to see.) Leave on unlit stove burner until flame dies down.

Per cupcake: 263 cal., 14 g total fat (9 g sat. fat), 54 mg chol., 173 mg sodium, 31 g carb., 1 g dietary fiber, 20 g sugar, 3 g protein.

Tip

Bananas Foster Topping is very hot when first removed from the stove and will melt the whipped cream when you pipe it on top. To prevent this, cool the mixture slightly.

Fresh Rosemary and Lemon Cupcakes

Prep: 30 minutes **Stand:** 30 minutes **Bake:** 22 minutes at 350°F **Cool:** 45 minutes

Makes 15 (2½-inch) cupcakes

½ cup butter

2 eggs

1¾ cups cake flour

2 teaspoons finely snipped fresh rosemary

1½ teaspoons baking powder

½ teaspoon salt

1 cup sugar

1½ teaspoons lemon extract

½ teaspoon vanilla

⅔ cup milk

2 teaspoons finely shredded lemon peel

3 tablespoons lemon juice

1 recipe Lemon Glaze

1. Allow butter and eggs to stand at room temperature for 30 minutes. Meanwhile, line fifteen 2½-inch muffin cups with paper bake cups. In a medium bowl stir together cake flour, rosemary, baking powder, and salt. Set aside.

2. Preheat oven to 350°F. In a large mixing bowl beat butter with an electric mixer on medium to high speed for 30 seconds. Add sugar, lemon extract, and vanilla. Beat on medium-high speed about 2 minutes or until light and fluffy, scraping sides of bowl occasionally.

3. Add eggs, one at a time, beating well after each addition. Alternately add flour mixture and milk to butter mixture, beating on low speed after each addition just until combined. Stir in lemon peel and lemon juice.

4. Spoon batter into prepared muffin cups, filling each about three-fourths full. Use the back of a spoon to smooth out batter in cups. Bake for 22 to 25 minutes or until a wooden toothpick inserted in centers comes out clean. Cool cupcakes in muffin cups on wire racks for 5 minutes. Remove cupcakes from muffin cups. Cool completely on wire racks.

5. Spread Lemon Glaze onto tops of cupcakes. Let stand until glaze is set.

Lemon Glaze

In a small bowl combine 1 cup powdered sugar and 5 teaspoons lemon juice. If necessary, stir in an additional ½ teaspoon lemon juice to reach spreading consistency. Stir in ½ teaspoon finely shredded lemon peel.

Per cupcake: 213 cal., 7 g total fat (4 g sat. fat), 45 mg chol., 159 mg sodium, 35 g carb., 0 g dietary fiber, 3 g protein.

Mochaccino Cupcakes

Prep: 40 minutes **Stand:** 30 minutes **Bake:** 18 minutes at 350°F **Cool:** 45 minutes
Makes 30 (2½-inch) cupcakes

¾ cup butter

3 eggs

1¾ cups all-purpose flour

1 cup unsweetened cocoa powder

1 teaspoon baking soda

¾ teaspoon baking powder

½ teaspoon salt

1 cup milk

½ cup strong brewed coffee, cooled

2 cups sugar

2 teaspoons vanilla

1 cup dark, bittersweet, or semisweet chocolate pieces

1 recipe Coffee Buttercream

30 crème-filled rolled wafers, such as Pirouettes

Unsweetened cocoa powder or ground cinnamon (optional)

1. Allow butter and eggs to stand at room temperature for 30 minutes. Meanwhile, grease and flour thirty 2½-inch muffin cups or line with paper bake cups. In a medium bowl stir together flour, the 1 cup cocoa powder, the baking soda, baking powder, and salt. In a 2-cup glass measuring cup combine milk and coffee. Set aside.

2. Preheat oven to 350°F. In a large mixing bowl beat butter with an electric mixer on medium to high speed for 30 seconds. Gradually add sugar, about ¼ cup at a time, beating on medium speed until combined. Scrape sides of bowl; beat for 2 minutes more. Add eggs, one at a time, beating well after each addition. Beat in vanilla. Alternately add flour mixture and milk mixture to butter mixture, beating on low speed after each addition just until combined. Stir in chocolate pieces.

3. Spoon batter into prepared muffin cups, filling each about three-fourths full. Use the back of a spoon to smooth out batter in cups.

4. Bake about 18 minutes or until tops spring back when lightly touched. Cool cupcakes in muffin cups on wire racks for 5 minutes. Remove cupcakes from muffin cups. Cool completely on wire racks.

5. Spoon Coffee Buttercream into a pastry bag fitted with a star tip. Pipe frosting onto tops of cupcakes. Insert wafers. If desired, dust with additional cocoa powder.

Coffee Buttercream

Allow ⅓ cup butter to stand at room temperature for 30 minutes. In a large mixing bowl beat butter with an electric mixer on medium speed until smooth. Gradually add 1 cup powdered sugar, beating well. Beat in 3 tablespoons cooled, strong brewed coffee and 1 teaspoon vanilla. Gradually beat in an additional 3 cups powdered sugar. If necessary, beat in additional strong brewed coffee until buttercream reaches spreading consistency.

Per cupcake: 285 cal., 12 g total fat (6 g sat. fat), 42 mg chol., 167 mg sodium, 45 g carb., 2 g dietary fiber, 32 g sugar, 3 g protein.

Cranberry-Chai Cupcakes

Prep: 40 minutes **Stand:** 30 minutes **Bake:** 15 minutes at 350°F **Cool:** 45 minutes

Makes 20 to 24 (2½-inch) cupcakes

½ cup butter

2 eggs

2 cups all-purpose flour

1 tablespoon Chai Spice Seasoning

1½ teaspoons baking powder

½ teaspoon baking soda

¼ teaspoon salt

1½ cups sugar

½ teaspoon vanilla

1¼ cups buttermilk or sour milk (see tip, page 11)

¾ cup chopped fresh or frozen cranberries

1 recipe Chai Cream Cheese Frosting

Sugared Cranberries (optional)

1. Allow butter and eggs to stand at room temperature for 30 minutes. Line twenty to twenty-four 2½-inch muffin cups with paper bake cups. In a medium bowl stir together flour, Chai Spice Seasoning, baking powder, baking soda, and salt. Set aside.

2. Preheat oven to 350°F. In a large mixing bowl beat butter with an electric mixer on medium to high speed for 30 seconds. Gradually add sugar, about ¼ cup at a time, beating about 2 minutes or until light and fluffy. Beat in vanilla. Add eggs, one at a time, beating well after each addition. Alternately add flour mixture and buttermilk to butter mixture, beating on low speed after each addition just until combined. Stir in chopped cranberries.

3. Spoon batter into prepared muffin cups, filling each about two-thirds full. Use the back of a spoon to smooth out batter in cups.

4. Bake for 15 to 20 minutes or until a wooden toothpick inserted in centers comes out clean. Cool cupcakes in muffin cups on wire racks for 5 minutes. Remove cupcakes from muffin cups. Cool completely on wire racks.

5. Spread Chai Cream Cheese Frosting onto tops of cupcakes. If desired, garnish with Sugared Cranberries. Store frosted cupcakes in the refrigerator.

Chai Spice Seasoning

Using an electric spice grinder, small food processor, or clean coffee grinder, finely grind 1 teaspoon fennel seeds and 1 teaspoon whole cloves. Transfer to a small bowl. Stir in 2 teaspoons ground cardamom, 1 teaspoon ground ginger, 1 teaspoon ground cinnamon, and pinch freshly ground black pepper. Store in an airtight container in a cool, dry place for up to 1 month.

Chai Cream Cheese Frosting

Allow two 3-ounce packages cream cheese and ⅓ cup butter to stand at room temperature for 30 minutes. In a large mixing bowl beat cream cheese, butter, 1½ teaspoons Chai Spice Seasoning, and 1½ teaspoons vanilla with an electric mixer on medium speed until light and fluffy. Gradually beat in 1½ cups powdered sugar. Gradually beat in an additional 2½ to 2¾ cups powdered sugar until frosting reaches spreading consistency.

Sugared Cranberries

Roll frozen cranberries in sugar to coat. Place on waxed paper; let stand until dry.

Make-Ahead Directions:

Store unfrosted cupcakes in a single layer in an airtight freezer container in the freezer for up to 1 month. Thaw at room temperature before frosting.

Per cupcake: 312 cal., 11 g total fat (7 g sat. fat), 51 mg chol., 193 mg sodium, 51 g carb., 1 g dietary fiber, 40 g sugar, 3 g protein.

Graveyard Cupcakes, page 266

Bye

Boo!

Holidays

Christmas and Halloween take the cake when it comes to dolled-up decorations, but every holiday deserves the same love. Work up a passion for each special occasion with a cleverly cute cupcake design, whether it be for a tree-trimming party, a Thanksgiving feast, or a Fourth of July blowout. No matter what time of year, we have a goodtime cupcake waiting to go center stage.

Christmas Ornament Cupcakes

Start to Finish: 1 hour 30 minutes
Makes 12 (2½-inch) cupcakes

1 cup Creamy White Frosting (see recipe, page 15) or canned creamy white frosting

12 2½-inch cupcakes in paper bake cups (any flavor)

12 ounces Easy Homemade Fondant (see recipe, page 15) or white rolled fondant icing*

Desired colors paste food colorings**

Powdered sugar

12 1½-inch pieces black licorice laces

6 white gumdrops, halved

Luster dust (optional)

1. Spread a thin layer of Creamy White Frosting onto tops of cupcakes. Let stand until set.

2. Divide Easy Homemade Fondant into several portions. Use a toothpick to add a small amount of desired food coloring to each portion of fondant. Knead fondant until color is evenly distributed.*** If desired, leave one portion of fondant white. (Keep fondant covered with plastic wrap when not using.) Add more food coloring as needed to reach desired shade.

3. On a work surface lightly dusted with powdered sugar, roll out one portion of the fondant to ⅛-inch thickness. Using a 3-inch cookie cutter or a sharp knife, cut out circles to fit tops of cupcakes. Place fondant circles on tops of frosted cupcakes, gently molding them over the edges of cupcake tops and smoothing the edges of fondant. Repeat with other colors of fondant, cutting a total of 12 circles.

4. Reroll scraps to ¼-inch thickness or thinner. Use a fluted pastry wheel or knife to cut strips; use a straw or pastry tip to cut dots or small circles out of fondant scraps. Lightly moisten backs of strips and dots with water; attach strips and dots to fondant-covered cupcakes. To give cupcakes a three-dimensional effect, curve strips slightly.

5. For ornament hangers, bend a licorice piece in half and insert ends into the top of a gumdrop half; attach hangers to cupcakes with frosting. If desired, brush cupcakes with luster dust for shine.

*Test Kitchen Tip:
Rolled fondant icing can be found in the cake decorating department of many hobby and crafts stores. Or instead of fondant icing, you can use rolled fruit leather in various colors.

**Test Kitchen Tip:
To achieve the colors shown in photo, for red fondant, combine pink and red-red paste food colorings. For the green fondant, combine leaf green and brown paste food colorings. For blue fondant, combine cornflower blue and sky blue food colorings.

***Test Kitchen Tip:
If you like, wear plastic gloves to keep from discoloring your hands.

Per cupcake: 425 cal., 13 g total fat (6 g sat. fat), 45 mg chol., 150 mg sodium, 74 g carb., 0 g dietary fiber, 60 g sugar, 3 g protein.

Tip

For a more creative twist, you can also use tiny aspic or cookie cutters to create the cutouts in the fondant for the ornament cupcakes.

Mini Gingerbread House Cupcakes

Start to Finish: 1 hour

Makes 12 (2½-inch) cupcakes

2 cups Creamy White Frosting (see recipe, page 15) or canned creamy white frosting

12 Gingerbread Cupcakes (see recipe opposite) or other 2½-inch cupcakes in paper bake cups

Chocolate-covered peanut butter wafer sandwiches

Honey and oats chewy granola bars

Frosted mini shredded wheat biscuits

Small decorative candies

Fresh herb sprigs

Crystallized ginger

Clear edible glitter or powdered sugar (optional)

1. Set aside ⅓ cup of the Creamy White Frosting. Spread the remaining frosting onto tops of cupcakes.

2. For chalet-style houses, cut 2-inch pieces from chocolate-covered peanut butter wafer sandwiches. At top of each piece make an angled cut on each side to create a place to attach roof. For each roof, cut two ¾-inch pieces of granola bar; attach roof pieces to house with reserved frosting. For regular houses, cut a square piece from a wafer sandwich. For the roof, cut a large triangle from wafer sandwich. Attach roof with frosting.

3. Add shredded wheat for doors and candies for doorknobs, using frosting to attach.

4. Carefully place houses on cupcakes. Decorate with fresh herb sprigs as desired, using rosemary sprigs for evergreen trees and other herb sprigs for garlands. Use frosting to attach pieces of ginger to each roof to create a chimney. If desired, sprinkle tops of cupcakes with edible glitter for snow.

Per cupcake: 421 cal., 20 g total fat (4 g sat. fat), 16 mg chol., 220 mg sodium, 61 g carb., 1 g dietary fiber, 43 g sugar, 3 g protein.

1. For chalet-style roof, cut two pieces off the top of the wafer at different angles.

2. Use a sharp knife to cut granola bar into ¾-inch pieces.

3. Before placing house on the cupcake, firmly attach the two roof pieces to the house (and together) with dabs of frosting.

Gingerbread Cupcakes

Preheat oven to 350°F. Line twenty-seven 2½-inch muffin cups with paper bake cups. Prepare 1 package 2-layer-size vanilla or yellow cake mix according to package directions, except omit one of the eggs. Add 1 tablespoon pumpkin pie spice and 1 teaspoon ground ginger to cake mix. Add ⅓ cup molasses and 1 tablespoon cider vinegar with the eggs. Fill muffin cups; bake according to package directions for cupcakes. Cool cupcakes in muffin cups on wire racks for 5 minutes. Remove cupcakes from muffin cups. Cool completely on wire racks. Place extra unfrosted cupcakes in a single layer in airtight containers or resealable freezer bags; seal. Store at room temperature for up to 3 days or freeze for up to 3 months.

Winter Wonderland Cupcakes

Prep: 1 hour **Bake:** 20 minutes at 350°F **Cool:** 45 minutes
Makes 12 (2½-inch) cupcakes

3 cups Cream Cheese Frosting (see recipe, page 14) or canned cream cheese frosting

Blue food coloring

12 Cookie Surprise Cupcakes or other 2½-inch cupcakes in paper bake cups

Clear and/or blue coarse sugar (optional)

Tiny marshmallows

Red rolled fruit leather

Black candy-coated chocolate pieces

Black candy-coated sunflower kernels*

Nonpareils

Gumdrops, cut into tiny slivers

Pine tree sprinkles

Snowflake sprinkles

12 chocolate wafer cookies (optional)

1. Tint half of the Cream Cheese Frosting a light sky blue color with blue food coloring. Spread half of the top of each Cookie Surprise Cupcake with blue frosting, swirling slightly. Spread the other half of each cupcake top with white frosting, swirling slightly. If desired, roll edges of cupcakes in coarse sugar.

2. For each snowman cupcake, press 2 tiny marshmallows together and flatten into a large disk. Flatten a single tiny marshmallow into a smaller disk. Position the smaller disk above the larger disk on a frosted cupcake to create a snowman.

3. For scarves, unroll red fruit leather and cut into strips. Decorate each snowman with a scarf. Press candy-coated chocolate pieces and sunflower kernels into frosting above small marshmallow disk for a hat. Attach nonpareils for eyes and a gumdrop sliver for nose. Arrange pine tree and snowflake sprinkles around snowman for a winter scene.

4. If desired, to make cupcakes look like snow globes, place each cupcake on its side on a chocolate wafer cookie, letting a little of the cookie stick out in front. Secure cupcakes to cookies with white frosting.

Cookie Surprise Cupcakes

Preheat oven to 350°F. Line twenty-four 2½-inch muffin cups with paper bake cups. Cut one 16.5-ounce tube refrigerated peanut butter cookie dough into 24 pieces. Roll dough pieces into balls. In a large mixing bowl combine 1 package 2-layer-size chocolate cake mix; 4 ounces cream cheese, softened; 1 cup water; ½ cup vegetable oil; and 3 eggs. Beat with an electric mixer on medium speed according to package directions. Set aside about 1 cup of the batter. Spoon the remaining batter into prepared muffin cups, filling each about one-half full. Press a peanut butter cookie ball into batter in each cup. Top each with about 1 teaspoon of the reserved batter. Bake about 20 minutes or until tops spring back when lightly touched. Cool cupcakes in muffin cups on wire racks for 5 minutes. Remove cupcakes from muffin cups. Cool completely on wire racks. Place extra unfrosted cupcakes in a single layer in airtight containers or resealable freezer bags; seal. Store at room temperature for up to 3 days or freeze for up to 3 months.

*Tip

Candy-coated sunflower kernels are often available at crafts and hobby stores.

Winter Wonderland Cupcakes with Christmas Trees

Frost cupcakes as directed in step 1. For Christmas trees, unroll green rolled fruit leather. Use small tree-shape cookie cutters to cut out trees. Press trees into green edible glitter. Press trees, glitter sides up, onto frosted cupcakes. Attach multicolor confetti sprinkles on trees with frosting. If desired, make cupcakes look like snow globes as directed in step 4.

Per Snowman and Christmas Tree cupcake variations: 563 cal., 26 g total fat (11 g sat. fat), 72 mg chol., 352 mg sodium, 80 g carb., 1 g dietary fiber, 61 g sugar, 5 g protein.

Winter Wonderland Cupcakes with Gingerbread People

Frost cupcakes as directed in step 1. For each gingerbread person, in a microwave-safe bowl microwave 2 or 3 vanilla caramels, unwrapped, on 100% power (high) for 5 to 10 seconds or until softened. Press caramels together into a flat disk; use a 1-inch gingerbread person-shape cutter to cut out a gingerbread person. Pipe white frosting bands onto arms and legs; pipe hair, eyes, and nose. Attach small red decorative candies for buttons. Press one or two gingerbread people onto each cupcake. If desired, make cupcakes look like snow globes as directed in step 4.

Per Gingerbread People cupcake variation: 621 cal., 28 g total fat (12 g sat. fat), 72 mg chol., 394 mg sodium 89 g carb., 1 g dietary fiber, 68 g sugar, 6 g protein.

Jolly Little Elf Cupcakes

Start to Finish: 2 hours

Makes 12 (2½-inch) cupcakes

12 Peppermint Fudge Cupcakes (see recipe opposite) or other 2½-inch cupcakes

5 ounces white baking chocolate

1 recipe Creamy White Frosting (see recipe, page 15) or two 16-ounce cans creamy white frosting

12 vanilla wafers, cut in half

8 ounces white candy coating with color flecks*

12 rolled sugar ice cream cones
   Yellow food coloring
   Brown paste food coloring

1 tube blue icing

1 tube green icing
   Red candy decorating balls
   Assorted candies and/or nonpareils

1. If necessary, remove paper bake cups from cupcakes. Line one very large baking sheet with waxed paper. Set aside. Using a serrated knife, trim cupcakes so tops are level. In a medium saucepan melt white chocolate over medium-low heat, stirring constantly. Stir in 1⅓ cups of the Creamy White Frosting (or 1 can frosting). Heat over low heat until mixture is smooth, stirring constantly.

2. Place cupcakes, cut sides down, on the prepared baking sheet. Spread sides with frosting mixture to evenly coat. Dip vanilla wafer halves in frosting mixture to coat; place on prepared baking sheet. Let stand until set.

3. In a separate bowl melt white candy coating according to package directions. Spread ice cream cones with melted coating, spreading over the sides to coat completely. Place on prepared baking sheet. Let stand until set.

4. With cupcakes cut sides up, cut a slit on both sides of each cupcake. Insert wafer halves, pointed ends up; secure with frosting mixture. Place ⅔ cup of the remaining frosting mixture in a bowl; tint with yellow food coloring. Place ⅔ cup frosting mixture in another bowl; tint with brown food coloring. Spoon frosting mixtures into separate heavy resealable plastic bags. Snip off a small piece from one corner of each bag. Pipe yellow hair over tops of six

cupcakes; repeat with the remaining cupcakes and the brown frosting.

5. Place ice cream cones, pointed ends up, on top of cupcakes. Spoon the remaining white frosting mixture into a heavy resealable plastic bag. Snip off a tiny piece from one corner of bag. Pipe two white dots onto the front side of each cupcake for the eyes. Use blue and green icing to add an accent dot to each eye. Using the green icing, add medium-size round dots around bases of six of the ice cream cones. Place red candy decorating balls around the bases of the remaining ice cream cones. Pipe green icing onto top of each ice cream cone or top cone with a candy ball. Arrange candy balls or assorted candies on each face for nose and cheeks. Use brown frosting to pipe mouths.

*Test Kitchen Tip:

The elf hats in the photo were made using a special kind of candy coating called Colorburst Brights Candy Melts available from Wilton. If you are unable to locate this product, you can spread hats with plain white candy coating and sprinkle with desired-color small sprinkles or sugars. Or for another festive look, spread melted red candy coating on half of the ice cream cones and melted green candy coating on the remaining ice cream cones.

Per cupcake: 969 cal., 48 g total fat (17 g sat. fat), 39 mg chol., 285 mg sodium, 131 g carb., 1 g dietary fiber, 111 g sugar, 4 g protein.

Peppermint Fudge Cupcakes

Preheat oven to 350°F. Grease and flour twenty-four 2½-inch muffin cups or line with paper bake cups. Prepare 1 package 2-layer-size chocolate cake mix according to package directions, except add 1 additional egg, one 4-serving-size package instant white chocolate or vanilla pudding and pie filling mix, and 1 to 1½ teaspoons peppermint extract. Fill muffin cups; bake according to package directions for cupcakes. Cool cupcakes in muffin cups on wire racks for 5 minutes. Remove cupcakes from muffin cups. Cool completely on wire racks. Place extra unfrosted cupcakes in a single layer in airtight containers or resealable freezer bags; seal. Store at room temperature for up to 3 days or freeze for up to 3 months.

1. Evenly spread melted candy coating on ice cream cones, covering each cone completely.

2. After cutting slits into both sides of each cupcake, insert one dipped wafer into each slit, pointed ends up. If necessary, secure in place with frosting.

O Tannenbaum Cupcakes

Start to Finish: 1 hour 30 minutes

Makes 12 (2½-inch) cupcakes

1 recipe Creamy White Frosting (see recipe, page 15) or two 16-ounce cans creamy white frosting or vanilla frosting

1½ cups powdered sugar

12 Pine Cupcakes or other 2½-inch cupcakes

12 rolled sugar ice cream cones

Green and brown paste food colorings

White and/or green edible glitter or sprinkles

Small pearl candies or other small candies

Fresh thyme leaves (optional)*

1. In a large bowl combine Creamy White Frosting and powdered sugar. Spread a layer of frosting onto tops of each Pine Cupcake.

2. Place an ice cream cone, pointed end up, on each cupcake. Tint remaining frosting forest green with green and brown food colorings. Spoon frosting into a large pastry bag fitted with a small open star tip. Starting at the bottom of the cones, pipe short bursts of frosting onto cones to cover cones completely.**

3. Sprinkle edible glitter around rims of cupcakes. Decorate the cone trees with pearl candies and, if desired, thyme leaves.

Pine Cupcakes

Preheat oven to 350°F. Grease and flour twenty-four 2½-inch muffin cups or line with paper bake cups. Prepare 1 package 2-layer-size white cake mix according to package directions, except stir in 1 tablespoon snipped fresh rosemary. Fill muffin cups and bake according to package directions for cupcakes. Cool cupcakes in muffin cups on wire racks for 5 minutes. Remove cupcakes from muffin cups. Cool completely on wire racks.

*Test Kitchen Tip:
If you choose to use fresh thyme on your Christmas trees, you'll probably want to remove the herb before eating the Christmas tree cone.

**Test Kitchen Tip:
If you prefer not to pipe frosting, frost cupcakes as directed in step 1. For step 2, tint the remaining frosting forest green with green and brown food colorings. Place frosting in a microwave-safe bowl; microwave on 100% power (high) until smooth and melted but still a little thick. Holding each ice cream cone upside down over bowl, spoon melted frosting over outside of cone to coat completely, allowing excess to drip into bowl. Place coated cones on a wire rack set over waxed paper. Let stand until set. Place cones on top of cupcakes. Continue as directed in step 3.

Per cupcake: 524 cal., 22 g total fat (5 g sat. fat), 27 mg chol., 190 mg sodium, 80 g carb., 1 g dietary fiber, 66 g sugar, 2 g protein.

Tip

Elaborately decorated cupcakes don't travel as well as those with small decorations. If you do tote them to a party, pack extra icing and candies to fix any features that fall off.

Frosty the Snowman

Start to Finish: 1 hour 30 minutes
Makes 12 cupcakes

1   recipe Creamy White Frosting (see recipe, page 15) or two 16-ounce cans creamy white frosting
12 2½-inch cupcakes in paper bake cups (any flavor)
1   cup shredded coconut
12 1¾-inch cupcakes (any flavor)
    Pretzel sticks
12 large marshmallows
    Miniature semisweet chocolate pieces
    Orange chewy fruit-flavor square candies, such as Starburst
12 black gumdrops, small black candies, or milk chocolate kisses
    Rainbow-color rolled fruit leather

1. Spread some of the Creamy White Frosting onto tops of the 2½-inch cupcakes. Place coconut in a pie plate. Dip cupcake tops into the coconut, rolling gently to coat.

2. If necessary, remove paper bake cups from the 1¾-inch cupcakes. Spread some of the remaining frosting onto all sides of the small cupcakes. Roll small cupcakes in coconut until coated. Spear each small cupcake through the center with a pretzel stick. Place one small cupcake onto the frosted top of each large cupcake, holding it in place with the end of the pretzel stick.

3. In a microwave-safe bowl microwave about ¾ cup of the remaining frosting on 100% power (high) for 10 to 20 seconds or until melted but still thick enough to coat. Using a fork, dip each marshmallow into warm frosting; spoon frosting over marshmallow to coat. Place marshmallows on a sheet of waxed paper; cool slightly to set frosting. Roll marshmallows in coconut until coated. Attach a marshmallow on its side to each small cupcake by spearing it with a pretzel stick and inserting the other end into a small cupcake. Patch with additional frosting.

4. Attach miniature chocolate pieces for the eyes and mouths. For the nose, cut orange candies into small triangles. Gently press into the marshmallow.

5. Attach a gumdrop to the top of each marshmallow for hat. For arms, insert two pretzel sticks into sides of each 1¾-inch cupcake. For scarves, cut strips from fruit leather. If desired, cut short ends of strips to make fringe. Wrap fruit leather strips around the necks of the snowmen.

Per cupcake: 618 cal., 30 g total fat (13 g sat. fat), 65 mg chol., 211 mg sodium, 85 g carb., 1 g dietary fiber, 66 g sugar, 4 g protein.

1. Spear a small coated cupcake with a pretzel; insert the other pretzel end into a large cupcake until the pretzel is no longer visible.

2. For the head, hold marshmallow on tines of a fork to dip. If necessary, spoon icing over marshmallow to coat.

3. Place icing-coated marshmallow in shredded coconut; roll to coat completely.

4. Snip fringe into ends of the fruit leather strips.

Giant Christmas Tree

Start to Finish: 1 hour 30 minutes

Makes 12 (2½-inch) cupcakes

½ to 1 teaspoon almond extract

3 cups Butter Frosting (see recipe, page 14) or canned vanilla frosting

Green paste food coloring

12 2½-inch Almond Cupcakes or Pine Cupcakes (see recipe, page 250)

Sliced almonds, toasted

5 lemon-flavor chewy candy logs, such as Tootsie Fruit Rolls

1. Beat almond extract into Butter Frosting; tint 2½ cups of the frosting forest green with green food coloring. Generously spread green and white frostings onto tops of 10 cupcakes, swirling frostings together. Set aside.

2. Frost the remaining 2 cupcakes with the remaining white frosting. Arrange sliced almonds on 1 of the white frosted cupcakes. For the yellow star, in a microwave-safe bowl microwave candy logs on 100% power (high) for 15 seconds to soften. Knead candies together; roll out to ¼-inch thickness. Using a 2-inch star-shape cutter, cut out a star shape. Place star on the remaining white frosted cupcake. On a large serving platter arrange the green cupcakes to form a pyramid shape, with cupcakes just touching each other. Place the almond-topped cupcake at the bottom of the pyramid for the trunk of the tree. Place the cupcake with the yellow star at the top of the pyramid.

Almond Cupcakes

Preheat oven to 350°F. Line twenty-four to thirty 2½-inch muffin cups with paper bake cups; set aside. Prepare 1 package 2-layer-size yellow cake mix according to package directions, adding ½ teaspoon almond extract. In a small mixing bowl beat one 8-ounce can almond paste, ¼ cup sugar, and 1 egg with an electric mixer on low speed until combined. Spoon a rounded teaspoon of the almond paste mixture into the bottom of each prepared muffin cup. Spoon batter over almond mixture in muffin cups, filling each about two-thirds full. Use the back of a spoon to smooth out batter in cups. Bake for 15 to 18 minutes or until tops spring back when lightly touched. Cool cupcakes in muffin cups on wire racks for 10 minutes. Remove cupcakes from muffin cups. Cool completely on wire racks. Place extra unfrosted cupcakes in a single layer in airtight containers or resealable freezer bags; seal. Store at room temperature for up to 3 days or freeze for up to 3 months.

Per cupcake: 386 cal., 15 g total fat (5 g sat. fat), 52 mg chol., 192 mg sodium, 63 g carb., 1 g dietary fiber, 54 g sugar, 3 g protein.

Cauldron Cupcakes

Start to Finish: 1 hour
Makes 12 (2½-inch) cupcakes

1 4-serving-size package vanilla pudding and pie filling mix

Green food coloring

1 cup finely crushed chocolate sandwich cookies with white filling (about 10 cookies)

12 2½-inch Chocolate Cupcakes (see recipe, page 10)

1 cup Chocolate Butter Frosting (see recipe, page 14) or canned chocolate frosting

1 tube green decorating gel

Small green candies, such as candy-coated chocolate pieces, nonpareils, or jimmies

Black licorice laces

1 recipe Cauldron Stirrers

1. Prepare pudding mix according to package directions, except stir in several drops of green food coloring with the milk until desired color is reached. Chill as directed.

2. Meanwhile, place crushed sandwich cookies in a shallow dish. Remove paper bake cups from Chocolate Cupcakes. Using a spoon or sharp knife, hollow out centers of cupcakes to form cauldron shapes, leaving ½ inch around the edges and about 1 inch on the bottom of each. Spread Chocolate Butter Frosting onto the sides of cupcakes. Holding each cupcake by the top over the dish, sprinkle cookie crumbs around the base to coat. Spread the remaining chocolate frosting around the top rims of cupcakes. Sprinkle with remaining cookie crumbs; shake off excess.

3. Spoon a generous tablespoon of the green vanilla pudding into the center of each cupcake. Decorate pudding with decorating gel and sprinkle with small green candies. Cut twenty-four 3-inch lengths of licorice. Using two licorice pieces for each cupcake, push the ends of licorice pieces into opposite sides of each cupcake rim to make a handle. Press one Cauldron Stirrer at an angle into each cupcake.

Cauldron Stirrers

Set a wire rack over waxed paper. In a small microwave-safe bowl combine ½ cup semisweet chocolate pieces and ½ teaspoon shortening. Microwave on 100% power (high) for 1 to 2 minutes or until melted, stirring every 10 seconds. Place a pretzel stick on the tines of a fork. Spoon melted chocolate over pretzel to coat completely. Place pretzel on rack. Repeat with 11 more pretzel sticks and the remaining melted chocolate. Let stand until chocolate is set.

Per cupcake: 412 cal., 15 g total fat (8 g sat. fat), 53 mg chol., 328 mg sodium, 67 g carb., 2 g dietary fiber, 51 g sugar, 5 g protein.

Monster Cupcakes

Start to Finish: 45 minutes

Makes 12 (2½-inch) cupcakes

1 recipe Creamy White Frosting (see recipe, page 15) or two 16-ounce cans creamy white frosting

Brown and leaf green paste food colorings*

Black, orange, and purple paste food colorings*

12 2½-inch cupcakes** in paper bake cups (any flavor)

6 large gumdrops, halved crosswise

Toasted coconut

Assorted black candies, such as licorice laces and candy-coated sunflower kernels

Marshmallows

Large and/or small gumdrops

White small oval mints, such as Tic Tacs (optional)

Rolled fruit leather

Candy circus peanuts, halved crosswise

1. Divide Creamy White Frosting into five portions. Tint one portion mossy green (using brown and leaf green food colorings). Tint a second portion black.*** Tint a third portion dark orange. Tint a fourth portion purple. Do not tint the fifth portion; use for attaching monster parts.

2. Cut the rounded tops off cupcakes. Spread cut surfaces of cupcakes with some of the black frosting. Place a large gumdrop half in the center on top of each cupcake.

3. Spread green, orange, and purple frostings onto cupcake tops. Place frosted tops over gumdrop halves on cupcakes, tipping each top back slightly to form a mouth.

4. Decorate cupcakes using toasted coconut and monster parts as follows: For eyes, attach a small piece of black candy to a slice of marshmallow; insert a small piece of black licorice into bottom of marshmallow slice. Press into cupcake. (Or make eyes from gumdrop pieces and small black candies and/or marshmallow halves, gumdrop pieces, and small black candies.) For teeth, cut marshmallows into pieces or use white small oval mints. For tongues, lay a fruit leather roll flat; fold and press together to make four layers. Use scissors to cut out tongue shapes. Attach candy circus peanut pieces to the fronts of cupcakes for feet.

*Test Kitchen Tip:
Look for special shades of paste food coloring in the cake decorating departments of hobby and crafts stores.

**Test Kitchen Tip:
If desired, tint cupcake batter bright green or purple. Use about ¼ teaspoon paste food coloring for every 2 cups of batter. Or use Red Velvet Cupcakes (see recipe, page 34).

***Test Kitchen Tip:
To achieve a rich black color without using excessive black food coloring, stir 1 to 2 tablespoons unsweetened cocoa powder into the frosting before adding the food coloring.

Per cupcake: 512 cal., 18 g total fat (7 g sat. fat), 43 mg chol., 281 mg sodium, 81 g carb., 0 g dietary fiber, 64 g sugar, 3 g protein.

1. Place end of fruit-leather tongue on gumdrop.

2. Replace cupcake top at an angle.

3. Add an eyeball, hair, and/or other features.

Pumpkin Patch Cupcakes

Start to Finish: 2 hours 15 minutes
Makes 12 (2½-inch) cupcakes.

¼ cup sour cream

¼ cup butter, softened

2 teaspoons vanilla

½ teaspoon ground cinnamon

½ teaspoon freshly grated nutmeg or ¼ teaspoon ground nutmeg

5 cups powdered sugar

Green and brown food colorings

Milk

12 Sugar and Spice Cupcakes or other 2½-inch cupcakes in paper bake cups

Candy pumpkins

1. For frosting, in a large mixing bowl beat sour cream, butter, vanilla, cinnamon, and nutmeg with an electric mixer on medium speed until combined. Beat in powdered sugar until smooth. Tint frosting with green and brown food colorings to reach desired grass color. Beat in enough milk until frosting reaches desired consistency.

2. Set Sugar and Spice Cupcakes on a wire rack. Spoon frosting into a large pastry bag fitted with a multi-opening (grass) tip. Using quick upward motions, pipe frosting to look like grass on tops of cupcakes.

3. Place two or three candy pumpkins on top of each cupcake. If desired, change pastry bag tip to a small round tip; pipe up and over the green stem end of each candy pumpkin, forming tendrils.

Sugar and Spice Cupcakes

Preheat oven to 350°F. Line twenty-six 2½-inch muffin cups with paper bake cups. In a large mixing bowl combine 1 package 2-layer-size yellow cake mix; 4 ounces cream cheese, softened; 4 eggs; ¾ cup water; ½ cup vegetable oil, ¼ cup packed brown sugar; 1 to 1½ teaspoons ground cinnamon; 1 teaspoon freshly grated nutmeg or ½ teaspoon ground nutmeg; 1 teaspoon ground ginger; 1 teaspoon vanilla; and ¼ teaspoon ground cloves. Beat with an electric mixer on medium speed about 1 minute or until combined. Spoon batter into prepared muffin cups, filling each about three-fourths full. Use the back of a spoon to smooth out batter in cups. In a small bowl combine ½ cup packed brown sugar and ½ teaspoon ground cinnamon. Sprinkle about 1 teaspoon brown sugar mixture over each cupcake. Bake for 18 to 20 minutes or until a wooden toothpick inserted in centers comes out clean. Cool cupcakes in muffin cups on wire racks for 10 minutes. Remove cupcakes from muffin cups. Cool completely on wire racks. Place extra unfrosted cupcakes in a single layer in airtight containers or resealable freezer bags; seal. Store at room temperature for up to 3 days or freeze for up to 3 months.

Per cupcake: 417 cal., 13 g total fat (5 g sat. fat), 50 mg chol., 194 mg sodium, 76 g carb., 0 g dietary fiber, 65 g sugar, 2 g protein.

Wicked Witch Cupcakes

Start to Finish: 1 hour 30 minutes
Makes 12 (2½-inch) cupcakes

1 12-ounce package semisweet chocolate pieces

2 teaspoons shortening

12 rolled sugar ice cream cones

Black edible glitter

2 10.75-ounce packages frozen pound cake, thawed

1 recipe Creamy White Frosting (see recipe, page 15) or two 16-ounce cans creamy white frosting

Green and black paste food colorings

12 2½-inch Vanilla Cupcakes (see recipe, page 10) or other 2½-inch white cupcakes in paper bake cups

1 cup shredded coconut, toasted*

12 chocolate wafer cookies

Green and yellow log-shape fruit-flavor chewy candies, such as Tootsie Fruit Rolls

1 tube white frosting with tip

1 tube black frosting with tip

1. In a small saucepan heat chocolate and shortening over low heat until melted, stirring occasionally. Meanwhile, place ice cream cones, pointed ends up, on a wire rack set over waxed paper. Spoon some of the melted chocolate over each cone. Using a small metal spatula or butter knife, spread chocolate to cover cones completely. Sprinkle with edible glitter. Let stand until set. If necessary, chill cones in the refrigerator about 30 minutes or until set.

2. Cut each pound cake in half horizontally and lay halves flat. Using a 1¾-inch round cookie cutter, cut 12 rounds from the pound cakes (save cake scraps for another use).

3. Tint half of the Creamy White Frosting green and half black with food colorings.** Frost cupcakes with black frosting. Frost sides of pound cake rounds with green frosting. Place pound cake rounds on the tops of cupcakes. (If necessary, press long wooden picks through centers of cupcakes to help hold pound cake pieces in place while frosting.) Frost tops of pound cake rounds with green frosting. (If using wooden picks, remove them.)

4. Sprinkle toasted coconut around backs and sides to resemble hair. Place a chocolate wafer cookie on top of each frosted pound cake round; place chocolate-coated cone on top of wafer cookie, using melted chocolate to attach, if necessary.

Place several green log-shape candies on a sheet of waxed paper. Microwave on 100% power (high) about 10 seconds or just until softened. Cut off pieces of the softened candy and shape into long, pointy, hooked noses. Use the remaining softened candy to make warts. Push noses into faces (if necessary, use a toothpick to start the hole). Add warts. Use frosting to secure all.

5. Fit the tube of white frosting with a round tip; pipe the bases of the eyes on cupcakes. Fit the tube of black frosting with a round tip; pipe a pupil onto each eye. Pipe black arched "evil" eyebrows over eyes and draw a mouth. Place several yellow log-shape candies on a sheet of waxed paper. Microwave on 100% power (high) about 10 seconds or just until softened. Cut tiny pieces from yellow candy for teeth; use frosting to secure onto cupcakes, creating a snaggletooth look.

*Test Kitchen Tip:

To toast coconut, preheat oven to 350°F. Spread coconut evenly in a large baking pan. Bake for 10 to 12 minutes or until golden, stirring frequently.

**Test Kitchen Tip:

To achieve a richer black color without using a great deal of black food coloring, stir 1 to 2 tablespoons unsweetened cocoa powder into the frosting before adding the food coloring.

Per cupcake: 987 cal., 47 g total fat (25 g sat. fat), 199 mg chol., 586 mg sodium, 134 g carb., 3 g dietary fiber, 96 g sugar, 9 g protein.

1. Place the frosted pound cake round on a frosted cupcake.

2. Press toasted coconut around back and sides of head, leaving room for a face.

3. Press a chocolate wafer cookie into frosting on top of the head.

4. Top wafer cookie with a chocolate-coated cone, using melted chocolate to attach if necessary.

Owl Cupcakes

Prep: 45 minutes **Stand:** 30 minutes
Number of Servings 18 (2½-inch) cupcakes

1 recipe Creamy Vanilla Frosting

18 2½-inch cupcakes in paper bake cups (any flavor)

18 1½-to 2-inch round raspberry and vanilla crème sandwich cookies, split*

36 green candy-coated milk chocolate pieces

18 whole cashews

¾ to 1 cup sliced almonds

1. Spread Creamy Vanilla Frosting onto tops of cupcakes, reserving a small amount of frosting for attaching candies.

2. For eyes, arrange two of the cookie halves, bottom sides up, side by side on top of each cupcake. Use frosting to attach candy-coated chocolate pieces to centers for eyes.

3. For a beak, insert a cashew between the eyes on each cupcake.

4. Cover the rest of each cupcake top with overlapping rows of sliced almonds.

Creamy Vanilla Frosting

Allow ⅓ cup butter to stand at room temperature for 30 minutes. In a medium mixing bowl beat butter and ⅓ cup shortening with an electric mixer on medium speed until creamy. Add 1 cup powdered sugar, beating well. Beat in 1 tablespoon milk and 1 teaspoon vanilla. Gradually beat in an additional 1 cup powdered sugar. If necessary, beat in additional milk to make frosting smooth and creamy.

*Test Kitchen Tip:
If you prefer, use vanilla wafers and pipe a large dot in the center of each wafer.

Per cupcake: 382 cal., 19 g total fat (8 g sat. fat), 52 mg chol., 190 mg sodium, 49 g carb., 1 g dietary fiber, 35 g sugar, 4 g protein.

Graveyard Cupcakes

Start to Finish: 2 hours
Makes 12 (2½-inch) cupcakes

12 chocolate sandwich cookies with white filling

1½ cups Creamy White Frosting (see recipe, page 15) or canned creamy white frosting

⅓ cup chocolate-flavor candy coating disks

12 Cookies and Cream Cupcakes or other 2½-inch cupcakes in paper bake cups

Candy pumpkins (optional)

Green food coloring (optional)

1. Split cookies in half. Scrape off and discard filling. Using a serrated knife, cut three sides from each of 12 of the cookie halves to make tombstone shapes. Crush remaining cookies and trimmings. Spoon about ¼ cup of the Creamy White Frosting into a heavy resealable plastic bag. Snip off a small piece from one corner of bag. On the flat sides of tombstones, pipe "RIP," "BOO!," or other messages.

2. Place a sheet of waxed paper on a large baking sheet. In a small microwave-safe bowl microwave candy coating on 100% power (high) for 30 seconds. Stir; microwave for 20 to 30 seconds more or until completely melted. Spoon into a heavy resealable plastic bag. Snip off a small piece from one corner of bag. Pipe 12 small leafless trees, each 3 to 4 inches tall (make them thick so they won't break when hardened) onto prepared baking sheet. If desired, make extra trees in case one or two break. Chill in the refrigerator until chocolate hardens.

3. Meanwhile, generously spread frosting onto tops of cupcakes. Carefully insert a cookie tombstone into frosting on each cupcake. Using a toothpick or wooden skewer, make a small hole in each cupcake top. Carefully peel chocolate trees from waxed paper and insert into holes on cupcake tops; if necessary, use frosting to secure trees. If desired, place a candy pumpkin on top of some of the cupcakes.

4. If desired, tint about ¼ cup of the frosting with green food coloring. Spoon green frosting into a heavy resealable plastic bag. Snip off a small piece from one corner of bag. Using quick upward motions, pipe grass accents on either side of the tombstones and around trees and on pumpkins. Sprinkle cupcakes with crushed cookies. Serve immediately or store at room temperature for 1 to 2 hours.

Cookies and Cream Cupcakes

Preheat oven to 350°F. Line twenty-four 2½-inch muffin cups with paper bake cups. Place 12 chocolate sandwich cookies with white filling in a resealable plastic bag; use a rolling pin or the flat side of a meat mallet to coarsely crush cookies. Prepare 1 package 2-layer-size white cake mix according to package directions, except use milk in place of the water. Stir crushed cookies into cake batter. Fill muffin cups; bake as directed for cupcakes. Cool cupcakes in muffin cups on wire racks for 5 minutes. Remove cupcakes from muffin cups. Cool completely on wire racks.

Per cupcake: 354 cal., 16 g total fat (5 g sat. fat), 1 mg chol., 249 mg sodium, 52 g carb., 1 g dietary fiber, 36 g sugar, 3 g protein.

1. To make the trees, fill a resealable plastic bag with melted chocolate. Snip a small piece off one corner of the bag; pipe chocolate onto waxed paper.

2. After trees have hardened in the refrigerator, carefully remove them from the paper.

3. Working quickly to prevent melting, gently press tree trunks into frosting.

Scary Faces Cupcakes (Werewolf, Medusa, Mummy)

Start to Finish: 30 minutes
Makes 18 cupcakes (6 werewolves, 6 Medusas, and 6 mummies)

2¼ cups canned chocolate or chocolate fudge frosting

18 2½-inch cupcakes in paper bake cups (any flavor)

12 large black gumdrops

1 red rolled fruit leather

24 small round white candies

1 cup canned white frosting

18 to 24 gummy worms or gummy rings

12 green candy-coated sunflower kernels

1. Spread some of the chocolate frosting onto tops of cupcakes.

2. For werewolf cupcakes, cut 6 of the black gumdrops almost in half, starting from the top of each gumdrop. Open slightly and attach to centers of 6 of the cupcakes for mouths. For each wolf, cut 2 triangle-shape ears from another black gumdrop; attach ears to cupcake. Cut small tongues from fruit leather; stick tongues inside mouths. Add round white candies for eyes. Spoon chocolate frosting into a pastry bag fitted with a star tip. Pipe fur all around faces. Spoon ¼ cup of the white frosting into a small heavy resealable plastic bag. Snip off a very small piece from one corner of bag. Pipe teeth on edge of mouths.

3. For Medusa cupcakes, cut gummy worms or rings into long, thin strips. Curl and pile the strips on top of 6 cupcakes. For eyes, use chocolate frosting to attach round white candies (partially bury eyes in the piles of worms) on each medusa.

4. For eyes on mummy cupcakes, use chocolate frosting to attach two green sunflower kernels to each of the remaining 6 cupcakes. Spoon the remaining white frosting into a pastry bag fitted with a ribbon tip. Pipe strips of white frosting back and forth to cover top of each cupcake, leaving eyes showing.

Per cupcake: 362 cal., 13 g total fat (6 g sat. fat), 43 mg chol., 237 mg sodium, 58 g carb., 0 g dietary fiber, 40 g sugar, 3 g protein.

Creepy Spider Cake

To make this cake, frost a round 2-layer cake with orange-tinted frosting. Spoon additional orange frosting into a pastry bag fitted with a round tip and pipe dots around the base of the cake. Fill a pastry bag fitted with a coupler and a small round tip with black-tinted frosting. Pipe frosting onto cake in a spider web design. For the spiders, cut the tops off one 2½-inch cupcake and two 1¾-inch cupcakes. Place cupcake tops on cake. Pipe stars onto bodies of spiders with black-tinted frosting in a pastry bag fitted with a small star tip. For legs, use pieces of black shoestring licorice. For eyes, cut small marshmallows into slices and add a dot of black frosting for the pupils.

Ghostly Cupcakes

Prep: 45 minutes **Bake:** 20 minutes at 350°F **Cool:** 45 minutes
Makes 12 cupcakes

12 2½-inch White Chocolate Cupcakes or other 2½-inch white cupcakes in paper bake cups*

1 16-ounce can vanilla frosting

12 1¾-inch White Chocolate Cupcakes or other 1¾-inch white cupcakes

12 small glazed or plain doughnut holes

1 recipe Easy Homemade Fondant (see recipe, page 15) or 16 ounces white rolled fondant icing

Black candy-coated sunflower kernels or 1 tube black icing

1. Set the 2½-inch White Chocolate Cupcakes on a flat surface. Spoon vanilla frosting into a pastry bag fitted with a small round tip. Pipe some of the frosting onto tops of cupcakes. If necessary, remove paper bake cups from the 1¾-inch White Chocolate Cupcakes. Place them upside down on the tops of the large cupcakes. Generously pipe some frosting onto top of each small cupcake. Top each with a doughnut hole. If desired, pipe a little frosting on the tops of the doughnut holes. If necessary, use frosting to secure any unstable parts of stacks.
2. Shape Easy Homemade Fondant into 1½-inch-diameter balls. (Work with one ball of fondant at a time and keep remaining fondant covered until needed.) On parchment paper, roll one ball into a 6-inch-diameter circle. Drape fondant circle loosely over a cupcake stack, pressing or creasing the fondant in places to make the stack look more ghostly. Repeat to make 12 ghostly cupcakes.
3. For faces, use frosting to attach sunflower kernels to the fondant for eyes and mouths or use black icing to pipe eyes and mouths.

White Chocolate Cupcakes

Preheat oven to 350°F. Line sixteen 2½-inch and twelve 1¾-inch muffin cups with white paper bake cups.* In a large mixing bowl beat 4 ounces cream cheese, softened, with an electric mixer until fluffy. Add 1 package 2-layer-size white cake mix, 1 cup milk, ½ cup vegetable oil, and 4 eggs. Beat on medium speed for 2 minutes, scraping sides of bowl occasionally. Stir in 1 cup finely chopped white baking chocolate with cocoa butter or miniature white baking pieces. Spoon batter into prepared muffin cups, filling each about three-fourths full. Bake about 20 minutes for 2½-inch cupcakes, about 14 minutes for 1¾-inch cupcakes, or until a wooden toothpick inserted in centers comes out clean. Cool cupcakes in muffin cups on wire racks for 10 minutes. Remove cupcakes from muffin cups. Cool completely on wire racks. Place extra unfrosted cupcakes in a single layer in airtight containers or resealable freezer bags; seal. Store at room temperature for up to 3 days or freeze for up to 3 months.

*Test Kitchen Tip:

If you prefer to make only one size cupcakes for another use, use twenty-two 2½-inch or forty-eight 1¾-inch muffin cups. If you don't have enough muffin cups or if all of the cupcakes do not fit into the oven at one time, store the remaining batter in the refrigerator while the first batch bakes.

Per cupcake: 748 cal., 30 g total fat (11 g sat. fat), 72 mg chol., 461 mg sodium, 113 g carb., 0 g dietary fiber, 92 g sugar, 5 g protein.

1 Pipe some of the frosting onto the top of a large cupcake; place one of the smaller cupcakes, top side down, on the frosting.

2 Pipe additional frosting on the second cupcake. Place a doughnut hole onto the frosting on the smaller cupcake.

3 Carefully drape a 6-inch circle of fondant over the stack of cupcakes and doughnut holes.

Turkey Tom Cupcakes

Prep: 2 hours 30 minutes **Bake:** 19 minutes at 350°F **Cool:** 45 minutes
Makes 12 (2½-inch) cupcakes

2 cups Chocolate Butter Frosting (see recipe, page 14) or two 16-ounce cans chocolate frosting

12 Pumpkin Cupcakes or other 2½-inch cupcakes in paper bake cups

6 large marshmallows, halved crosswise

Candy corn

Gold sparkling decorating gel*

Crème-filled rolled wafer cookies, such as Pirouettes

¼ cup Creamy White Frosting (see recipe, page 15) or canned creamy white frosting

24 miniature semisweet chocolate pieces

12 small orange gumdrops, halved

Stick a toothpick into the uncut top of a marshmallow half. Holding onto the toothpick, dip marshmallow halves into melted frosting. If necessary, use a spoon to drizzle frosting over top of marshmallows. Place marshmallows on waxed paper. Carefully pull out toothpicks.

1. Line a baking sheet with waxed paper. Set aside. Spread half of the Chocolate Butter Frosting onto tops of Pumpkin Cupcakes. In a microwave-safe bowl microwave ½ cup of the remaining chocolate frosting on 100% power (high) for 10 to 20 seconds or until frosting is melted, stirring every 5 seconds. Stick toothpicks into uncut tops of marshmallow halves. Dip marshmallow halves into melted frosting, turning to coat; let excess drip off into bowl. (If frosting thickens, microwave for a few seconds more.) Place marshmallows, pick ends up, on prepared baking sheet. Carefully remove picks. Let stand until set.

2. Cut a small slit in the center of each marshmallow half. For beak, insert a candy corn into each slit, with pointed end sticking out. Using decorating gel, carefully pipe a turkey wattle up and over each beak.* Place a coated marshmallow half slightly off-center on each frosted cupcake. For feathers, break wafers into pieces; insert pieces into each cupcake in a half circle around the marshmallow head.

3. Spoon Creamy White Frosting into a heavy resealable plastic bag. Snip a small piece from one corner of bag. Pipe small rounds on the marshmallows for eyes. Press a miniature chocolate piece into

each white round. Spoon remaining chocolate frosting into a pastry bag fitted with a star tip. Pipe chocolate frosting around the edges of marshmallow heads. For the feet, press 2 gumdrop halves below the head on each cupcake.

Pumpkin Cupcakes

Preheat oven to 350°F. Line twenty-four 2½-inch muffin cups with paper bake cups; set aside. Prepare 1 package 2-layer-size yellow cake mix according to package directions, except use ¾ cup water and ⅓ cup oil. Stir 1 cup canned pumpkin, ½ cup sour cream, and 1 teaspoon pumpkin pie spice into batter. Spoon batter into prepared muffin cups, filling each two-thirds to three-fourths full. Bake as directed for cupcakes. Cool cupcakes in muffin cups on wire racks for 5 minutes. Remove cupcakes from muffin cups. Cool completely on wire racks. Place extra unfrosted cupcakes in a single layer in airtight containers or resealable freezer bags; seal. Store at room temperature for up to 3 days or freeze for up to 3 months.

*Test Kitchen Tip:
If you prefer, tint about ½ cup white frosting with red food coloring and use to pipe wattles.

Per cupcake: 386 cal., 14 g total fat (6 g sat. fat), 16 mg chol., 206 mg sodium, 66 g carb., 1 g dietary fiber, 52 g sugar, 1 g protein.

Easy Pumpkin Pies

Start to Finish: 30 minutes

Prepare one 7.2-ounce package fluffy white frosting mix according to package directions or prepare Sweetened Whipped Cream Frosting (page 15). Remove 1½ cups of the frosting; stir in the ½ teaspoon cinnamon and the orange food coloring. Spread the orange frosting onto twelve 2½-inch cupcakes. Sprinkle with graham crackers. Spoon a small amount of the white frosting on top of each cupcake. If desired, sprinkle with additional cinnamon and/or nutmeg.

New Year's Toast

Prep: 1 hour **Bake:** 18 minutes at 350°F **Cool:** 45 minutes
Makes 24 (2½-inch) cupcakes

1 package 2-layer-size white cake mix

Champagne

1 recipe Champagne Frosting

Easy Homemade Fondant (see recipe, page 15) or white rolled fondant icing

Pink or white luster dust

Pink pearl candy beads*

1. Line twenty-four 2½-inch muffin cups with paper bake cups.
2. Preheat oven to 350°F. Prepare cake mix according to package directions, substituting champagne for the water. Fill muffin cups; bake as directed for cupcakes. Cool cupcakes in muffin cups on wire racks for 5 minutes. Remove cupcakes from muffin cups. Cool completely on wire racks.
3. Spoon Champagne Frosting into a pastry bag fitted with a large star tip. Pipe frosting onto cupcakes while dragging the tip across the top of each cupcake to create waves for a "bubbly" look.
4. Use your hands to shape Easy Homemade Fondant into balls ranging in size from ¼ to ¾ inch. (You'll need several dozen balls.) Use a clean, dry artist's paintbrush to paint luster dust onto balls.
5. Arrange fondant balls on cupcakes, placing several balls on each cupcake. Arrange candy beads on cupcakes. If desired, serve cupcakes in shallow champagne glasses.

*Test Kitchen Tip:

Pearl candy beads can be found in the cake decorating departments of hobby and crafts stores. If you can't find the beads, create small bead-size balls from pink-tinted Easy Homemade Fondant or rolled fondant icing.

Champagne Frosting

Prepare Creamy White Frosting (see recipe, page 15) as directed, except substitute 2 tablespoons champagne for 2 tablespoons of the water. If desired, use red and brown food colorings to tint frosting a creamy deep pink.

Per cupcake: 245 cal., 10 g total fat (3 g sat. fat), 0 mg chol., 146 mg sodium, 36 g carb., 0 g dietary fiber, 28 g sugar, 1 g protein.

1. Break off pieces of Easy Homemade Fondant and use your hands to roll into smooth balls.

2. Dip a clean artist's paintbrush into luster dust and spread it evenly over each fondant ball.

Easy Confetti Celebration Cupcakes

Start to Finish: 45 minutes

Spread or pipe canned vanilla frosting onto tops of twenty-four
2½-inch cupcakes. Sprinkle with multicolor confetti sprinkles. Tint
the remaining vanilla frosting with food colorings to desired colors.
Place each color of frosting in a separate heavy resealable plastic
bag. Snip off a very small piece from one corner of each bag. Pipe
strands of the colored frostings over cupcakes and serving plate to
look like streamers.

Love Note Cupcakes

Prep: 50 minutes **Bake:** at 350°F per package directions **Cool:** 45 minutes
Makes 24 (2½-inch) cupcakes

1 package 2-layer-size German chocolate cake mix

1 2-ounce bottle red food coloring (¼ cup)

1 recipe White Chocolate Whipped Cream (see recipe opposite)

1 recipe Mascarpone Frosting (see recipe opposite)

2 cups Chocolate Buttercream (see recipe, page 14) or canned chocolate frosting

1. Line twenty-four 2½-inch muffin cups with paper bake cups.

2. Preheat oven to 350°F. Prepare cake mix according to package directions, except use a mixture of red food coloring and water to equal the amount of water called for in the package directions. Fill muffin cups; bake as directed for cupcakes. Cool cupcakes in muffin cups on wire racks for 5 minutes. Remove cupcakes from muffin cups. Cool completely on wire racks.

3. Spoon White Chocolate Whipped Cream into a pastry bag fitted with a large round or star tip. Insert tip into the top of each cupcake. Squeeze some of the whipped cream into the center of each cupcake.

4. Spread some of the white Mascarpone Frosting, pink Mascarpone Frosting, and Chocolate Buttercream onto tops of cupcakes. Spoon the remaining frostings into separate pastry bags fitted with small round tips or small star tips. Pipe messages or draw hearts onto cupcakes. Store in the refrigerator.

Per cupcake: 374 cal., 16 g total fat (8 g sat. fat), 57 mg chol., 181 mg sodium, 56 g carb., 1 g dietary fiber, 47 g sugar, 3 g protein.

Easy Rose Bouquet

Start to Finish: 40 minutes

Frost twelve 2½-inch chocolate, white, or strawberry cupcakes with canned chocolate, vanilla, or strawberry frosting. Unwrap and peel open 6 to 9 sheets red rolled fruit leather. Cut sheets into 1-inch-wide strips. Coat each strip with granulated sugar. To make each rose, loosely coil a strip, pinching coil together at the bottom and allowing top edge to remain loose. Gently turn down some of the top edge to open up the rose. Pinch the bottom of the rose together to make a point. Arrange a rose on each cupcake.

White Chocolate Whipped Cream

In a small saucepan combine 3 ounces white baking chocolate with cocoa butter, chopped, and ¼ cup whipping cream. Cook and stir over low heat until chocolate is nearly melted. Remove from heat; stir until smooth. Cool for 15 minutes. In a chilled large mixing bowl beat ¾ cup whipping cream with the chilled beaters of an electric mixer on medium speed until soft peaks form (tips curl). Add cooled white chocolate mixture. Beat on medium to high speed just until stiff peaks form (tips stand straight). If desired, cover and chill for up to 24 hours before using.

Mascarpone Frosting

In a large mixing bowl beat ½ cup mascarpone cheese or cream cheese, softened, and 2 tablespoons butter, softened, with an electric mixer on medium to high speed until smooth. Beat in ½ teaspoon vanilla. Gradually add 4 cups powdered sugar, beating well. Beat in enough milk (2 to 4 teaspoons), 1 teaspoon at a time, until frosting reaches spreading consistency. Use red food coloring to tint desired amount of frosting pink.

Bird's Nest Cupcakes

Prep: 1 hour 30 minutes Stand: 30 minutes Bake: 15 minutes at 350°F Cool: 45 minutes

Makes 28 (2½-inch) cupcakes

1 cup butter

4 eggs

2¾ cups cake flour

2 teaspoons baking powder

½ teaspoon baking soda

¼ teaspoon salt

1 8-ounce carton sour cream

⅓ cup orange juice

1 tablespoon finely shredded lemon peel

2 tablespoons lemon juice

1¼ cups sugar

1 recipe Citrus Frosting or 1½ cups other frosting

6 ounces vanilla candy coating

4 cups chow mein noodles

½ to ⅔ cup (about 84) pastel-color candy-coated egg-shape milk chocolate candies or jelly beans

1. Allow butter and eggs to stand at room temperature for 30 minutes. Line twenty-eight 2½-inch muffin cups with paper bake cups. In a medium bowl stir together cake flour, baking powder, baking soda, and salt. In a small bowl combine sour cream, orange juice, lemon peel, and lemon juice. Set aside.

2. Preheat oven to 350°F. In a very large mixing bowl beat butter with an electric mixer on medium to high speed for 30 seconds. Gradually add sugar, about ¼ cup at a time, beating on medium speed about 3 minutes or until light and fluffy, scraping sides of bowl occasionally. Beat in eggs, one at a time, beating well after each addition. Alternately add flour mixture and sour cream mixture to butter mixture, beating on low speed after each addition just until combined.

3. Spoon batter into prepared muffin cups, filling each about three-fourths full. Use the back of a spoon to smooth out batter in cups.

4. Bake for 15 to 17 minutes or until a toothpick inserted in centers comes out clean. Cool cupcakes in muffin cups on wire racks for 5 minutes. Remove cupcakes from muffin cups. Cool completely on wire racks.

5. Spread Citrus Frosting onto tops of cupcakes. In a small microwave-safe bowl microwave candy coating on 100% power (high) for 30 seconds. Stir; microwave for 20 to 30 seconds more or until completely melted. In a large bowl combine chow mein noodles and the melted candy coating. Shape chow mein noodle mixture into a nest on top of each cupcake.*

6. Add 3 candy-coated milk chocolate candies to each nest.

Citrus Frosting

In a medium bowl stir together one 16-ounce can cream cheese or vanilla frosting and ½ teaspoon finely shredded lemon peel.

*Test Kitchen Tip:

If mixture begins to set up, heat it in the microwave on 100% power (high) for 10 seconds at a time until softened.

Per cupcake: 303 cal., 14 g total fat (8 g sat. fat), 52 mg chol., 194 mg sodium, 41 g carb., 0 g dietary fiber, 26 g sugar, 3 g protein.

Easy Easter Bunny Bites

Start to Finish: 40 minutes

Spoon frosting into a pastry bag fitted with a multiopening tip. Pipe frosting onto tops of twelve 2½-inch cupcakes. On a work surface sprinkled with granulated sugar, use a rolling pin to flatten large white gumdrops; cut or shape flattened gumdrops into triangles to use for ears. Press ends of two gumdrop triangles into the frosting near top of each cupcake head; press into frosting to attach. Use pink icing to pipe insides of ears. Use black icing to pipe whiskers. Add a pink jelly bean nose. Pipe vanilla frosting for eyes (or use large white round candies); pipe a pupil onto each eye with black icing.

Sparkler Cupcakes

Prep: 45 minutes **Stand:** 1 hour **Bake:** 20 minutes at 350°F **Cool:** 45 minutes
Makes 12 (2½-inch) cupcakes

½ cup red candy coating disks

½ cup blue candy coating disks

½ cup white candy coating disks

2½ cups Creamy White Frosting (see recipe, page 15) or canned creamy white frosting

12 Confetti Cupcakes or other 2½-inch cupcakes in paper bake cups

Red, white, and blue sprinkles and/or jimmies (optional)

1. Place colored candy coating disks in three separate small microwave-safe bowls. Microwave one bowl on 100% power (high) for 30 seconds. Stir; microwave for 20 to 30 seconds more or until melted. Repeat, one at a time, with the remaining bowls of candy coating. Spoon melted candy coatings into three small heavy resealable plastic bags. Snip off a small piece from one corner of each bag. On sheets of waxed paper, make 8- to 9-inch-long sticks (about ¼-inch thickness) of each color candy coating by piping back and forth over waxed paper in a zigzag pattern. Let stand about 1 hour or until firm. (If necessary, place the sticks of candy coating in the freezer until firm.)

2. Meanwhile, spoon Creamy White Frosting into a disposable pastry bag fitted with a medium star tip. Pipe frosting onto tops of Confetti Cupcakes.

3. Break the zigzag sticks of candy coating into 3- to 4-inch lengths. Insert the candy sticks into frosting, radiating out from the center like sparklers. If desired, sprinkle with colored sprinkles.

Confetti Cupcakes

Preheat oven to 350°F. Line twenty-four to twenty-six 2½-inch muffin cups with paper bake cups. In a large mixing bowl beat 1 package 2-layer-size white cake mix, one 4-serving-size package instant cheesecake pudding and pie filling mix, 1 cup water, 3 eggs, ½ cup sour cream, and ⅓ cup vegetable oil with an electric mixer on low speed until combined. Beat on medium speed for 2 minutes more, scraping sides of bowl occasionally. Stir in ½ cup red, white, and blue sprinkles or jimmies. Spoon batter into prepared muffin cups, filling each two-thirds to three-fourths full. Use the back of a spoon to smooth out batter in cups. Bake for 20 to 22 minutes or until a wooden toothpick inserted in centers comes out clean. Cool cupcakes in muffin cups on wire racks for 5 minutes. Remove cupcakes from muffin cups. Cool completely on wire racks.

Per cupcake: 493 cal., 25 g total fat (8 g sat. fat), 32 mg chol., 230 mg sodium, 64 g carb., 0 g dietary fiber, 54 g sugar, 3 g protein.

Easy Berry Cheesecakes

Start to Finish: 25 minutes

Spoon frosting into a pastry bag fitted with a large star tip. Insert tip into tops of twelve 2½-inch cupcakes. Squeeze about 2 teaspoons of the frosting into the center of each cupcake. Pipe swirls of the remaining frosting onto tops of cupcakes. Arrange fresh blueberries and strawberry halves on cupcakes. Store in the refrigerator. If desired, dust with powdered sugar just before serving.

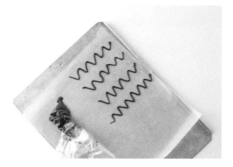
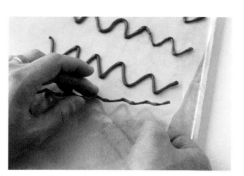

1. Cut a small hole from corner of bag; pipe zigzag patterns onto waxed paper.

2. Once zigzag sticks of candy coating are hardened (place in the freezer if necessary), gently peel sticks from paper.

Metric Information

The charts on the facing page provide a guide for converting measurements from the U.S. customary system, which is used throughout this book, to the metric system.

Product Differences

Most of the ingredients called for in the recipes in this book are available in most countries. However, some are known by different names. Here are some common American ingredients and their possible counterparts:

Sugar (white) is granulated, fine granulated, or castor sugar.

Powdered sugar is icing sugar.

All-purpose flour is enriched, bleached, or unbleached white household flour. When self-rising flour is used in place of all-purpose flour in a recipe that calls for leavening, omit the leavening agent (baking soda or baking powder) and salt.

Light-color corn syrup is golden syrup.

Cornstarch is cornflour.

Baking soda is bicarbonate of soda.

Vanilla or vanilla extract is vanilla essence.

Green, red, or yellow sweet peppers are capsicums or bell peppers.

Golden raisins are sultanas.

Volume and Weight

The United States traditionally uses cup measures for liquid and solid ingredients. The chart, top right, shows the approximate imperial and metric equivalents. If you are accustomed to weighing solid ingredients, the following approximate equivalents will be helpful.

1 cup butter, castor sugar, or rice = 8 ounces = ½ pound = 250 grams

1 cup flour = 4 ounces = ¼ pound = 125 grams

1 cup icing sugar = 5 ounces = 150 grams

Canadian and U.S. volume for a cup measure is 8 fluid ounces (237 ml), but the standard metric equivalent is 250 ml.

1 British imperial cup is 10 fluid ounces.

In Australia, 1 tablespoon equals 20 ml, and there are 4 teaspoons in the Australian tablespoon.

Spoon measures are used for smaller amounts of ingredients. Although the size of the tablespoon varies slightly in different countries, for practical purposes and for recipes in this book, a straight substitution is all that's necessary. Measurements made using cups or spoons always should be level unless stated otherwise.

COMMON WEIGHT RANGE REPLACEMENTS

IMPERIAL / U.S.	METRIC
½ ounce	15 g
1 ounce	25 g or 30 g
4 ounces (¼ pound)	115 g or 125 g
8 ounces (½ pound)	225 g or 250 g
16 ounces (1 pound)	450 g or 500 g
1¼ pounds	625 g
1½ pounds	750 g
2 pounds or 2¼ pounds	1,000 g or 1 Kg

OVEN TEMPERATURE EQUIVALENTS

FAHRENHEIT SETTING	CELSIUS SETTING*	GAS SETTING
300°F	150°C	Gas Mark 2 (very low)
325°F	160°C	Gas Mark 3 (low)
350°F	180°C	Gas Mark 4 (moderate)
375°F	190°C	Gas Mark 5 (moderate)
400°F	200°C	Gas Mark 6 (hot)
425°F	220°C	Gas Mark 7 (hot)
450°F	230°C	Gas Mark 8 (very hot)
475°F	240°C	Gas Mark 9 (very hot)
500°F	260°C	Gas Mark 10 (extremely hot)
Broil	Broil	Grill

*Electric and gas ovens may be calibrated using Celsius. However, for an electric oven, increase Celsius setting 10 to 20 degrees when cooking above 160°C. For convection or forced air ovens (gas or electric) lower the temperature setting 25°F/10°C when cooking at all heat levels.

BAKING PAN SIZES

IMPERIAL / U.S.	METRIC
9×1½-inch round cake pan	22- or 23x4-cm (1.5 L)
9×1½-inch pie plate	22- or 23×4-cm (1 L)
8×8×2-inch square cake pan	20×5-cm (2 L)
9×9×2-inch square cake pan	22- or 23×4.5-cm (2.5 L)
11×7×1½-inch baking pan	28×17×4-cm (2 L)
2-quart rectangular baking pan	30×19×4.5-cm (3 L)
13×9×2-inch baking pan	34×22×4.5-cm (3.5 L)
15×10×1-inch jelly roll pan	40×25×2-cm
9×5×3-inch loaf pan	23×13×8-cm (2 L)
2-quart casserole	2 L

U.S. / STANDARD METRIC EQUIVALENTS

⅛ teaspoon = 0.5 ml	⅓ cup = 3 fluid ounces = 75 ml
¼ teaspoon = 1 ml	½ cup = 4 fluid ounces = 125 ml
½ teaspoon = 2 ml	⅔ cup = 5 fluid ounces = 150 ml
1 teaspoon = 5 ml	¾ cup = 6 fluid ounces = 175 ml
1 tablespoon = 15 ml	1 cup = 8 fluid ounces = 250 ml
2 tablespoons = 25 ml	2 cups = 1 pint = 500 ml
¼ cup = 2 fluid ounces = 50 ml	1 quart = 1 liter

Index

Page numbers in *italics* indicate illustrations